John Milton
A Biography

For James and Alice and the families connected to all of us.

John Milton
A Biography

NEIL FORSYTH

LION

A Lion Book
an imprint of
Lion Hudson plc
Wilkinson House, Jordan Hill Road,
Oxford OX2 8DR, England
www.lionhudson.com
ISBN 978 0 7459 5310 6

First edition 2008
10 9 8 7 6 5 4 3 2 1 0

The text paper used in this book has been made from wood
independently certified as having come from sustainable forests.

A catalogue record for this book is available
from the British Library

Typeset in 10/12 Bembo
Printed and bound in Malta
by Gutenberg Press

Contents

Abbreviations

Campbell Gordon Campbell. A Milton Chronology. Basingstoke: Macmillan, 1997.

Carey John Milton: Complete Shorter Poems, ed. John Carey. London: Longman, 1971; second ed. 1997.

CM The 'Columbia Milton', i.e. The Works of John Milton, ed. F. A Patterson, et al. 18 vols in 21. New York: Columbia University Press, 1931–38.

DDD 1 The Doctrine and Discipline of Divorce. First edition. Quoted from J. Max Patrick, ed. The Prose of John Milton. New York: Doubleday Anchor, 1967.

DDD 2 The Doctrine and Discipline of Divorce. Second edition. Quoted from YP.

EL The Early Lives of Milton, ed. Helen Darbishire. New York: Barnes and Noble, 1965

Flannagan The Riverside Milton, ed. Roy Flannagan. Boston and New York: Houghton Mifflin, 1998.

Fowler John Milton: Paradise Lost, ed. Alastair Fowler. London: Longman, 1971; second ed 1998

Lewalski Barbara Lewalski. The Life of John Milton. Oxford: Blackwell, 2003.

Leonard John Milton: The Complete Poems, ed. John Leonard. London: Penguin, 1998.

LR Life Records of John Milton, ed. J.M. French, 5 vols. New Brunswick, NJ: Rutgers UP, 1949–58.

MQ Milton Quarterly

PL Paradise Lost

PMLA. Publications Of The Modern Language Association

PR Paradise Regained

SA Samson Agonistes

YP 'Yale Prose', i.e. the Complete Prose Works of John Milton. Gen ed. Don M. Wolfe. 8 vols. New Haven: Yale University Press, 1953–80.

Preface

In the dream I am wearing white gloves, like Alice's White Rabbit. I am touching a precious book. There is only one copy in existence of this book, which seems to be the first edition of Milton's tribute to his beloved friend Charles Diodati. (The book is in the British Library in London, along with many other texts of which there is only one copy, such as Milton's family Bible.) After some straightforward negotiations, I am allowed to see the book, though I have to wear the white gloves to avoid spoiling it with my sweaty hands. I am grateful for the staff's obvious care, and hope that it was not just my shifty eyes that kept a guardian present the whole time. In a variant of the same dream, it takes a good deal longer for me to be allowed to see the bound manuscript in which Milton kept a record of his earlier writings and projects. (This must be in the library of Trinity College, Cambridge.) The staff are not really polite, merely haughty – something I learned to expect of officials during my undergraduate years at that university, which was also Milton's. (He, too, did not like it much.) Before I can open the book or even touch the manuscript, I wake up.

These are guilt dreams, I know. I have not done the proper legwork in order to write this book; I have not spent hours in the archives, crossing the Atlantic several times to view manuscripts and pictures (such as the lovely portrait of the ten-year-old Milton in the Pierpoint Morgan Library in New York). It is at least temporarily reassuring that many such documents have been on view in the major exhibitions celebrating the four hundredth anniversary of Milton's birth, at the Bodleian in Oxford, at Milton's college in Cambridge as well as at the University Library, and at the New York Public Library. This book is, as a former student told me in a kindly but firm tone, a work of 'haute vulgarisation'. That is, I have tried to transmit to as wide a readership as possible the results of the scholarly researches of others, along with some of my own opinions. My task, as I saw it, was to write a biography of Milton that would excite readers who might be merely curious, and who would like to know why Milton is so widely loved and admired, and even, sometimes, detested. I hope you who are reading will begin to see why Wordsworth wrote a sonnet in 1802, at a moment of political turmoil, which begins:

Milton, thou shouldst be living at this hour
England hath need of thee.

I must thank in particular Gordon Campbell, both for his 1996 re-edition of William Riley Parker's 1968 elegant and learned *Milton: A Biography*, and for his painstaking and meticulous 1997 *Chronology*. I have made especial use, as everybody should, of Barbara Lewalski's recent and authoritative *Life of John Milton* (2000, revised edition 2003). I feel rather nervous about the occasions I have found myself disagreeing with her (especially regarding how early Milton became a radical), and I know I have borrowed too much from her magisterial book. If you want to follow up anything from this book, go first to Lewalski or Campbell. Other accounts I have found stimulating in different ways include those by Anna Beer, Cedric Brown, Steven Fallon, Roy Flannagan, Peter Levi and Angus Wilson. The endnotes will sometimes give the necessary references, but I have tried to keep those to a minimum. For quotations from Milton's poetry I have not been able to resist the old-spelling texts of Roy Flannagan's Riverside edition (or occasionally the texts available online at the Milton Reading Room). They may seem a little strange at first, but you soon get used to them, and they open the reading world of Milton's contemporaries directly to our experience. I have sometimes used John Leonard's translations of the Latin in the Penguin *Complete Poems*, and I have regularly consulted, and occasionally quoted, the richly annotated Longman editions of John Carey and Alastair Fowler. For the prose I use, as everybody now does, the *Complete Prose Works*, published by Yale University Press. I also have to thank Princeton University Press for their habitual generosity in allowing me to rework several pages from my book on *Paradise Lost*, entitled *The Satanic Epic*.

Good friends have been kind enough to read through earlier drafts of this book: Lukas Erne, Indira Ghose, Elizabeth Kaspar, John Leonard, Richard Waswo. Many changes have resulted from their suggestions and vigilance. I trust the reader will remember that the errors and infelicities that remain are all my own achievement. I am also happy to be able to thank the staff at Lion Hudson for the invitation to write this book, and for their helpful patience in seeing it to completion.

Many other debts must go unrecorded. The community of Milton scholars lives in a world of constant exchange, and I hope my friends and colleagues in that world will forgive any unacknowledged thefts they recognize. For those of you who may be coming to Milton for the first time, I wish you as much pleasure in the reading of this book as I have had in the writing of it.

Introduction:

Blind Love

It is customary these days to begin a biography not with the hero's birth, indispensable as that event is, but with a revealing and typical incident, one which quickly opens a window onto the life, and into the psyche, of the subject. I here violate the custom only slightly, since the representative moment I have chosen is not quite an incident but two lines of poetry about a dream. At the end of a sonnet in which Milton recounts a dream of his dead wife, whom he had never seen because they were married after his blindness became total, he writes:

> But O as to embrace me she enclin'd,
> I wak'd, she fled, and day brought back my night.

The lines have moved me on every reading since the first, when I was a young student. All the harsh, negative and often foolish things that are said or believed about Milton evaporate next to the felt intensity of these words. Frustrated love, the inability to reach what one most desires, the slight and touching note of self-pity at the inevitability of forever waking to see nothing, all these and many other feelings are suggested. Yet the lines, intensely personal as they are, conceal a learned allusion to Aeneas's vision of his wife Creusa in Virgil, and the poem begins with an explicit reference to Euripides' tragedy *Alcestis*, in which the heroic bride is brought back to her undeserving husband from the dead. Not being able to have what one desires is a standard topic in Petrarchan sonnets. This combination of profound emotion and alignment with great predecessor poets to express that emotion is characteristic of Milton at his best.

Those who already know something about Milton will recognize that in beginning my story at this point, I have stacked the deck. Milton's feelings about women are a perennial topic of often vicious, but mostly intelligent and rewarding, conversation. Eve, Dalila and a bizarre invented female called

'Sin' are the normal examples from his poetry in that discussion, and we will explore all three later in this book. The biographical perspective requires, though, that we begin from this personal statement of mourning for a lost love. I have also stacked the deck in another way. The book that was regarded until recently as the leading biography of Milton, by William Riley Parker, claims that this poem is not about Katherine Woodcock, Milton's second wife, at all, but about his first wife, Mary Powell. Both women had indeed died, as the poem implies, shortly after childbirth, Mary almost immediately, Katherine some three months later.

Two things, though, incline me to agree with almost all other commentators. One is practical: there is no evidence that Jeremy Picard, the scribe who wrote out the poem for the blind Milton, had worked for him before the 14 January 1658, yet Mary died in 1652; Katherine died on 3 February 1658. The record of her death in the family Bible is also apparently in Picard's hand. The other reason is more subjective: the poem mentions purity, which is what Katherine's name means in Greek, and although Mary gave Milton the three children who eventually survived the frightening conditions of birth and infancy in the period, their troubled marriage does not lead me to imagine that a poem that begins by evoking his wife as 'my late espoused saint' was written for her, or even – though here the grounds are even more subjective – that it is likely to have been written so soon after Milton's blindness became total in 1652. Milton's nephew, Edward Phillips, who wrote one of the first biographies of his uncle, simply says that both women 'died in Childbed' and does not mention the sonnet.

The poem points to one of the key difficulties in writing Milton's biography. A great deal is known about his life, both about his public roles as a pamphleteer and as an important aide to Oliver Cromwell, and even many details of his private world have been discovered, whether from the few surviving letters or from those early biographies known collectively as the 'Early Lives'. But it is not always easy to connect all this biographical detail with the emotional world behind it. That there was such an emotional world is obvious, not only from this sonnet but from many, many passages throughout the great poems like *Paradise Lost* or *Samson Agonistes*. It is impossible not to connect the blindness of Samson with Milton's own, not to hear Milton's anguish in Samson's cry 'O dark, dark, dark, amid the blaze of noon'. And most readers hear an autobiographical reference when Adam suddenly inserts into a speech bewailing his fate a gratuitous passage about the difficulty of finding a good wife. We need to follow up such passages because the precise connections between Milton's emotional interior and public self are usually lacking. He wrote, or left, no diary. We have to leave behind the world of hard fact and speculate, as in the case of the sonnet, and the biographer must trace out for himself the network of such connections.

If it is the biographer's decision, though one shared with most sensible readers nowadays, to connect that sonnet with Milton's second wife, the choice entails further decisions about how to represent the evidence for Milton's first marriage to Mary Powell. In one of the divorce tracts that he wrote after Mary left him to return to her Royalist parents, Milton argues that, unless divorce is allowed, the blessing of matrimony has changed 'into a familiar and co-habiting mischiefe; at least into a drooping and disconsolate household captivitie, without refuge or redemption'. It is temptng to read this personally, but everything in the divorce tracts takes the form of a general argument: there is nothing explicit about Milton's own marriage. We must also reckon with the power of the imagination to construct a world that the man himself did not know in his own life.

In the same tract Milton represents this unhappy husband as committed to forced labour, since he must 'grind in the mill of an undelighted and servile copulation'.[1] The image of an enslaved man required to perform unwilling sex is clear. Much later Milton applies this language in a more general way to Samson: he complains that he must 'grind in brazen fetters under task'[2] (though this is not a sexual task) and must labour 'Eyeless in Gaza at the mill with slaves' (*SA* 41), and he refuses, almost with an electric charge, to allow his wife, Dalila, to touch him. But in neither case is Milton writing about himself. We must infer the connection, and not all will be happy with the inference. Add to these a third instance of the same language in another early tract – that the 'strumpet flatteries' of those wicked priests of the Church of England seduce the king 'as those Philistins put out the fair, and farre-sighted eyes of his natural discerning, and make him grind in the prison house of their sinister ends and practices'[3] – and we begin to discern a 'grinding' obsession. This latter quotation, with the king as Samson, actually predates Milton's first marriage by a few months. So it is difficult to pin down the precise biographical implications, if obsession there were. The passage also predates his blindness by several years.

There is some evidence, though mostly of this same indirect kind, that Milton saw himself as susceptible to a woman's beauty. According to an early and playful Latin poem, Elegy VII, he was, like Adam in *Paradise Lost*, liable to be 'fondly overcome with female charm' (*PL* IX 999). Perhaps as a result Milton aspired to an altogether unrealistic chastity in his youth. The tensions, both erotic and psychological, generated by this opposition of charm and chastity are evident throughout much of his writing. And this gives me another reason to attach the 'espoused saint' sonnet to his second wife. Unlike Mary Powell, whom Milton married in relative haste soon after they met when she was a girl of seventeen, Milton married his second wife

Katherine after he was blind. The love that grew between them could not thus be dependent on whatever visual appeal she may have had.

So the first Milton I invite my readers to imagine, complicated as he certainly was, is a man for whom what mattered most in daily life, apart from God, was not politics or rhetoric or the church but how men and women find and understand each other. Milton felt that most people in his time had got it wrong. What a man wanted in a wife was a fit companion, 'the copartner of a sweet and gladsome society'; he imagined marriage as a loving conversation. If it turned out that you had made a mistake in choosing your partner, then you should be free to divorce (women too) – a very unpopular idea at the time. He was not immune to the standard reasons for marriage, bodily satisfaction and raising children, but he was a sexual idealist: he felt that true marriage should transcend these physical needs. The Eve Milton imagined for *Paradise Lost*, in some ways a typical male fantasy, has a good deal of erotic appeal: she

> half imbracing leand
> On our first Father, half her swelling Breast
> Naked met his under the flowing Gold
> Of her loose tresses hid. (IV 494-7)

She is also more than capable of understanding Adam and taking an interest in what moves him. Yet Milton's sense of their relationship goes further. He chose to retell the Genesis story by putting the first man and the first woman at the centre, and making it clear they were in love with each other. But, as in most such stories, one of them is more in love than the other. Adam, after all, had asked for a wife, whereas Eve just found herself alive and – at first – alone. She likes what she sees in the lake, her own reflection, and has to be led back to discovering Adam and what he is worth. Milton makes her growing sense of inferiority (inspired by Satan) partly responsible for her disobedience in eating the apple and then giving it to Adam. And later she knows instinctively how to deflect his anger and how to begin the process of trying to reconstruct their love for each other. The Bible story becomes a love story.

The Satan who tempts Eve to her disobedience is easily Milton's most famous and fascinating invention. We'll be spending some time with him later, although I have written another book, *The Satanic Epic*, about how and why he is so important. But there are many other Miltons as well as the poet who invented all these extraordinary characters. If we are to understand him, we need to follow him into the satirical outbursts of his attacks on bishops as well as the eloquence of his defense of liberty. The bishops are those, he claims, 'that spend their youth in loitering, bezzling, and harlotting, their studies in unprofitable questions, and barbarous sophistry, their middle age in ambition and idlenesse, their old age in avarice, dotage, and diseases' (*YP* I 677). This is the Milton who, in the intensity of pamphlet warfare, will not let his opponents' poor grammar pass without comment: 'This tormentor of semi-colons is as good at dismembering and slitting sentences, as his grave Fathers the prelates have bin at stigmatizing & slitting noses' (*YP* I 894). There is another Milton who can write in defense of the liberty of the press, 'as good almost kill a Man as kill a good Book; who kills a Man kills a reasonable creature, Gods Image; but hee who destroyes a good Booke, kills reason it selfe, kills the Image of god, as it were in the eye... a good Book is the pretious life-blood of a master-spirit, imbalm'd and treasur'd up on purpose to a life beyond life'.[4] (Did Milton remember these words later when his own books were publicly burned, and he was imprisoned?)

There is a Milton who not only had the temerity, some say the folly, to put speeches into the mouth of God, but who has God congratulating himself that his Hell-hounds can 'lick up the draff and filth' shed upon the Earth by sin after the Fall, 'Till cramm'd and gorg'd, nigh burst/ With suckt and glutted offal' (*PL* X 630-3) they will, at the end of time, be overthrown and sent back to Hell by the Son. We must always allow for the difference of seventeenth-century culture: Samuel Pepys, who left us a marvellous diary of the time, tells how he went to visit one of the women he most admired, Lady Sandwich, walked in to her drawing room and found her sitting on the chamber pot that she had just received as a present. Nonetheless, in a different version of Christianity it would be indelicate to have God talking in such physical Anglo-Saxon words about filth or offal, but in Milton's it is exactly right.

Whether in verse or prose Milton's language is, to say the least, strong. It is also at times so heart-stoppingly beautiful as to have bedevilled English literature ever since. Listen as Milton imagines for us one of the pagan gods, Hephaestus (Vulcan), thrown out of heaven:

> How he fell
> From Heav'n, they fabl'd, thrown by angry Jove
> Sheer o'er the Chrystal Battlements; from Morn
> To Noon he fell, from Noon to dewy Eve,
> A Summers day; and with the setting Sun
> Dropt from the Zenith like a falling Star,
> On Lemnos the Aegean Ile. (*PL* I 740-46)

If you notice only how Milton arranges the verse to get the word 'Dropt' at the beginning of the line, you will have begun to appreciate what it is that has made poets turn back to him in admiration ever since. You may also notice, perhaps, how lovely a word Lemnos is. There was no need to mention the name of the island here, or even the place where the god fell; it is a gratuitous addition, but it shows how Milton had been enchanted by the sounds of classical languages since he was a young boy.

For all of the points I have just raised Milton has been attacked, both in his own lifetime and in ours. Part of the pleasure of reading him, and reading about him, is the intensity of the passions he arouses, whether positive or negative, and the sheer importance of the issues he wrote about. But it is time now to turn back to the beginning of the story and imagine Milton as that young boy already in love with learning.

1

St Paul's

On July 14, 2008, at 11.45 a.m. a bizarre open-air ceremony took place amid the turmoil and noise of modern London. On one edge of a building site in the city, briefly allowing a splendid view of St Paul's from the back, a small group of locals and other enthusiasts gathered to hear the Lord Mayor of London, resplendent in his red robes, make a short speech and then pull a cord hanging down the side of building in Bread Street. After a couple of unsuccessful tugs, the action eventually unveiled a blue plaque announcing that the poet and statesman John Milton was born here on December 9, 1608. There were a few cheers, and the crowd repaired to the interior of the building next door, owned by the Mitsubishi corporation, for a champagne reception and a few more speeches, including a rather lugubrious reading of two of Milton's sonnets by the poet laureate. The construction workers who had paused at the unusual sight of the Lord Mayor and other dignitaries went back to their tasks. No one mentioned that the date of the ceremony was oddly appropriate, since Milton had an important influence on the French Revolution.

In spite of the sign, screwed in place that very morning, which names as 'John Milton Passage' the short gap in the corporate blocks of modern Bread Street that leads through to St Mary-le-Bow, the London in which these events took place would be unrecognisable to Milton. His London was still a medieval walled town with gates remembered only in modern names like Aldersgate, Ludgate or Newgate. Streets were called after the principal shops gathered there: Threadneedle Street, Fish Street, Bread Street. Even St Paul's cathedral, just around a corner or two from his birthplace, was not the baroque masterpiece of Sir Christopher Wren we know but the crumbling Gothic structure, one of the largest in Europe, that was destroyed in the Great Fire of London in 1666.

Yet even then, according to one of the most useful books to have survived from the early modern period, John Stow's *Survey of London*, the area was 'wholly inhabited by rich merchants'. Milton's family was no exception. His father was a scrivener, which means he was an expert in financial matters – part notary, part contract lawyer, even part money-lender (at high rates, in the era before modern banking). He invested money for others, drew bonds between borrowers and lenders, bought and sold property for himself as well as others and gave depositions in legal cases. The house in Bread Street was called the Spread Eagle because of the sign that hung outside the downstairs shop, the emblem of the Worshipful Company of Scriveners. John Milton describes his father carefully as a man of 'supreme integrity' in one of several autobiographical passages in his works (*YP* IV.1, 612). Yet he does not refer at all to his grandfather, perhaps because he had been a Roman Catholic and paid fines for Recusancy, the offence of refusing to convert to the Church of England. A family story had it that grandfather Milton found his son reading an English Bible, a sign of his conversion to Protestantism, and disinherited him. Thus John Milton senior became that classic figure of the new capitalist and bourgeois world, a self-made man. And he did well at it, even lending money to aristocrats like Sir Fulke Greville or Sir Francis Leigh, nephew of the earl of Bridgewater. He was at work signing documents on the day of his son's birth, though only our modern perspective would find anything surprising in that.

He was also a considerable musician, and appears in collections alongside such composers as Thomas Morley and William Byrd. He provided settings for psalms in Thomas Ravenscroft's popular collection, as did John Tompkins, the organist at St Paul's, and he also had more than a financial interest in theatre: he became a trustee of Blackfriars Playhouse (the indoor theatre for which Shakespeare had written in his last years) in 1620. He passed on his musical passion to his son, who learned to play both the small organ and the bass-viol. There was much singing and music practice as the young John was growing up.

Although he mentions his father often, Milton says of his mother, Sara née Jeffrey, only that she was 'a woman of purest reputation, celebrated throughout the neighbourhood for her acts of charity' (*YP* IV.1, 612). Since he wrote these words, like the remark about his father's 'supreme integrity', in the context of a (Latin) defense of his own virtue against the attacks of his Royalist opponents, they may be taken for what they are worth. She too was a member of the emerging Protestant bourgeoisie, the daughter of a merchant tailor of St Swithin's parish, London. An early biographer, Cyriack Skinner, a pupil of Milton's who knew him well, but not his mother, calls her 'a prudent virtuous Wife'. She 'had very weake eies, & used spectacles' after the age of thirty, whereas the scrivener 'read without spectacles at 84'[1], says

John Aubrey, who collected information about Milton after the famous man's death. Milton's later blindness aligned him in his own mind with Homer and Tieresias, but he does not mention his mother in that connection. He must, nonetheless, have imagined where his own problem came from, having seen his mother reading, or more likely sewing, with some difficulty throughout his childhood.

Three of the six children born to Milton's parents survived infancy; at the time only one child in two made it to the age of five. His older sister, Anne, married a man in the legal profession, Edward Phillips. John himself was born when his father was forty-six and his mother thirty-six. His brother Christopher was a late child, seven years younger, also destined to be a lawyer. He would eventually be knighted near the end of his life.

The church of All Hallows, where Milton was baptised, was just down the road, and he went there regularly as a boy. The minister was Richard Stock, a respected and eloquent puritan – a word to beware of. At the time it meant simply that he wanted to continue the Protestant mission of *purifying* the church from Roman Catholic ceremony and trappings. There was never a separate sect known as Puritans, which is why the word is often written with a lower-case *p*. As we shall see, puritans often quarrelled fiercely among themselves. Stock catechized the local children daily before school and demanded strict observance of the Sabbath and continuous reading of the Bible. Milton retained his anti-Papist views and his dislike of rich, morally lax aristocrats throughout his life, but he would later repudiate the minister's conservative views on marriage, his Sabbatarianism (an insistence on dour Sundays) and his defense of tithes, the practice of paying a tenth of one's income to maintain the church and pay the minister's salary. Indeed, later in his life, Milton did not even attend church. He had learned to question all its teachings to the point that he seems to have regarded himself, some have suggested, as the only true Christian.

Milton probably began learning Latin at the age of seven, the usual age, from various home tutors, including Thomas Young, a Scot of Presbyterian background who gave his pupil a Hebrew Bible, and whom Milton refers to later with gratitude for having introduced him to classical literature. Another of these tutors was perhaps the Patrick Young who was the Prebendary and Treasurer of St Paul's. When the boy was ten, his parents did what well-to-do and doting parents have often done: they had his portrait painted. It now hangs in the Pierpont Morgan Library in New York and shows a serious, attractive boy dressed as the young gentleman his parents' status warranted. His hair is cropped, but he has an embroidered doublet and a rather fancy lace collar. The distinction of Roundhead and Cavalier had not yet come into being.

At some point, probably in 1620, Milton began attending the school attached to the cathedral. So keen was his appetite for literature, he says, that, from the age of twelve at least (that is, in the same year of 1620), he scarcely ever left his 'studies before the hour of midnight' (*YP* IV.1, 612). At the age of twelve, Jesus, in Luke's gospel account, stayed behind in the temple and started talking to the learned 'doctors' (Luke 2.43-47). That may be why Milton chose to remember being twelve as such a significant year in his own life. He admits that these late-night studies were 'the first cause of injury to my eyes, whose natural weakness was augmented by frequent headaches'.

St Paul's school was probably the best in London at the time. It had been founded in 1512 by John Colet, one of the first English humanists, who made it obligatory to teach both classical (as opposed to medieval) Latin and Greek. In Milton's time, the high master was Alexander Gil, a noted scholar who defended the use of reason in religion, and who wrote a grammar of English which illustrates the various tropes of rhetoric by quotations from the poets, referring to Spenser as 'our Homer' or to Philip Sidney as 'our Anacreon'; his son, also Alexander, a junior teacher or usher, became a long-standing friend of Milton's. The younger Gil was himself a poet, and – a sign of the times – wrote a Latin poem in 1623 in celebration of the collapse of a chapel in Blackfriars which killed ninety Roman Catholics. The poem imagines the deaths as revenge for the attempted murder of the king and destruction of Parliament on 5 November 1605, and suggests that it is providential that the date would have been the same in the new Gregorian calendar which was being used in Catholic countries (though not adopted in Britain till 1756). Milton himself would write a poem on the Gunpowder Plot in which he depicts the pope as an agent of Satan thwarted by Providence. And in one of his last poems, he imagines the massacre of the Philistines by Samson as he pulls down the temple around them. These were not peaceful times.

The closest friend Milton made at St Paul's was Charles Diodati, the son of a wealthy Protestant family in voluntary exile from Italy. His uncle, whom Milton later visited, was a distinguished scholar in Calvinist Geneva and the first translator of the Bible into Italian. Charles was an even more precocious scholar than the young Milton, and went off to Oxford at age thirteen. The curriculum they both followed included the major classical authors; the pupils had to write imitations of each. They would have started with Aesop and Caesar in prose and Terence and Ovid in verse. Quite soon they would have composed a letter, like Cicero, or translated a satire of George Wither's, say, into Juvenalian Latin (something ridiculed by the learned playwright Ben Jonson but a useful exercise for mastering various styles). Greek soon followed, including first the New Testament and then

Homer, Hesiod and Pindar, as well as Plutarch's *Moralia* and Demosthenes. Milton quickly became good at double translation exercises, that is, turning Greek into Latin or vice versa. He also learned to read Hebrew, as well as French and Italian.

Two of his early school exercises survive in a manuscript page found in 1874. They include a brief poem, 'Ignavus satrapam', which is based on an episode in the *Aeneid* in which two young friends or lovers, Nisus and Euryalus, slaughter the Rutulians in their sleep (IX 314-449). The episode is famous for its pathos, since Euryalus is killed as he escapes, dying, in a famous simile, like a poppy cut down by a plough (IX 435-6), while Nisus, blind with grief, rushes into the fray and is killed himself. We shall see Milton's fascination with mass slaughter again, and also the intensity of his feeling for a friend. Milton was heart-broken when he heard of Charles Diodati's early death. But this juvenile eight-line poem focuses simply on the fact that the leader of the Italian forces, Turnus, was asleep during the attack, and advises the reader (himself?) to learn from the episode. The other poem in the manuscript (now at the University of Texas in Austin) also celebrates the virtue of getting up early, a virtue Milton would practice throughout his life.

When he looked back on this first period of his education, Milton chose to emphasize his immunity to all the sex in his reading. Whether in fables and romance, or in erotic poets like Ovid or Propertius, Milton claims to have found only 'what a noble virtue chastity must be'. It is what true knights are sworn to protect. The body is sacred to the Lord, he says, and so, 'if unchastity in a woman whom Saint Paul termes the glory of man, be such a scandal and dishonour, then certainly in a man who is both the image and glory of God, it must, though commonly not so thought, be much more deflouring and dishonourable' (*YP* I 892). Such feelings are common enough in early adolescence, and in Milton's case the link with the passage in Paul's first Letter to the Corinthians – 'For the man is not of the woman; but the woman of the man' – would be a constant point of reference all his life as a way of accounting for differences between men and women (I Corinthians 11:8). He was aware of the double standard, and inclined to invert it.

Milton's earliest English poems are psalm paraphrases, obviously written under his father's influence, and one of them will be familiar to anyone with even the slightest Christian upbringing. It converts the words of Psalm 136, 'O give thanks unto the Lord, for he is good, for his mercy endureth forever', into

> Let us with a gladsome mind
> Praise the Lord for he is kind.

> For his mercies aye endure,
> Ever faithful, ever sure.

The chief example of God's goodness in that psalm is the Exodus, the story of deliverance from the Egyptian Pharaoh and arrival in the Promised Land. In the Jewish context the legend is the founding myth of Israel, and in Christianity it had long been an example of redemption. The other paraphrase is of Psalm 114, also a reference to the escape of the sons of Abraham from Egypt and across the Jordan, which stresses the power of God over 'the troubled sea' and 'Jordan's clear streams'. These themes are common in the psalms, where the struggle of God with mighty waters of various kinds is an Old Testament vestige of the ancient combat myth as well as allusion to the history of Israel, and such ideas recur regularly in Milton's mature poetry. But here, as the headnote says, when he published the poems in his first collection, they 'were done by the author at fifteen years old'. Some ten years later he translated the same psalm into Greek verse and sent it to Alexander Gil, saying that it was the first poem he had written in Greek since leaving school.

2

Cambridge

Milton was disappointed by Cambridge University. He went there intending to become a minister of the church, but in his writings from those years he refers to himself only as a scholar or poet, never as preparing for ordination. It is true that the established church was in trouble, riven by the royal insistence on High Anglican ritual, and these troubles were then exacerbated by the rise of the controversial and unpopular bishop William Laud. Milton would soon have a great deal to say about church governance. Whether or not (or when) these troubles put him off a career in the cloth, he turned more and more towards what he soon came to see as his real vocation – poetry. Most of it is in Latin, the language students were supposed to speak to each other and to their tutors (if not Greek, or Hebrew), at least during formal instruction. He also composed various speeches, normal university assignments, which would teach him how to write polemical prose.

Milton registered at Christ's College, Cambridge on 12 February 1625, though he was probably already in residence. He was sixteen, not an unusual age for college entry at the time. Like others from middle-class families he paid £50 per year. The college is sometimes said to have had a Reformist tradition, and Richard Stock, his parish priest from All Hallows, was a graduate, but in the 1620s it was caught up in the growing conflicts between Laudians and the more strongly Calvinist and puritan tendencies.

Soon after Milton's admission to the college, James I died, on 27 March, to be succeeded by his son Charles I. In a way, this man was to be as important as any other in Milton's life. But for now there were other more immediate preoccupations. The summer of that year, 1625, saw a bad outbreak of plague in which as many as a sixth of the population of London died. Milton probably stayed in Cambridge during that first summer, but when the plague hit the university too, he went back to London.

When he returned to Cambridge for his second year, the university was soon embroiled in a contest over elections for the new chancellor. The

House of Commons wanted one man, Thomas Howard, earl of Berkshire, but the king backed his favourite, the duke of Buckingham. ('Favourite' was sometimes a euphemism for homosexual lover, and there were indeed rumours to that effect.) The Master of Christ's went for Buckingham, but the Fellows were divided. Eventually, amid accusations of vote-rigging and with many abstentions, a slight majority of the university electors went for Buckingham. This was merely one among a series of issues that separated Calvinists and the ceremonially inclined Laudians, who believed that the power of the liturgy could stimulate the congruence of God's grace and man's free will that was at the heart of high-church Arminian theology[1].

We have no evidence to show that Milton involved himself in these matters, but noticeably absent from all his writing in these years is any poem or discourse celebrating any of the many royal or courtly events that attracted other university poets; nothing on the births and deaths of royal children, the coronation of Charles, or even his visit or Buckingham's to Cambridge. But Milton did write a Latin elegy for the bishop of Ely (d. 6 October 1626) who had spoken at Cambridge in support of Berkshire against Buckingham.

The continuing plague in England coincided with disasters in the military campaigns on the Continent. Breda in the Netherlands fell to the Spanish General Spinola in June after a siege of eleven months. In the poem Milton soon wrote (Elegy III) for the death of the bishop of Winchester, Launcelot Andrewes (d. 25 September 1626), he represents Libitina, goddess of corpses, as encamped throughout England, even in the palaces of the nobility, and links the plague with the military situation. He appears to lament the death of Ernst von Mansfeld (d. 29 November 1626), whose troops, many of them English, had failed to relieve the siege of Breda. Mansfeld had visited London and been cheered as a hero by the people. Milton would later criticize Andrewes for his high-church defense of the role of bishops (*YP* I 768-74), but for the moment at least this poem shows no more than that Milton was taking a keen, and Protestant, interest in the politics of the international situation.

At almost exactly the same time, Milton wrote his longest Latin poem to date, 'In quintum Novembris', an oddly truncated mixture of heroic poetry (in 226 hexameters) and mockery of the attempt of a group of Roman Catholic nobles on 5 November 1605, to blow up the king and the Houses of Parliament. The poem was probably occasioned by what had become the standard and enforced celebration of Guy Fawkes Day, but it has also been read as a covert call to more militant Protestant action following the disasters he refers to in the elegy for Launcelot Andrewes. The poem contains the first of Milton's portrayals of Satan.

If these are signs of a growing sympathy on Milton's part for the international Protestant cause, it may have been under the influence of Joseph Mede, a distinguished fellow of Christ's from 1613 till his death in 1639, who worked out a series of correspondences between the biblical apocalypse and contemporary history. Mede was in close touch with that wider European world, and his scholarship served to legitimate the millenarianism that was common among puritans. He was also an opponent of Laud. Unfortunately there is no record of a contact with Milton, though as Milton grew older he belonged to intellectual circles which overlapped with Mede.

Milton did maintain contact with a former tutor, Thomas Young. He wrote a Latin verse letter (*Elegy* IV) to Young, who in 1627 was now in voluntary exile in Hamburg because of his Presbyterian views. Milton imagines him living in poverty and loneliness, surrounded by the horrid noise of what we know as the Thirty Years War (1618–48). He addresses his own country, England, as a hard-hearted parent exposing its innocent children to danger. He urges Young to live in hope, to triumph over his misfortunes.

Milton was still a young man, looking about him. Another of his Latin poems from this time, *Elegy* VII, is far away from all this conflict both in subject and in tone. It is about an amorous adventure in London. The poem is playfully Ovidian, but I think some real-life experience lies behind it. Indeed Milton was probably in London twice in the spring of 1627 to sign legal documents with his father in order to secure his finances. The poem's speaker resists Cupid's darts at first; indeed, he almost seems to challenge Cupid by walking wild and free in London. But then he sees a beautiful girl out for a stroll among a crowd – 'in such a form Venus herself might choose to appear' (63) – and Cupid makes him fall for her at first sight of her eyelashes, her lips, her cheek. 'I burned inwardly with love: my whole being was aflame' (74). The girl disappears, and the speaker is unsure whether to seek release from the pain or to bask in his delicious misery. 'Only be gracious enough to grant,' he begs Cupid at the end, 'if any maiden is ever to be mine in the future, that one arrow may pierce us both, making us lovers' (101-2). The poem is in Latin, and is full of literary allusions. Latin was a way to write up fantasies that could not be explored in English. But the poem presents the speaker ('ego') as a naive young man who cannot stop himself looking at the girls and meeting their eyes – a credible image of Milton at this age. Granted that, once he sees the young woman, he compares himself to the god Vulcan, thrown out of heaven for his passion (an image that recurs years later in *Paradise Lost* I 740-46). And granted that the sudden sight of the beloved echoes Dante and Petrarch. But it is not, I hope, only the biographer's hunger for the inner life of his subject that leads me (and many others) to find a potentially amorous Milton in the young *flâneur* of this poem.

Though he was clearly a successful and extraordinary student, Milton was rarely happy at Cambridge. He had a problem with his first tutor, William Chappell. The man seems to have been a popular teacher, but soon, perhaps as early as Milton's first year, more likely at this time, the spring of 1627, a serious difference arose between them and Milton was rusticated, that is, sent home for a time. That would explain why he was able to be in London in May and June in order to sign those documents with his father.[2] Exactly what happened we do not know. It is possible that Milton was disappointed academically by Cambridge since his school, St Paul's, had been so good a place to learn, and his irritation got the better of him. It may have been a theological dispute, since Chappell was, like Laud, a follower of Arminius and thus a believer in limited free will. At this time Milton was still a strongly Calvinist predestinarian. Such a conflict would also, and necessarily for the times, be political. In his notes an early biographer, John Aubrey, even says that Chappell 'whip't him'. The words are inserted above the line, perhaps because this was an item Aubrey picked up later from a different source than Milton's brother Christopher, from whom he is recording information at this point. It would have been unusual for a student, to be whipped like a schoolboy, so the story may have been untrue. But clearly something serious had happened, and when he returned Milton was, exceptionally, allowed to change tutors; his new tutor was Nathaniel Tovey. (Tovey later became Christopher's tutor also.)

During his rustication, Milton probably wrote a charming Latin poem (Elegy I) to his friend from St Paul's, Charles Diodati, in which he mentions the threats of a stern tutor and his delight at being back in London among his books. He is able to go to the theatre (apparently entirely classical theatre, that is, Greek or Roman – a sign of Milton's St Paul's- or Cambridge-induced cultural snobbery) when he is tired, or to look at pretty girls, and to take walks in the country. On the basis of no evidence whatever, but with many classical references, he says that English women are the most beautiful in the world, contrasting them with what he does know well, descriptions in the texts of Latin poets. The poem ends abruptly, though with no apparent irony, because the writer suddenly has to return to Cambridge, just as Odysseus has to leave Circe and move on, with the help of the mysterious plant 'moly'. For William Riley Parker this is the most amusing part of the poem, though unintentionally so. Milton struggles to find a transition but knows he must end quickly and send the poem off: 'irony is occasionally lost on youth, and a poem composed is a poem composed. We can be glad that he did not destroy this intimate revelation, for it is a pleasant reminder in Latin elegiacs that Milton was once seventeen.'³ And with all that, the poem poses a characteristic puzzle to the biographer: all these 'beautiful, golden maids who shine' through London streets, are they what Milton saw and desired in his free periods from Cambridge discipline, or are they what his extensive reading in the classical poets invited him to imagine? Almost certainly both.

Whether or not he had to produce poems like these for his tutors, Milton also had to produce prose exercises for various university assignments. He preserved some of these, and eventually published them near the end of his life. They are known as *Prolusions*, and are either disputations upholding one side of a position in a debate or are logical declamations. One, the longest, Prolusion VI, is in part a parody of all such discourses. It may not be easy to think of Milton, even in his student years, as a licensed jester or stand-up comedian, but that is John K. Hale's description of his role as entertainer in a Christ's College 'salting', an elaborate initiation rite which was the occasion for this Prolusion, delivered at the beginning of the long vacation of 1628.⁴ He played the 'Father' or master of ceremonies, aping the role and regalia of the college tutors, during a feast of misrule that inducted freshmen into their second year of studies. Salt would be added to a fresher's beer if his performance were judged inadequate (and so needing more *sales*, Latin for wit). The text contains endless puns on salt (*salire*, to leap, *saltare*, to dance), as well as language that has embarrassed some of Milton's editors, and which Phyllis Tillyard left untranslated in her 1932 edition. Milton suggests, for example, that one member of his audience may refrain from laughing because he has stuffed his belly too full at the feast and may express some gastric riddle not from his Sphinx but his sphincter. The Latin speech also included the English poem, 'At A Vacation Exercise', that Milton later cut out and printed separately. Read in this context, the famous opening words of the poem take on another, perhaps lesser, meaning. 'Hail native Language, that by sinews weak/ Didst move my first endeavouring tongue to speak' are not the student poet's first tentative foray, but simply signal the switch from Latin prose to English verse. His stated wish to write on 'some graver subject' (30) is also less resonant, since it may encompass just about everything after that sphincter.

At one point in this merry performance, Milton refers to an earlier oration which he had thought would provoke his fellow students to dislike him. This was probably Prolusion I, in which it was Milton's job to argue for Day in the debate over 'Whether Day or Night is the Most Excellent'. He there insults anyone who would oppose him in this kind of exercise without the proper learning since they soon run out of things to say, 'as dumb as the frogs of Seriphus'. Elsewhere he also compares such people to Shakespeare's foolish Trinculo in *The Tempest* (YP I 887). We can see why Milton thought his audience might be hostile to this kind of treatment, but it turns out that they rather enjoyed his wit, or so Prolusion VI implies. This speech is the occasion for much juvenile joking, playing on the names of college officials and students and poking fun at the students' sexual urges to play the 'father' in Cambridge town. In the same breath he refers to his own role as 'Father' for the occasion, and jokes about the change from his habitual nickname of 'The Lady of Christ's' – the first reference to this sobriquet, which recalls, he claims, what the people called Virgil. He gamely rejects the gender assumptions which that name implies: to be a man he does not have to drink great bumpers of wine like a prize-fighter, or show a horny hand from ploughing or visit brothels. Evidently he had been hurt by the nickname, and is stung to a characteristically thoughtful and aggressive reply. He ends the speech, curiously and significantly, by reminding his audience of the failure of an English naval expedition to rescue the Huguenots, French Protestants, besieged in La Rochelle in October 1627: the commander of that fleet had been the new university chancellor, Buckingham.

Also in July 1628, Milton wrote to his old friend from St Paul's, Alexander Gil, that he had been invited by the college fellows to supply comic verses for the graduation ceremony. These poems were probably earlier versions of what we know as 'Naturam non senium pati' and 'De Idea Platonica'. In the one Milton aligns himself with the forward-looking world of science, opposing the idea that Nature is growing old and decaying, and in the other Milton, as feisty student satirist, attacks the Plato whom he later claims to admire.

This same Alexander Gil was soon in deep trouble. Buckingham, the king's favourite, whom Milton had just impugned, had become so unpopular that he was assassinated on 23 August. Gil toasted the event and wrote some ill-judged verses calling him the king's Ganymede. This reference to the beautiful youth snatched by Zeus to live on Olympus was bad enough, but he also called the king and his son Charles 'the old fool and the young one'. The Star Chamber soon sentenced him to be defrocked and to have his ears cut off. Gil's father, Milton's old headmaster at St Paul's, managed to get the mutilation remitted, but Gil stayed over two years in prison.

In spite of his speechifying fun, Milton was no happier with the tasks assigned students at Cambridge. In Prolusion III he directly attacks the sterile scholasticism of the authorities with their constant admiration for Aristotle, and now expects his fellow students (not insulted this time) to share his boredom. Instead of working in tormented anxiety over unreal problems the students should be following the muses and studying serious subjects: history, geography, science, moral philosophy. The university was the first of many institutions that Milton attacked in his life: its scholastic (that is, medieval, and therefore old-fashioned) methods produced crabbed and ignorant politicians and ministers of the church. He thought that the church was so badly governed because of what the gentry, who supported the status quo, had learned at university. The 'monkish and miserable sophistry' of that education incapacitated them for 'all true and generous philosophy', as he wrote later in 1642 in *The Reason of Church Government* (*YP* I 854). In the treatise *Of Education* of 1644 he charged the universities with bringing students to a 'hatred and contempt of learning', and making people who could not think for themselves susceptible to tyranny.

Milton was awarded his Bachelor's degree on 29 March 1629, and continued on towards his Master of Arts degree from 1629 to 1632. He was automatically required to sign three Articles of Religion, and registered no objection: the king is the head of the church, the Book of Common Prayer is the lawful liturgical text, and the Thirty-Nine Articles, which had defined the Church of England since the Elizabethan compromise, contained nothing contrary to the word of God. A few years later, Milton could not have agreed to any of those propositions. Unless he signed with his fingers crossed, it does not look as if he was yet committed to the puritan cause[5].

Most probably in April 1629 he wrote Elegy V, 'On The Approach of Spring', the most sensual and creative of his Ovidian poems. The earth 'voluptuously bares her all-sustaining breasts, breathes out the perfumes of Arabian harvests and pours sweet spices and scent of Paphian roses from her lovely lips' (57-60). A little later, the 'lascivious Earth sighs out her passionate longing, and the throng of creatures rush to follow the Mother's example' (95-6). Amid all the frolic, 'Lustful Faunus seizes one of the Oreads, while the Nymph seeks safety on trembling feet. Now she hides, but hiding, ill-concealed, she wishes to be seen; she flees, but fleeing yearns to be caught' (127-30). There is more in the same vein. And Milton's Muse is awakened to 'madness and sacred ecstasy': he will sing like a nightingale. He also celebrates the nightingale in what he later published as his first English sonnet, switching from Ovidian to Petrarchan terms and defining himself as both lover and poet.

On 9 December 1629 Milton turned twenty-one. Perhaps it was to celebrate this, or his graduation with a BA earlier that year, that the so-called Onslow portrait was painted. The original has been lost since the eighteenth century, but a copy is in the National Portrait Gallery in London. The portrait is said to have come from Milton's widow, who had returned to her native Cheshire after his death, and kept it 'in her chamber till her death'. She told her executor that 'her husband gave it to her to show her what he was in his youth when he was about 21 years of age.' It shows an attractive, serious, and rather wistful young man, one, we know, who was already something of a poet.

3

Early Signs of Genius

At the time of his twenty-first birthday, Milton was in London and bought an Italian book, mostly sonnets, by Giovanni della Casa. He also received a letter from his friend Charles Diodati to which he replied with the urbane Elegy VI, which was both playful and serious in tone. Evidently Diodati, wintering in Cheshire, complained (probably in Greek as usual) that because of all the festivities he was unable to write decent poetry. In his reply Milton celebrates the power of wine and feasting to inspire the creative urge. Diodati need not worry about his Christmas merriment if he wants to write merely light elegy (like this poem itself). It is the epic poet who sings of wars and heaven or hell and its dog Cerberus, who must live frugally. This is an interesting hint about how the future author of *Paradise Lost* conceived of the poet's life – but in case we might take such hints too seriously ('the poet is sacred to the gods, he is their priest', 77), it is also worth noting that the savage dog of hell is there because Milton, as often, cannot resist a pun: in Latin *canis* means dog, and the poet sings, *canit*. Nonetheless Milton offers himself as instance of this kind of poet, and introduces parallels that will always haunt him: he is Pythagoras drinking water as purified priest for a ritual, he is the blind Tiresias, Orpheus grown old, Homer bringing Odysseus over the wide seas. The poem ends by describing his own 'Ode on the Morning of Christ's Nativity' as a mixture of the epic and pastoral modes.

That poem, Milton's first major achievement, he had written for Christmas Day of 1629. It adapts the Virgilian idea of a new golden age in his famous fourth eclogue to that which truly heralds a new millennium. Just as the infant Hercules strangled Typhon in his cradle, so the divine child ends the reign of the old dragon. By witty conceit, marking an idea that became common in Milton's poetry, two ages are made to overlap: 'Time will run back, and fetch the age of gold.' When Milton published the poem in his collection of 1645, he placed it first, as if it were a dedication; the muse must hasten to present the ode, even the whole book, to the new Christ before the magi come with their own gifts. Beside the title, Milton placed the words 'Composed 1629'. Since this was the year, indeed the month, when Milton turned twenty-one, the poem thus relates the birth of Christ to the poet's own coming of age. Modesty was never Milton's strong suit. A long catalogue of pagan gods expelled from their shrines has been thought to register a certain puritan anxiety at the increasing influence of Laud and his Popish practices over the English Church, but there is some doubt whether Milton had yet developed any serious antagonism to Laud.

During the spring of the next year, 1630, plague closed the university and Milton probably lived back in London. A newer and more light-hearted mood produced an Elizabethan-style lyric song, 'On May Morning', and then a sequence of Petrarchan poems, sonnets and a brief canzone, all but the first in Italian. Clearly, Milton is experimenting with poetic form. One of the sonnets plays with the fact that rhyming in Italian is so much easier than in English: the eight words of the octave use two rhymes all ending in '-a', the six of the sestet in '-o'. Three of these Italian sonnets use the final rhyming couplet characteristic of the English or Shakespearean rather than the Petrarchan structure. Another sonnet is addressed to Diodati, and the whole set implies a graceful and amorous compliment to a kinswoman of his, apparently a certain Emilia, to whom Milton may have been attracted. This dark foreign beauty contrasts with the earlier English girls celebrated at a distance in the Elegies. But no one really knows who these young women were, and they may have been largely a poet's necessary fantasies. The main audience for the poems is after all Milton's beloved friend Diodati.

The first poem Milton actually published was probably written at this time. Milton dates it to 1630, but that is an approximate date, probably a year early. (He tends to predate his work throughout his life.) The poem appeared in the Second Folio of Shakespeare's plays in 1632. It is not obvious why the as yet unknown Milton should have been asked to write something for this volume. The connection may have been through his father, as trustee of Blackfriars' theatre, and it has even been argued that the otherwise unknown 'I. M.' whose poem appears in the First Folio was Milton senior. This poem shows great respect, as the context requires, for Shakespeare, but also a certain need to establish distance, for this newly arriving poet to carve out some space for himself.

> What needs my Shakespeare for his honour'd Bones,
> The labour of an age in piled Stones,
> Or that his hallow'd reliques should be hid
> Under a Star-ypointed Pyramid?
> Dear Sonne of Memorie, great heir of Fame,

What need'st thou such dull witnes of thy name?
Thou in our wonder and astonishment
Hast built thy self a lasting Monument.
For whilst to th' shame of slow-endeavouring art,
Thy easie numbers flow, and that each part
Hath from the leaves of thy unvalu'd Book,
Those Delphick lines with deep impression took,
Then thou our fancy of her selfe bereaving,
Dost make us Marble with too much conceaving;
And so Sepulcher'd in such pomp dost lie,
That Kings for such a Tomb would wish to die.

The dominating idea is that Shakespeare needs no stone monument, since his works are his best monument, that is, this very book, the Second Folio. The poem contrasts two ways of writing: one is Shakespeare's, in which 'easie numbers flow' (*numbers* are metrical verses); and this puts the other, 'slow-endeavouring art', to shame. There is perhaps a hint of rivalry, or envy, if Milton is thinking of his own slowness at producing poetry. And though the poem mentions our 'wonder and astonishment', it goes on to imply that too much respect for Shakespeare can petrify you, or turn you to 'Marble with too much conceaving'. Thus the word 'astonishment' carries a buried meaning. It appears that the poem had a model in another epitaph that circulated at the time in manuscript and was even attributed to Shakespeare – so Milton started his published career by adapting a poem he may have thought of as Shakespeare's.[1]

There is another admiring reference to Shakespeare in the delightful poem 'L'Allegro', probably written during a further restful summer the next year, 1631, in Hammersmith, where his father had moved. Milton makes a contrast of Jonson and Shakespeare similar to the one in the Second Folio poem, and it became integral thereafter to the English way of approaching Shakespeare. While Jonson wears a 'learned Sock', a reference to the standard footwear of actors in classical drama, we can hear

Sweetest Shakespear, fancies childe
Warble his native Wood-notes wilde. (133-4)

Whereas Jonson is learned in classical texts, takes those authorities seriously and often expects his audiences to respect the allusions, Shakespeare is seen as a 'natural', someone who 'with small Latin and less Greek' (as Jonson said in his own poem on Shakespeare, reappearing alongside Milton's in the Second Folio), simply creates his wonderful works as if from nothing, or from 'nature' (whatever that complex word signifies), like a bird singing. There is love here, in Milton's attitude, but also, once again, a certain distancing of himself. Milton, we might say, was already more like Jonson, a learned bird. Though there are many obvious allusions to and imitations of Shakespeare at certain moments in his later work, Milton quickly moved on beyond this early influence and became a very different poet.

'L'Allegro' is actually one of two poems; it is answered by an equally brilliant companion piece, 'Il Penseroso'. They are the best possible answer to all that disputation at Cambridge in which Milton had been required to take one side or the other in a debate. They are dramatic monologues invoking certain opposing character types. The second, spoken by a contemplative, even reclusive, man answers the youthfully gregarious persona of the first. It is 'mirth' versus 'melancholy'. Each offers a fantasy of an ideal, 'such sights as youthful poets dream', represented as a kind of day-in-the-life. L'Allegro begins his day as he hears the lark from his bed. He comes to the window and greets the sun as the distant cocks crow, then goes walking while ploughmen whistle and milkmaids sing. His eyes play on a fantasy of romantic castles at secluded heights, while in a nearby shepherd's cottage, as in pastoral fiction, Corydon and Thyrsis eat vegetarian meals served by Phyllis. After haymaking the young and old listen to fairy tales together. Or perhaps in the city of high romance with knights and jousts and ladies, the talk is all of feasts and marriages. Finally to the theatre, to that comedy of Shakespeare or Jonson.

All this is spoken in a marvellously subtle four-beat iambic metre, eight-syllable lines often alternating with seven-syllable lines to produce trochaic variation (which means that the stress often falls on the first syllable of the line). The more serious 'Il Penseroso' has more purely iambic lines, while there are twice as many trochees, as befits their common effect in English, in the lighter poem, 'L'Allegro':

> Haste thee nymph, and bring with thee
> Just and youthful Jollity,
> Quips and Cranks, and wanton Wiles,
> Nods and Becks, and Wreathed Smiles...
> Com, and trip it as you go
> On the light fantastick toe. (25-34)

The mood is that of *A Midsummer Night's Dream*, or Ariel in *The Tempest*. Il Penseroso, on the other hand, the Melancholy man, prefers to go to a tragedy. He seeks no company, and prefers to walk alone at night or a morning after rain. He stays up late reading, or letting the mind fly upwards to metaphysical heights. His favourite places are dimly lit churches, perhaps like the great cathedral near Milton's London home that he knew so well, or the magnificent 'chapels' of some Cambridge colleges such as King's,

>   – storied Windows richly dight,
>   Casting a dimm religious light.
>   There let the pealing Organ blow
>   To the full voic'd Quire below
>   In Service high, and Anthems cleer,
>   As may with sweetnes, through mine ear,
>   Dissolve me into extasies,
>   And bring all Heav'n before mine eyes. (159-66)

He loves these studious cloisters, and, with a charming and lightly ironic smile at Milton's own aspirations, counts on finding in his old age

>   some peacefull hermitage,
>   The Hairy Gown and Mossy Cell,
>   Where I may sit and tightly spell
>   Of every Star that Heav'n doth shew,
>   And every Herb that sips the dew;
>   Till old experience do attain
>   To something like Prophetic strain.

Milton will indeed attain that prophetic strain, but we should not miss the odd juxtaposition of monkish cell and an interest in the rapidly advancing sciences of astronomy and botany.

The titles of the poems are Italian, and may imply a similar audience to that of the Italian sonnets, his accomplished friend Charles Diodati. The playful contrast is similar to that of the elegiac and epic poets in the Latin Elegy VI, also addressed to Diodati, but we need not imagine that the cheerful and serious characters are similarly divided between the two poets: both are clearly Milton. His next poem proves it.

On New Year's Day of 1631, Thomas Hobson, the man who had driven generations of Cambridge students to London and back died. He was in his eighties. Several university wits, Milton included, wrote affectionate poems for this man, who had built up a successful business. The phrase 'Hobson's choice' refers to his habit of telling students that they could choose any horse so long as it was the one by the stable door. These light-hearted verses yet contain a pleasant description of mortality:

[Death] lately finding him so long at home,
And thinking now his journeys end was come,
And that he had tane up his latest Inne,
In the kind office of a Chamberlin
Shew'd him his room where he must lodge that night,
Pull'd off his boots, and took away the light.
If any ask for him, it shall be sed,
Hobson has supt and's newly gone to bed.

Milton, or his readers, enjoyed this so much that he even wrote another poem for Hobson. Milton's career was launched. A few months later he wrote a more serious memorial poem for Jane Savage, marchioness of Winchester – apparently as a poetic exercise, since he seems not to have known her. She, like Hobson, was mourned by others as well. And Milton willingly joined in these occasions for trying out his abilities.

In 1632, his final year at Cambridge, Milton fulfilled the residence requirements for his Master's degree. Probably Prolusion VII, the most elaborate of the speeches, was the requisite oration. It makes the proposition that 'Learning brings more Blessings to Men than Ignorance'. Milton presents himself not as a prospective clergyman, a career he may already have privately renounced, but as a scholar and poet. Combining the two personae of L'Allegro and Il Penseroso, the speech wittily celebrates his summer memories of green fields and meditative walks. Once again he denounces the university, including the constant interruptions to study like the present occasion, and praises the newer kinds of learning, especially history and natural science – the true rewards of study. The speech is indebted to Bacon's well-known 'Advancement of Learning' for its rejection of scholastic logic and its praise of the value of education both to the individual and to the state. Love of learning, he also says, tends to produce solitary men uneasy with social life. Yet for such people (and he is surely thinking of himself), even if totally absorbed in study, it is possible to form one or two strong friendships with other wise and learned men. Exactly whom he has in mind is uncertain, since we know of no special friend he made at Cambridge (Diodati had gone to Oxford). Even Edward King, for whom he would soon write 'Lycidas', was apparently not a close friend. Perhaps the reference is to be taken by his audience as a general compliment, or even a buried reproach. After all, the only example he gives of this kind of friendship is a dialogue of 'the divine Plato', in which Socrates and Phaedrus converse 'in the shade of that famous plane-tree' – and the subject of which is love. Does he imply he found no such love here?

This farewell to Cambridge imagines a very different life for the man of learning from what he had known there. He can live through his books in all periods and places. He can grow 'to be the oracle of many nations, to find one's home regarded as a kind of temple, to be a man whom kings and states invite to come to them, whom men from near and far flock to visit, while to others it is a matter of pride if they have but set eyes on him once' (*YP* I 297). Much later, such a life would indeed be Milton's.

4

Studious Retirement

After he graduated with his MA from Cambridge in July 1632, Milton went to live with his parents in Hammersmith, at the time a pleasant village six miles up the Thames from London. Milton's family had moved here in 1631, and his father became a churchwarden by May 1633 at the new 'chapel of ease', which had been consecrated (on 7 June 1631) by that same Bishop Laud who was provoking all the trouble within the established church. The documents that establish this were found only in 1996 in the Hammersmith and Fulham Record Office, and dispose of any lingering sense that Milton senior had puritan leanings, whatever his son may have felt by now. Some three to four years later (by May 1636 at the latest), the family moved further out, to the village of Horton on the Buckinghamshire–Berkshire border, perhaps because of yet another outbreak of the plague. No one yet knew that plague was carried by fleas on rats; it was thought to be the result of bad-smelling city air, or miasma.

On or around his twenty-fourth birthday on 9 December 1632 Milton wrote another Petrarchan sonnet, VII. It is strictly Petrarchan in form ('in strictest measure even', 10) but hardly in subject. It is not about love but a kind of psychological crisis: 'How soon hath time the subtle thief of youth / Stolen on his wing my three and twentieth year.' Milton is twenty-four and has not begun his real working life. All he can do is hope, as the sestet proposes, that Time and the will of heaven are leading him toward something, and something that is even now seen 'in my great task-master's eye'. Nothing Milton wrote shows quite so clearly the anxiety induced by the need to serve this puritan God, who here sounds like Orwell's Big Brother. Milton included the poem in a letter to a friend, probably Thomas Young, who had criticized his delay in taking holy orders – something he could now do, having passed twenty-four years of age. The carefully drafted letter survives in two different manuscript versions, suggesting that he had some trouble in formulating what he wanted to say. He again admits to his doubts about his 'tardie moving', and knows he is 'unserviceable to mankind' in this 'affected solitarinesse', and confesses to feeling dissatisfied. He too would like to have a family and 'immortall fame'.

There is an especially revealing moment in this letter when Milton refers to the parable of the vineyard. In Matthew 20:1–16, the master of the vineyard contracts with workers in the morning for a day's labour, but then hires more workers through the day, even at the eleventh hour. At the end of the day he pays them all the same, which is regarded as unfair by those who 'have borne the burden and the heat of the day'. Jesus seems to interpret the parable as a rebuke to those who expect more from God's grace than others. Indeed, the text concludes by reiterating the saying that 'the last shall be first, and the first last; for many are called but few are chosen'. Milton, however, interprets the parable to justify his delay, as if it is somehow better to wait till the eleventh hour. In this way he overcomes the accusation implied in another important parable, that he has hidden his talent. The man who does that, in Matthew 25:30, is 'the unprofitable servant', and he is 'cast into outer darkness: there shall be weeping and gnashing of teeth'. These ideas nagged at Milton, and he returned to them later, after his blindness.

Yet Milton was obviously in no hurry to take up the profession for which he had supposedly been preparing, the ministry, and he would soon have to negotiate seriously with his father about this. He preferred to live at leisure, and to prepare for the life of a poet, as he tried to explain in a Latin poem, 'Ad Patrem', that must have been written during these years (1632 or 1633). How quickly this became his settled goal we do not know exactly, but a marvellous and short religious ode perhaps written soon after the sonnet on Time, entitled 'At a Solemn Music' (that is, a sacred concert), shows him celebrating the relation of music and poetry in something like his mature lyric style. We might, he imagines, answer the singing Saints before God's throne with a song, perhaps even this one, which restores the harmony lost through sin. This idea about the mystic importance of music recurs in later poems.

Milton's father seems to have been a generous and understanding man. But in the psyche of a son, the father may well be hostile, tyrannical and indifferent. 'Ad Patrem' is direct evidence for Milton's feelings about his father, although since it is addressed to him, and given, it is unlikely to reveal much of the darker side of the relationship. But it shows quite a lot. The poem is a kind of protest, and it looks as if Milton senior had been insisting on some decision, one which would lead his son away from poetry. The son jollies him along: he can't be serious when he claims to despise the Muses, since he has learned his musical skills from them. Milton senior has not forced him into business or the law, but has encouraged him to lead the life of leisure. He has already achieved some small success, and hopes for more, perhaps even through this poem, which will preserve the memory of a beloved father.

Some have seen Milton as aligning himself with Phaethon, or even with the Prometheus who rebelled against Zeus. But no, on the surface at least, the passages so cited thank the father for having, like Hyperion, the sun god, given him his chariot. The reference to Phaethon is very indirect, even wry. And Prometheus is in the text as the giver of fire and wisdom to humankind, not as the Aeschylean rebel against Zeus. The speaker does not say to his father, as Willam Kerrigan would have it: 'In so far as I am a poet, I am not your son; my origins are divine, my authority is God, and it is with God that the struggle we are here engaged in must be adjudicated. Are you holding now in your hands my *Promethean* fire?'[1] On the contrary, in this passage he aligns himself with his father: it is the human mind which has a divine origin, the one revealed by poetry (17-20).

There is no external evidence for the dating of this poem, yet it has been taken as crucial by those who have some special theory about Milton's development.[2] We would like to know exactly what it was his father had said, and when, that made Milton sit down and compose this elaborate, formal, yet playful reply in dactylic hexameters. To me it looks as if Milton senior was pushing him to decide on a career, and probably still urging him towards the church. In the course of their discussion, father had said some rather harsh things to son about poetry – or, at least, about poets. He despises it or them (17), it is futile and useless (56-7),he hates it (67). The occasion may well have been some casual remark or question ('What are you going to do with yourself?') now that the family were settled in Hammersmith. Milton would no longer be going back to Cambridge in the autumn, and some tension may have arisen. At the very least, Milton felt that he owed his father some explanation – and rather than making it a negative assessment of the church, about which they almost certainly disagreed if they allowed themselves to talk frankly, he writes a positive defense of poetry, and praise for the father who has 'brought me here to this quiet retreat away from the noise of the city' ('Me procul urbano strepitu, secessibus altis/ Abductum'). Church and poetry could be combined of course, as the careers of both John Donne and George Herbert show. But the silence in the poem about the church may have been caused by more than a desire to spare his father's feelings.

Milton wrote later that he had been 'Church-outed by the Prelats' (*YP* I 823), by which he meant not that he was thrown out of the church, but that his distaste for the priests forced him to give up any idea of a career in the ministry. He does not say exactly when this happened, and in retrospect it may have seemed more like a decisive moment than the longer process it actually was. But the process had probably already started. In spite of his father's new role as local churchwarden, Milton's reluctance to enter the ministry was surely caused in part by the changes introduced by Laud, appointed archbishop of Canterbury on 6 August 1633. Under Queen Elizabeth I, bishops had often understood the Thirty-Nine Articles that defined the new Protestant Church of England in a Calvinist sense, and had been loath to impose strict compliance with elaborate ceremonies and rituals. But things were different now under Charles I. Laud feared puritanism and insisted on high-church rituals, including a full set of elaborate vestments, all of which seemed to be leading the Church of England back towards Rome. Very soon, on 18 October, James I's controversial *Book of Sports* was reissued as *The King's Majesty's declaration to his subjects concerning lawful sports to be used.* It listed those sports that were permissible, indeed encouraged, as soon as church was over on Sundays: these included 'dancing, either men or women, archery for men, leaping, vaulting, or any other such harmless recreation', along with 'May-games, Whitsun-ales and Morris-dances, and the setting up of May-poles'. The declaration rebuked puritans and other 'precise persons', and was issued to counteract the growing calls for strict abstinence on the Sabbath. Charles ordered that any minister who refused to read it out loud would be deprived of his position. This was an instance of the growing division in the country. Disputing doctrine in sermons was discouraged and 'correct' preaching enforced by ecclesiastical courts beyond the reach or protection of the Common Law. Puritan pamphleteers were liable for brutal punishments: William Prynne, for example, author of *Histrio-Mastix* of 1632, an attack on the Caroline fashion for public entertainments, masques, dancing and maypoles, especially the theatre, was tried by the Star Chamber (the infamous court used by Charles to suppress sedition) in 1633 and sentenced to imprisonment, a £5,000 fine and the removal of part of his ears.

Milton, however, was not yet a militant puritan. Indeed there was no one group or sect, at least in England, that could be identified by the title 'Puritan'. It was originally a term of abuse for those opposed both to high-church ceremonial and to the entertainments of the period (it is so used in *Twelfth Night* of Malvolio, for example). Those of puritan tendency often preferred to call themselves 'the godly'. They now came together in their opposition to Laud. One sign of where Milton stood at this period is that he had signed the subscription book for his Cambridge MA, and thus acknowledged the liturgy of the Anglican church and the king's supremacy. He was not averse to seeking friends, and perhaps patronage, within the aristocracy. He now accepted commissions for two entertainments: one a brief pastoral flurry for Alice, dowager countess of Derby, *Arcades*, performed at her Uxbridge household of Harefield, Middlesex, in 1632; the other the first of his major works, *A Masque Presented at Ludlow Castle,* for the family of the earl of Bridgewater, her son-in-law, who was married to her second daughter,

Frances. This connection was highly advantageous for the unknown young Milton. The dowager countess of Derby was now about seventy and had long been associated with poets. Her first husband had been the Fernando Stanley, earl of Derby (d. 1594), for whose company some of Shakespeare's early plays had been written. Edmund Spenser dedicated poems to her, and she participated in two of Ben Jonson's masques.

Masques, often expensively staged performances with much music, dance and special effects, had become popular with the royal court and under Charles were being used to promote an ideology of platonic love and pastoralism supporting the king's absolute and personal rule (from 1629–40 Charles ruled without Parliament). In some ways Milton's masque, which we know as *Comus* after the central character, is not so different. It was written for a festivity at Ludlow castle on the Welsh border (now a rather sad ruin) on Michaelmas night, 29 September 1634, to honour the official installation of John Egerton, earl of Bridgewater, as lord president of Wales. It contains much music, written by Henry Lawes, the king's music-master and an acquaintance of Milton's father, who planned the whole entertainment. It also contains some fashionable Platonism and pastoral allegory, while spirits descend on wires and sing. But the main implications of this Miltonic variant of the form are highly unusual.

Milton had probably never actually seen a masque, since they were private court and aristocratic entertainments. But he could have read the published texts and talked to Lawes, or his father, about them. Perhaps the distance of Ludlow from London, plus the Calvinism of Bridgewater himself, encouraged Milton covertly to challenge the cultural politics of the genre, although we should remember that Bridgewater was a friend and supporter of Charles and Buckingham (yes, the same as the corrupt chancellor of Cambridge University), and that later on, after civil war had broken out and the king had been beheaded, Bridgewater's son would be calling for that unconscionable rebel Milton to be executed. For the performance of *Comus* in 1634, however, it was still possible for a Royalist family to invite a puritan to work for them, especially an unknown young man like Milton. They may have known nothing about him. In any case it was chiefly the musician, Henry Lawes, who was responsible for the masque and who played the Attendant spirit. It was probably Lawes rather than the Bridgewater family who invited Milton to do the libretto (as it would be called if this were an opera). It was certainly Lawes who was responsible for publishing the first edition, anonymously, in 1637.

Comus is much longer than other masques, and the poetry clearly predominates over the musical parts. It tells the tale of three children, played by the earl's daughter, the Lady Alice, aged fifteen, and her younger brothers, aged eleven and nine, who are lost in a wood and threatened by Comus and his bestial rout. The boys are separated from their sister, who is lured by Comus and held fast in a chair. The boys discuss chastity and philosophy, while the Lady, like the nymphs pursued in classical mythology, is threatened with rape. The progression towards degeneracy begins already in Comus's first speech, written in the jaunty measure of 'L'Allegro':

> Meanwhile welcome joy, and feast,
> Midnight shout, and revelry,
> Tipsy dance and jollity

but soon moves into the licence and obscenity of Cotytto, 'Goddesse of Nocturnal sport' (528). In the main passage, Comus, played by a professional actor, delivers richly suggestive speeches, a parody of the court's philosophy but wonderful poetry, in which he denounces 'the lean and sallow abstinence' (709) and praises the Lady's looks: 'Beauty is Nature's brag' (745).

The way Comus leads up to this praise is easily the most seductive in English poetry since Shakespeare. It is hard not to be swayed by the language, which is clearly influenced by the rhythm and sparkle of a Shakespearean speech, but has its own inner logic, alien to Shakespeare's flourish. At one point, for example, Comus claims:

> Wherefore did Nature powre her bounties forth,
> With such a full and unwithdrawing hand,
> Covering the earth with odours, fruits, and flocks,
> Thronging the Seas with spawn innumerable,
> But all to please, and sate the curious taste?
> And set to work millions of spinning Worms,
> That in their green shops weave the smooth-hair'd silk
> To deck her Sons; and that no corner might
> Be vacant of her plenty, in her own loyns
> She hutch't th' all-worshipt ore and precious gems
> To store her children with; if all the world
> Should in a pet of temperance feed on Pulse,
> Drink the clear stream, and nothing wear but Frieze,
> Th' all-giver would be unthank't, would be unprais'd,
> Not half his riches known, and yet despis'd… (710-34)

The language is magnificently anti-puritan. The 'green shops' are a remarkable idea, transcending Shakespeare, as are those industrious spinning worms. We hear, behind the magnificently persuasive rhetoric, a young poet discovering his voice and articulating, among many other things, his father's profession as money-lending capitalist, one whose livelihood depends on the general ambition to exploit what the world gives, not to resist its pleasures.

It is a much longer speech, and I cut it off here only in the hope that the reader may be inclined to go and read the whole. This is the first real Milton, the one who echoes down the ages. The passage continues with further praise of nature's fertility, and with the important idea that will recur later in *Paradise Lost*, that mineral riches actually grow in the earth. If we do not make the best use we can of the natural world God has given us,

> we should serve him as a grudging master,
> As a penurious niggard of his wealth,
> And live like Natures bastards, not her sons,
> Who would be quite surcharg'd with her own weight,
> And strangl'd with her waste fertility;
> Th' earth cumber'd, and the wing'd air dark't with plumes,
> The herds would over-multitude their Lords,
> The Sea o'erfraught would swell, & th' unsought diamonds
> Would so emblaze the forhead of the Deep,
> And so bestudd with Stars, that they below
> Would grow inur'd to light, and com at last
> To gaze upon the Sun with shameless brows. (*Comus* 725-36)

The marvellous rhythms are Shakespearean ('the wing'd air dark't with plumes' is a characteristic variation), but the theme has reached beyond and behind Shakespeare, to the world of fairy lore that he exploited in *A Midsummer Night's Dream*, with its added layer of classical myth, and to the conflicts that were beginning to define the new world that had come into being since Shakespeare's death in 1616. It was no longer Shakespearean drama that dominated the cultural world, perhaps no longer even Jonson's city comedy or Middleton's odd mixture of courtly and puritan values. Milton's strange masque articulates a new voice. Eventually those 'unsought diamonds' will grow in the Deep 'inur'd to light', if not cultivated, until they come, like Satan, 'To gaze upon the Sun with shameless brow'. Comus's powerful evocation of 'unsought diamonds' will become a version, almost an allegory, of the cultural politics of the next crucial and destructive years through which England had to live.

Nonetheless, there is another hope. At 756–99 the Lady replies to Comus with a defense of chastity and then develops an argument that becomes almost a defense of a puritan socialism, a covert sermon about conspicuous expenditure in big houses like this one. Nature has enough for everyone if not exploited by the rich. Eventually the Lady is rescued from her frozen chair by the intervention of a higher power, Sabrina, a spirit who embodies the nearby River Severn. She sings, and there is music to accompany her, but she also represents the power of poetry to 'unlock/ The clasping charm and thaw the numbing spell' (851-2). The Lady is one of the few characters in Milton to resist temptation. And temptation, we shall see, is still Milton's principle theme in the great poems of his maturity.

The Bridgewater children, Alice in particular, had recently complained of demonic possession, and had been treated with protective amulets and St. John's wort by the well-known physician John Napier.[3] In a sense, then, the masque replays her cure. The earl himself, in his capacity as a judge, had recently given an extremely fair-minded ruling in a long drawn-out case of rape of a fourteen-year-old girl, Margery Evans, by a powerful local official.[4] This will have been in the minds of those present on this big occasion, more especially as Michaelmas was a holiday associated with public administration and justice. The lessons for the day, from Ecclesiasticus 38–44, are about greatness ('Let us now praise famous men'), about sitting on the judges' seat and the wisdom of ancient prophecies. The gospel for the day, Matthew 18, denounces the man who offends against children: 'it were better for him that a millstone were hanged about his neck, and that he were drowned in the depth of the sea'. Milton may not have known these details of the Bridgewater family when he first composed the masque, though he will probably have noticed the uncanny connections at the time of the performance.

But there was another reason why the subject of the masque was extremely risky and needed to be handled with great delicacy. An extraordinary sexual scandal had recently afflicted the family of the countess's eldest daughter, Anne. Her husband, the infamous earl of Castlehaven, had had his servants frequently rape both his wife and his step-daughter, who was married to his own son. He was also accused of sodomy and, even worse, Popery. He was executed in May 1631. The dowager countess was now supporting Anne and her daughter. Milton makes tactful reference to her role in *Arcades,* but in *Comus,* given the subject, he had to be careful not to insult his hosts, and especially not the young virgin playing the Lady. In particular he had to avoid having the references to rape and chastity seem ironic.[5]

The sensitivity of the topic is clear from the differences between the versions of the text preserved. Lady Alice's part is trimmed in the Bridgewater manuscript, closer to the acted version (perhaps to make the part more manageable for the girl), while Comus's argument against virginity and most of his explicit sexual threats are cut. These passages were all restored when the text was published anonymously in 1637, and again when it was included in Milton's first book of poetry in 1645. The masque is also preserved in the

Trinity manuscript, a precious record that Milton had started keeping of his work during the period of retirement at Hammersmith. (It is so named because it was left to Trinity College, Cambridge, where it remains.) There we can see Milton adding or altering stage-directions, for example, as he gained a better understanding of the craft and the resources available.

Chastity was an unusual topic for a masque, but very important for the young Milton. Several years later, in 1642, he still made much of his urge to chastity in one of his more revealing autobiographical statements already quoted in Chapter One: 'if unchastity in a woman whom Saint Paul termes the glory of man, be such a scandall and dishonour, then certainly in a man who is both the image and glory of God, it must, though commonly not so thought, be much more deflouring and dishonourable' (*Apology* in *YP* I 891-3) In the same passage he contrasts the 'thick intoxicating potion which a certaine Sorceresse the abuser of loves name carries about' with 'the charming cup' of chastity and love. Magic potions like these two contrasting drinks derive from the same world of folklore and romance as Circe or her son Comus. But in Milton's thinking their effects are elaborated by a lyrical devotion to philosophy, especially, he says, Plato and Xenophon. These references to his reading in the years of retirement when he wrote *Comus* give us a clue to what these sexual fantasies of scandal, dishonour or deflowering were really about. He is thinking especially of Socrates, and in particular of the speech in the *Symposium* that Plato puts into the mouth of the beautiful young Alcibiades about how he had tried unsuccessfully to seduce Socrates. The contrast of two kinds of Eros is one aspect of the speech that Socrates himself delivers.

The intensity of this commitment to chastity makes the Lady of *Comus* unnervingly like the 'Lady of Christ's', as Milton had been called at Cambridge. But it also implies an equally strong need to struggle with its opposite. The Elder Brother evokes that contrary state of the soul, with a remarkable profusion of liquid *l* sounds:

> When lust
> By unchaste looks, loose gestures, and foul talk,
> But most by lewd and lavish act of sin,
> Lets in defilement to the inward parts,
> The soul grows clotted by contagion,
> Imbodies and imbrutes, till she quite lose
> The divine property of her first being. (463-69)

He goes on to evoke the state of the carnally sensual soul, in a passage that recalls Plato's *Phaedo* 81D, as similar to the shadow one sees around new-made graves and Charnel vaults, 'loath to leave the body that it lov'd'. To which the Second brother replies with a line that must always raise a laugh in the theatre: 'How charming is divine Philosophy. (476).

When John Diodati, Charles's brother, was married at St Margaret's in Westminster on 28 July 1635, this would have been a chance for Milton to have a reunion with his friend. It is not clear how much of Milton's sexual attitudes at the time have to do with this friendship. In a couple of mildly flirtatious letters to Charles of 1637, he urges him to come back to London, where they could meet more often, and where Milton himself was thinking of moving, to the Inns of Court. But he also describes his love for his friend in language that oozes Platonic idealism and the quest for Beauty. At the same time he admits to a secret, indeed blushing, desire for immortal fame as a poet. The feelings are all mixed up and hard to measure. The intensity of the friendship makes it look homoerotic, though not what we nowadays call homosexual. Nonetheless, the ideal of chastity may well have emerged as strongly as it did from his struggles with strong but submerged feelings for Charles Diodati, and it probably affected his ideal of all close relationships in later life. In particular Milton's sexual idealism about marriage is evident here for the first time. At around the same time, late autumn 1637, Milton also added to the text of *Comus* a long and passionate speech in praise of 'the sun-clad power of Chastity' and 'the sage/ And serious doctrine of Virginitie', as well as Comus's response: 'She fables not, I feel and I do fear/ Her words set off by some superior power' (782-801).

In May 1636 Milton's father finally retired and left his scrivener's business, though he retained legal liabilities in two ongoing Chancery suits. The reason given was 'removal to inhabit in the country', which meant Horton. Here Milton seems not to have written much poetry, at least nothing he preserved. His inactivity has been likened to the state of the chaste Lady frozen in her chair, and may be a sign of the continuing indecision about a career. But it may also result from the obligation to care for his aging parents. Christopher was living only some of his time in Horton, since he spent his terms at the Inner Temple in London studying for the bar. There were other anxieties. Plague still infected even this remote village, and a few people died of it in Horton itself.

Instead of writing, Milton threw himself into a self-prescribed reading programme, mostly or 'entirely' (as he later claimed) in the Greek and Latin writers, both famous, like Plato or Terence, and more obscure, like Lycophron or Procopius. Some of these books survive: Milton's copy of Pindar (now in the Harvard Library), which he had bought on 15 November 1629, is very heavily annotated, and with suggestions for correction or addition to the index; and his Euripides (now in the Bodleian Library, Oxford), acquired in

1634, is marked up both for scansion and for staging effects. Milton's own writings soon reflected his extraordinary knowledge of classical literature. But he also read the church fathers (who he found disappointing not only for their lack of wisdom but also for their style of 'pampered metaphors, intricate and involved sentences... cross-jingling periods', *Of Reformation*, *YP* I 568) and taught himself some Hebrew in order to be able to read the Old Testament and even understand some rabbinic commentaries. In one of those letters to Diodati, of 23 November 1637, he says he has been reading a lot of history, including 'the obscure history of the Italians under the Longobards, Franks and Germans' up to their liberation under Rudolph, king of Germany in c. 1273. He asks Diodati to send him Giustiniani's work on the Venetians. No one would have doubted that Milton was a true scholar, but this is hard evidence that he was pursuing his lifetime habit.

At this time he also began keeping his Commonplace Book (now in the British Library), in which he would copy out appealing or useful passages from his reading. These give us an idea of his current preoccupations. He quotes passages from Tertullian and Cyprian (two of those church fathers he found so tedious) against public entertainments, and then refutes them. He also includes bits about marriage for the clergy, and polygamy or bigamy, indicating that he was already highly unorthodox in his thinking about marriage before his own problems and the divorce tracts. And he quotes a piece from Sulpicius Severus's world chronicle of about AD 400 on how kings are not welcome to God or to a free people. But his reading was not unrelievedly self-improving. At the same time, he was also taking notes on Italian literature: Dante, Boccaccio, Ariosto. And one of the early entries in the Commonplace Book concerns the great plague of Constantinople in 542, a preoccupation of all England again now after the bad summer of 1636, and one of the probable reasons for the family's move to Horton.

Among all the records of his intensive reading, there is no reference at all to contemporary poetry in English. And yet John Donne had become dean of St Paul's in 1621, while Milton was a boy at St Paul's school. He would have heard some of those remarkable sermons. Donne's Meditations, or *Devotions Upon Emergent Occasions*, were published in 1624. And the poems of 'the Deane of Pauls, Dr John Donne' were published in 1633, two years after his death, with a second, improved edition in 1635. George Herbert died in 1633, and his poems were then published as *The Temple*. Were they too insignificant to bother with in the midst of all this earnest self-improvement? Perhaps it was their attachment to the High Anglican Church, taken over by Laud from 1633, which put them out of reach for Milton. The poems had circulated for years in manuscript form before being printed, and many were serious meditations on religious issues. Yet, in spite of Milton's brief musical connection through Henry Lawes with the countess of Derby and the Egerton family, the milieu of these High Anglican priests, which included aristocrats like Lady Magdalene Herbert, clearly did not overlap with that of a young writer living as a studious recluse outside town. He was going quietly, but insistently, his own way.

5

Coping With Death: 'Lycidas'

Throughout his adolescence Milton had been practising poetry on corpses. He had written elegies for a marchioness, two bishops, a Cambridge University vice-chancellor and its carrier, a beadle and a 'fair infant dying of a cough'. But in the next few months several deaths occurred that brought important changes in his life. In April 1637 his mother Sara died, apparently after an illness. She is buried in the aisle of Horton Church. A bluestone still bears her name. Whatever obligations Milton may have had towards her care were now removed. The passing of a literary era was marked by the death of Ben Jonson in August. And then Milton heard about the death, also in August, of an old Cambridge acquaintance, Edward King. Slightly younger than Milton, King had already had a flourishing career: he had been appointed by royal fiat to a Cambridge fellowship at the absurdly young age of eighteen (presumably because his family owned large estates in Ireland and could exert influence at court); he had written some Latin poems; and he was preparing to take holy orders when he was drowned at sea as he crossed to Ireland. His Cambridge friends, perhaps in response to the volume that emerged for Ben Jonson from Oxford, proposed a memorial volume of poetic tributes to this young man, cut off in his prime at twenty-five, and Milton agreed to write one. The result is 'Lycidas'. It also contains explicit political comment for the first time in Milton's career, which is a measure of how English attitudes had developed and hardened in the three years since *Comus*. Milton signed it in the King volume only with his initials, perhaps because of the furious attack it contains on the established church.

If we are going to understand what makes Milton a great poet, this is the moment to pause and begin to do so, for it was now that he wrote, out of that quiet period of retirement, a 'monody', as he calls it, to which subsequent poems in English about the death of friends or fellow poets have to allude, or with which they must cope: Shelley on Keats in 'Adonais', Tennyson's 'In Memoriam', even Auden on Yeats. John Berryman, when visiting Robert

Lowell in the 1940s, stayed up night after night reading and reciting 'Lycidas' with his hosts: he later wrote several elegies to commemorate fellow American poets, and also a splendid story about the poem, 'Wash Far Away'. Yeats once asked Virginia Woolf if there were any poem she could return to unsated, and though she thought of Milton as 'the first of the masculinists', her answer was 'Lycidas'.

Other poems in the King volume imitate the fashionable metaphysical style, the witty legacy of John Donne ('my pen's the spout/ Where the rain-water of my eyes run out' as one poem puts it), but Milton's poem ignores all that and adopts the traditional genre of the pastoral elegy. 'Elegy' comes from the Greek *elegos*, meaning a song of mourning, though it was often used merely to describe a certain metre in classical poetry, alternating hexameters and pentameters. Milton had written seven such poems at Cambridge, as we have seen. But pastoral elegies, deriving from the Greek poet Theocritus's lament for Daphnis (Idyll I), are traditionally songs about the loss of a friend or lover. The term 'pastoral' means that the mourner and the subject are represented as shepherds. Milton alludes to three poets in particular, Theocritus, Virgil and the Italian Sannazaro, all of whom use the name Lycidas (and often for a poet or singer). Milton is inviting comparison with the best. Among English models, the poem is more heavily indebted to Spenser than to Shakespeare, presumably a conscious choice of style, but also a sign that Milton was moving away from the penumbra of Shakespeare that was evident in the many allusions of *Comus*. The shepherds of the poem are also allusions to the language of biblical parable. At John 10:11, for example, Jesus refers to himself as the good shepherd, who 'giveth his life for the sheep'. He contrasts himself with the hireling, who 'seeth the wolf coming, and leaveth the sheep, and fleeth: and the wolf catcheth them, and scattereth the sheep'. The poem makes explicit use of this reference to the wolf, as we shall see.

The conventions of pastoral poetry are so alien to us now that it is hard to overcome the strangeness of the poem, even when you have read it several times and know it well. Indeed the man who made the first and perhaps still the best study of this pastoral tradition in relation to 'Lycidas', James Holly Hanford, admitted that 'the mass of writing to which this artificial yet strangely persistent literary fashion gave rise seems unendurably barren and insipid'.[1] Within a hundred years, the fashion had died. By 1779, one of the greatest of English critics, Samuel Johnson, had entirely lost sympathy with the pastoral form to which, he thinks, Milton has reduced the emotions. Johnson is worth listening to. He admired Milton the poet but disliked Milton the man, and was especially and deliciously unpleasant about 'Lycidas'. He hated the form so much that he just could not hear the beauties of the poem at all.

One of the poems on which much praise has been bestowed is Lycidas; of which the diction is harsh, the rhymes uncertain, and the numbers unpleasing. What beauty there is we must therefore seek in the sentiments and images. It is not to be considered as the effusion of real passion; for passion runs not after remote allusions and obscure opinions.

Referring to the opening lines of the poem, in which Milton says he has been forced to come and pluck the berries of this poetic form before he feels ripe to do so, as well as the nymphs and other creatures that populate pastoral poetry, Johnson goes on:

Passion plucks no berries from the myrtle and ivy, nor calls upon Arethuse and Mincius, nor tells of rough *satyrs* and *fauns with cloven heel*… In this poem there is no nature, for there is no truth; there is no art, for there is nothing new. Its form is that of a pastoral; easy, vulgar, and therefore disgusting; whatever images it can supply are long ago exhausted; and its inherent improbability always forces dissatisfaction on the mind.

He extends the point with a typically balanced eighteenth-century Augustan sentence, very different from the kind of vibrant prose that Milton himself would soon be writing. 'He who thus grieves will excite no sympathy; he who thus praises will confer no honour.'[2]

Johnson especially loathed, as a staunch and conservative Christian, the overlap of 'ecclesiastical pastor' with classical shepherd-poets. Yet the relation was vital to Milton, since Edward King was both poet and priest, and Milton himself had only recently given up the possibility of combining the two in his own career. If we are to respond to the poem at all, then, we need to accept – or at least read across – those pastoral conventions. Indeed, the poem questions those conventions, as do many pastoral poems. The lamentation itself may be merely conventional, and it is not clear how well Milton knew King, but we need to see that Milton was facing, perhaps for the first time, the possibility that he too might die before he had achieved any of what he had promised his father.

It is hard to choose particular moments to pick out for emphasis, so well and widely known is the poem. The last words everyone can quote: 'Tomorrow to fresh woods and pastures new.' But the first words are also worth hearing clearly: 'Yet once more, O ye laurels, yet once more'. A largely monosyllabic line gets this extraordinary poem under way, hesitant, repetitive, ruminative. Ordinary, everyday language introduces the heightened world of pastoral poetry. And yet the opening words, so apparently unremarkable, conceal a biblical allusion of large implications. At Hebrews 12:26–7, God fulminates: 'Yet once more I shake not the earth only, but also heaven.' The passage continues with an explanation: 'And this word, Yet once more, signifieth the removing of those things that are shaken, as of things that are made, that those things which cannot be shaken may remain.' Like many such apparently innocuous phrases in the New Testament, this one is an allusion to a passage in the Old Testament, at Haggai 2:6–7, and it invokes a momentous cry, God's separation of things transitory from things eternal as he announces the building of the Second Temple of Jerusalem. This layering of reference is to be characteristic of Milton as his poetry develops. When you hear God's cry behind them, 'yet once more' cannot remain a quiet complaint about timing. Often enough in Milton, Bible thunder enriches simple statement.

The main point of the poem is a search for consolation in the face of death. Each possible consolation is tried out and then found wanting or partial. 'Fame', for example ('that last infirmity of noble mind', 71), which a young poet like Milton or Edward King might well imagine as a satisfying goal of his poetic endeavours, turns out to be deferred to the next world ('Fame is no plant that grows on mortal soil'), and the couplet which asserts this is shrill and so probably false, ironic at the least: as God 'pronounces lastly on each deed,/ Of so much fame in heaven expect thy meed'. Moreover the god who so pronounces, because of the classical conventions, is Jove. In this Christian context that makes the potential consolation doubly distant, if not illusory.

In the process of exploring this theme of false or problematic consolation, Milton discovered poetic devices that he was to use with increasing force and subtlety as his career developed. One is the long verse paragraph of irregular length that invites the reader in and then troubles him, a poetic form that Milton virtually invented. We wait for the verse paragraphs to resolve themselves: sometimes they do, sometimes they don't. Mainly iambic pentameters, the poem also contains occasional and surprising short lines, as well as an irregular rhyme scheme. Milton's musical training had made him one of the most subtle poets of sound in the language.

But there is much more to it. Take the structural method of moving between what the imagination can offer and what reality actually consists of – especially appropriate in a poem about a man who dies young and unfulfilled. The long and lovely flower passage, for example, which occupies lines 132 to 151, and which the Trinity manuscript shows Milton revised and extended, invites the 'Sicilian Muse' to call up from the vales, that is, the world of Sicilian pastoral poetry, a list of specific and magnificently named (and mostly English) flowers.

> Bring the rathe Primrose that forsaken dies,
> The tufted Crow-toe, and pale Gessamine,
> The white Pink...

and so on. These are then to be strewn across 'the Laureate Hearse where Lycid lies'. We read and enjoy the passage and picture the grand and powerful funeral image. Only one problem: there is no hearse, and so no flowers. Lycidas (Edward King) was drowned, and his body was not recovered. This whole spectacular flower sequence is, as lines 152–3 tell us explicitly, illusory: 'For so to interpose a little ease/ Let our frail thoughts dally with a false surmise'. We were absorbed in the flower idea, believing it perhaps, and were then coldly ejected into the reality of the drowned and unquiet corpse, 'where'er thy bones are hurled', at line 154.

In a sense we have been tricked, and Milton's poetic narrator is the one responsible. Pastoral visions will just not do in the face of the calamity of death. We are then left to imagine the angel on the peak of St Michael's Mount in Cornwall taking pity on the body ('Look homeward Angel now, and melt with ruth') and the possibility of local help: 'O ye *Dolphins*, waft the haples youth' (163-4). Whether angel or dolphins do help, we are never told.

Beneath the search for consolation, most readers recognize sooner or later, is Milton's fear of his own premature death. In that respect, the allusion to Orpheus becomes even more poignant. He was torn apart by Maenads (Milton comes back to this in *Paradise Lost*) and his severed head ('goary visage') floated down to the sea. This famous story is told by both Ovid and Virgil, and the allusion increases both the ambitious reach and the anxiety of the poem. Orpheus was a poet, and he was killed; Edward King had poetic ambitions too, and was killed. Milton acknowledges his own high ideals, and is afraid of his own early death. There are so many references to Orpheus in Milton's poetry and prose that it was clearly a story he took personally. This 'Lycidas' passage is much worked over and revised in the Trinity manuscript.

In the centre of the poem is an 'interlude' bracketed by two references to the Alpheus–Arethusa myth. It is in many ways the focal point of the poem, although at first it may seem to mark time in order to make an apparently intrusive, political point. Although satire and invective were sometimes a part of the pastoral tradition, as in Petrarch, Mantuan or Spenser's *Shepherd's Calendar*,[3] some readers have shared the view that this intrusive passage is so out of tune with the rest of the poem that it pulls it apart. 'Lycidas' is in fact the only pastoral *elegy* that includes ecclesiastical satire. It is even more than satire, it is full-blooded denunciation. Generations of critics have tried to neutralize the oddity of this passage, but it still sticks out and calls attention to itself. What is it doing there?

The excuse for it is that St Peter, swinging his keys at the heavenly gates, 'shakes his mitred locks' like the good first bishop he is, and tells the arriving Edward King that he'd rather he had not died (some consolation!). Instead he'd rather have spared

> Anow [enough] of such as for their bellies' sake
> Creep and intrude and climb into the fold. (114-5)

These animals, an educated reader of Milton will have recognized, allude to Spenser's false shepherds in the May eclogue of the *Shepherd's Calendar*, 'There crept in wolves'. These wolves, we soon learn, are the clergy who do not fulfil their proper function as pastors, that is, to feed their sheep, but instead, 'Blind mouths!',[4] offer a seriously unpleasant-sounding alternative to this pastoral verse.

> And when they list, their lean and flashy songs
> Grate on their scrannel Pipes of wretched straw. (123-4)

It is central to the pastoral convention of the poem that bad preaching should be equated to bad singing, and that the lines stand out vividly in the midst of this mostly mellifluous verse. The harsh English words in fact translate a line of Virgil ('to murder a rotten tune on a grating straw'[5]). The passage continues:

> The hungry Sheep look up and are not fed,
> But swoln with wind, and the rank mist they draw,
> Rot inwardly, and foul contagion spread:
> Besides what the grim Woolf with privy paw
> Daily devours apace, and nothing said. (125-9)

That conclusion is devastating. 'Nothing said'.[6] The whole passage is powerfully negative, and most of us will understand the point of its main image if we allow ourselves to read. The wind—well, yes, how does it get out of the 'swoln bellies'? One end or the other, and either way, it causes a bad smell ('foul contagion spread': the plague was thought to be spread by bad air). Small wonder, given the strength of this language, that reforming church governance soon became a focus of Milton's energy.

In fact in some cases of sheep-bloat, even more severe, the wind cannot be belched up ('rot inwardly') and the sheep die. The condition is usually precipitated by the rapid consumption of lush legume pasture (like clover) in spring. Gas builds in the stomach until it cannot be eructated normally. The increasing pressure causes heart and lung failure. The passage sounds as if Milton had seen actual cases of sheep-bloat, and indeed perhaps he had. The family was now living in a small village surrounded by farming country. But characteristically, Milton's lines echo two passages of Italian poetry. One is pastoral, the seventh *Eclogue* of Petrarch, where sheep-rot is an allegory of church corruption, the other is from Dante's *Paradiso*, where the people of Florence listen to their preachers like sheep that return unknowingly from pasture, fed on wind. We could probably extend the range of reference of this image a bit further, though still within clearly acceptable bounds, if we recall that the magnificent and classical idea of Typhon, the monster who does battle with the gods in Hesiod's mythological poem about the origins of the universe (*Theogony*), and to whom Milton refers several times, is occasionally likened to a vast and internally produced wind, a typhoon of the belly.

And that grim Wolf, the head of these foul priests, well, who is he? The answer to that question is surprising. Or answers, rather, since there are several. Obviously, the Roman Catholic Church is one solution, with its pervasive influence over the corrupt Church of England, especially through Charles I's French Catholic queen, Henrietta Maria. Particularly perhaps, the Jesuits, since their founder, Ignatius Loyola, had two grey wolves on his coat of arms. These men, spies as they had been in Donne's time, still carried on illegal proselytising in England and worked against the established Protestant state church. Jesuits were soon to be a special enemy of Milton's, as we shall see from his visit to Rome. The wolf is also kin to those fellow creatures just mentioned, who 'for their bellies' sake / Creep and intrude and climb into the fold', language which echoes the parable in John 10:1–28 about corrupt preachers as wolves and the long tradition about them.

So far it is fairly clear that the lines are an explicit attack on the established, bishop-centred church with its prelates. But take the wolf idea one more classical and etymological step. The Greek for 'wolf', *lykos*, is in the name of the poem's supposed hero, Lycidas, son of wolf, or 'wolf's whelp'. Apparent opposites in the poem, the two are reunited in their etymological origins. Could this be inadvertent. With *Milton*?

Governance of the established church through a paid clergy of bishops and priests was one of the chief points to which Milton and his puritan friends already objected. In fact, a majority of the young men graduating from Cambridge went into the ministry and collected a salary for doing not very much. They often lived elsewhere and left the parish in the care of uneducated or incompetent substitutes. But what does this denunciation have to do with the general theme of the poem and its frustrated search for consolation? Nothing very obvious, as an older generation of readers used to lament. Merritt Hughes is, as usual, marvellously typical:

> It is a fact [!] to be reckoned with that the more narrowly the 'digression' on the clergy is limited to reference to the quarrel of the Puritans with the English or with the Roman Catholic Church, the less interesting it is both from the historical and the literary point of view.[7]

But what if this secret etymological link suggests a more sinister but suppressed idea? Edward King, we know, was destined for the church, as Milton too had been in the very recent past. But which church? Does the absence of consolation suggest not simply a timeless impossibility, but also a less exalted idea, namely that Milton chose this particular name for his Cambridge contemporary not simply because it was a common pastoral name for a shepherd but instead because he knew he was already creeping off in the Royalist–Laudian direction of the wolf?

Perhaps his English name – King – is just as significant as the pastoral-classical 'Lycidas'. Of Edward King's ten extant Latin poems, seven were written to celebrate the birth of royal children. And in 1636 he had written of the holy serenity that the church gives to Italy. St Peter's digression appears to distinguish Lycidas from the wolves, but the names bring them back together. Surely a poet as alert to etymological implications as Milton will not have put a long bit about corrupt and predatory wolves into a poem whose title is 'son of wolf' without inviting his readers to speculate on the relationship, and so undo the purity of the image constructed for the dead and now sainted 'shepherd'?

Milton's greatness as a poet consists partly in an ability to articulate two opposing messages at the same time. The Romantics thought that, in Blake's famous words, he was 'a true Poet' and 'of the devil's party without knowing it'.[8] Is 'Lycidas' then an early instance of Milton's supposed sympathy for Satan in *Paradise Lost*? Is Milton giving away his unconscious preferences even while he insistently states the opposite? He may, I would argue, have just done that in *Comus,* the masque written for performance in 1634 and published now in 1637. The masque praises chastity and virginity. Yet the finest poetry is given to Comus the rogue. Of course, in a drama, we expect both sides of the story to be articulated. But the bad guy, the one who attacks the young girl's chastity, gets most of the good lines.

'Lycidas' is different in one obvious respect. It isn't a drama, though it contains several dialogues, and indeed keeps changing its main voice. The passage about the wolves is spoken by a special voice, a 'dread' one, St Peter's, founder of the church. He is no bad guy, in spite of his bishop's mitre. What he says carries authority. He is surely supposed to be genuinely sorry at the current state of his church. Yet in this context it is passing strange to make St Peter, of all people, the one to denounce the clergy, and one of Milton's boldest strokes. The only voice which rings true, which steps out of the pastoral world to denounce contemporary reality, belongs to the personification, indeed the founder, of what he denounces. The poem deploys its various voices as a kind of hall of echoes, one voice sounding behind the next, till we are not entirely sure whose voice to listen to. All of them, or none? St Peter's speaks up in the middle of a Chinese box-like structure. Perhaps we should allow for Milton's divided imagination, or at least the repressive political censorship, the need to make an implicit critique, linking, for those who have ears to hear, the hated career of priest in a Royalist church with what Edward King himself was preparing to do. No wonder, then, that Samuel Johnson thought it was not sincere.

When 'Lycidas' was republished in 1645, by which time the political situation had utterly changed, Milton added a headnote which explicitly calls attention to this passage. He summarizes the context of the poem and adds that it 'by occasion foretells the ruine of our corrupted Clergy then in their height'. The wolfish digression becomes the prophetic centre.

King had died before he could become a fully ordained minister of this corrupt church; a good thing, perhaps. He remained, that is, son of wolf rather than a wolf himself. St Peter welcomes him and distinguishes him from the hireling shepherds. Yet as everyone realizes, the poem is as much about Milton himself, apparently identifying with King but in reality separating himself from him and from Milton's youthful self, perhaps even turning against him. Milton, too, had escaped the grim wolf, that is, the entanglement and corruption of a career in the church. The poem says goodbye to that option as clearly as it says goodbye to Edward King. Milton too had risked becoming a son of wolf. Now he had finally killed off that wolf, he could look ahead to a journey. No doubt he already anticipated his departure when he penned those famous last word of 'Lycidas': 'Tomorrow to fresh woods and pastures new'.

There are three other aspects of the poem that are significant for Milton's biography. One is the reference to that typhoon of the belly, the 'swolln wind'. Milton later linked the onset of his blindness to his increasing digestive troubles, and this passage in 'Lycidas' may be the first symptom. These troubles with his belly also fertilized his language. From now on his satirical prose, and even his poetry, is often smeared with references to the lower bodily functions. He will soon invite the prelates to 'Wipe your fat corpulencies out of our light' (*YP* I 732)

Second, a careful reader will notice that the poem shows a narcissistic fascination with hair. Camus has a hairy mantle (104), St Peter shakes 'his Miter'd locks' (112), the pastoral tradition is called in a fine phrase 'the tangles of *Neara's* hair' (69), and strangest of all, the drowned Lycidas himself mounts to heaven and immediately washes his hair: 'With *Nectar* pure his oozy locks he laves' (174). Even the island of Anglesey has a 'shaggy top' (54). This preoccupation with hair (Milton's own seems to have been quite beautiful) will return soon in an image that recurs several times – that of Samson.

Third, there is the buried violence in the language. Apart from the severed head floating downstream and displaying its 'goary visage', there is the famous reference to a mysteriously apocalyptic 'two-handed engine at the door,' that 'Stands ready to smite once, and smite no more' (130-1). And there is some aggressive cutting. Just when a young man hopes for fame,

> Comes the blind *Fury* with th'abhorred shears,
> And slits the thin-spun life. (75-6)

The shears rhyme with 'trembling ears', as John Leonard has shown,[9] and in 1637, three prominent puritans, William Prynne (as I mentioned in Chapter Four), Henry Burton and John Bastwick, were sentenced by the infamous Star Chamber to having their ears cut off on the scaffold. At the time of the writing of the poem, two of them were in prison-ships on the Irish Sea. Prynne was having his ears cropped for the second time, and his face was branded with the letters S. L. This was supposed to signify 'seditious libeller', but like his later namesake Hester Prynne in Nathaniel Hawthorne's great novel *The Scarlet Letter*, he wore the letters proudly and joked they really meant *stigmata Laudis* (the marks of Laud). These were violent times, and Milton responds with both fear and defiance.

In one way Milton was lucky not to have become further involved in these political matters. Someone who did, John Lilburne, spent most of the rest of his life in and out of prison, mostly in. Lilburne met John Bastwick and was shocked that someone could be so severely punished for expressing their religious beliefs. He offered to help Bastwick in his struggle with Laud and the church. He went to Holland to organize the printing of a book that Bastwick had written. In December 1637 Lilburne was arrested and charged with printing and circulating unlicensed books. On 13th February 1638 he was found guilty and sentenced to be fined £500, whipped, pilloried and imprisoned. The following month he was whipped from the Fleet Prison to Palace Yard. When he was placed in the pillory he tried to make a speech praising Bastwick and was gagged.

While in prison Lilburne wrote about his punishments in *The Work of the Beast* (1638) and also an attack on the Anglican Church, *Come Out of Her, My People* (1639). A courageous man, Lilburne's career and writings were to be more and more important, representative of the radical tendency in the period. As we shall see, Milton's views were to move closer to his, even though his life took a very different course.

'Lycidas' was sent off and soon published in the commemorative volume for Edward King. Late in 1637 or early in 1638 Christopher Milton, who was as different from his older brother John as possible, married Thomasine Webber, and they came to live at Horton. Milton was thus free of obligations towards the care of his widowed father, who was now seventy-six. Indeed, his father had agreed to finance his departure on the Grand Tour. Henry Lawes helped him procure a passport. He was given letters of introduction for Paris by a new friend, Sir Henry Wotton, provost of Eton, to whom he had sent a copy of *Comus*. Wotton had been ambassador in several of the places Milton planned to visit, and regretted not having met Milton earlier. He offered him prudent advice for a young Protestant travelling in Catholic Italy: '*I pensieri stretti, il viso sciolto* [close thoughts, an open face] will go safely over the whole World.' Milton did not manage to follow this excellent counsel.

6

Foreign Parts

Milton set off on his Grand Tour in late April or early May 1638 and stayed away for well over a year. In the company of a servant, or gentleman's gentleman, he travelled first to Paris, where he presented his letter of introduction from Sir Henry Wotton to the English ambassador, and received fresh letters to various merchants which would assist him on the rest of his journey. He did not like either the France of Louis XIII and Cardinal Richelieu, or the French; when he later writes about reforming education in England, one benefit he imagines is that there will no longer be any need for 'the *Mounsieurs* of *Paris* to take our hopefull youth into thir slight and prodigall custodies and send them over back again transform'd into mimics, apes & Kicshoes.

This may have as much to do with his later dislike of Royalist fops as of the French, but it is true that the only two men he mentions meeting in Paris are not French. The ambassador, Viscount Scudamore of Sligo, introduced him personally to Hugo Grotius, renowned Dutch scholar and jurist, exiled from his native Holland as an opponent of strict Calvinism, who was living in Paris as ambassador of Queen Christina of Sweden. Grotius was a famous man and lived through the conflict that would become the Thirty Years War, on which he commented regularly and which he tried to bring to an end. He was also the author of several important treatises: on natural law, on the social contract, on religious toleration, on free will. Milton had read him, had long 'ardently desired to meet him' (*YP* IV.1, 615) and indeed soon adopted most of Grotius's views in the course of the pamphlet warfare in which he engaged when he returned to England. Grotius was also the author of the Latin dramas *Adamus Exul* (1601) and *Christus Patiens* (1617), on subjects Milton would later take up in his epic poems.

Travelling in Europe, even with a servant and letters of introduction to help, was still an arduous business. Carriages were not easy to come by, and much distance had to be covered on horseback or on foot; highwaymen were a danger; health and police certificates had to be obtained. Thus the journey from Paris to Nice took Milton about two weeks, and it was no doubt a relief to travel to Genoa and then to Livorno (Leghorn) by sea. He then made his way on land to Pisa and thence in June 1638 to Florence, the high point of his tour, to which he returned happily on his way back the following year.

Milton stayed in Florence for five months and made several new friends. He was also invited to frequent several private academies, Florentine institutions 'for promoting humane studies and encouraging friendly intercourse' as he later explained (*YP* IV.1 616). These academies were consciously modelled on Plato's Academy (the Athenian 'grove' where he walked and talked with his disciples), held regular debates on many different intellectual topics (justice, music, governance) and often held banquets like the one described in the *Symposium*. Milton admired the institutions and felt the lack of any such in England. They had self-consciously urbane names. The books of the Svogliati academy ('Will-less' or perhaps better 'unprejudiced', said to include the best wits in Florence) record Milton's attendance on September 6/16 (I give English Julian old-style / Italian Gregorian new-style dates) and his recitation from memory of a 'very learned Latin poem in hexameters', probably 'Naturam non pati senium' ('That Nature is not subject to old age') from his Cambridge days. A list of members of the Apatisti ('Passion-less' or 'Indifferent', that is, rational) academy that year includes 'Giovanni Milton inglese'. One of his new friends, the eighteen-year-old Carlo Dati, was the secretary. The esteem in which Milton was held is mentioned more than once in contemporary documents and letters, and may be measured by the fact that the poet Antonio Malatesti presented and dedicated to him a fifty-sonnet sequence, *La Tina*. Each of the sonnets is a kind of linguistic joke depending in part on erotic *double entendre*, which implies that these new Florentine friends recognized Milton's capacity to understand earthy humour in more than one language. *La Tina* is also an instance of the role accident plays in biography; the poems were not published at the time, it seems, but the manuscript was discovered on a London bookstall in 1750. The poems were then published, but the manuscript has since disappeared.[2]

Apart from attending these meetings, the highlight of his visit to Florence was meeting Galileo. Milton recalls him later, appropriately enough in *Areopagitica*, his tract on liberty of publication, as 'the famous Galileo, grown old, prisoner to the Inquisition, for thinking in Astronomy otherwise than the Franciscan and Dominican licencers thought' (*YP* II 538). He also recalls the meeting in *Defensio Secunda*. Formally under house arrest, Galileo was now almost totally blind and living in a villa at Arcetri, a short distance outside the town. Milton may have seen him there, or when he came in for medical treatment. In any case, the meeting made such an impression that Galileo is the only contemporary mentioned in *Paradise Lost,* as 'the Tuscan artist' (I 288) responsible for the telescope. Galileo's glass observes 'Imagined Lands and Regions in the Moon' (V 261-2). One of the members of the Svogliati Academy Milton met in Florence was Vincenzo Galilei, one of the great man's illegitimate sons, named after his grandfather, the music theorist Vincenzo. It is obvious how much more interesting these academies were than what Milton had known at cold and misty Cambridge. Among other things, these male societies seemed to value a meritocratic ideal of manhood, mixing commoner with aristocrat, and as political models, if Milton was thinking of this so early, were almost miniature republics.

In late September Milton travelled on to Siena and then Rome, where he stayed for two months. His account does not mention St Peter's, currently being remodelled by Bernini (though he probably remembered it when he later invented Pandemonium in *Paradise Lost,* I 710-98), but says he did view the famous antiquities and once again had the company of 'learned and ingenious men'. So much does he write about himself, including this trip, that even his silences have been taken to be significant. In all the many months Milton spent travelling through Italy (Florence, Rome, Naples) telling his readers at length about the trip, he never so much as mentions a painting. Why? Indifference? Residual puritan iconoclasm? Accident? We simply do not know. Nonetheless, the late Roland Mushat Frye wrote a big, often persuasive, book entitled *Milton's Imagery and the Visual Arts.*[3] The assumption, a large one, was that so sensitive a man as Milton could not possibly have ignored the visual wonders that surrounded him, whether in Italy or in England. But nary a word from Milton himself. Lord Arundel, like other contemporary travellers, created a special room back home to house the artistic loot he collected, including some 200 books of drawings by Leonardo, Michaelangelo and Raphael. John Evelyn, whose diary is a wonderful record of the time, employed a young man to make copies of the paintings he saw and coveted. Milton, however, collected – and later shipped home – books and letters and a good deal of music, but not even a hint of a painting.

He met prominent figures such as Cardinal Francesco Barberini, the pope's nephew, whose family dominated Rome: when Evelyn met him a few years later, Barberini loaned him a Correggio for his servant to copy. But we hear of no such idea from Milton. Nonetheless he also met the poet Giovanni Salzilli, who wrote an extravagant laudatory quatrain for him that Milton included among the commendations from Italian friends preceding the Latin section of his 1645 *Poems*, and to whom he addressed 'Ad Salsillum' on the occasion of an illness. Nothing is known of this illness, apart from the stomach disorder mentioned in the poem, but it is written in scazontics, a modification of iambic trimeters, and Milton plays on the literal meaning of the word *skazon* in Greek, 'limping'. Perhaps Salzilli had gout, like many men of the time, as Milton did later in his life. At the Jesuit College on October 20/30 Milton went to a dinner attended by other visiting Englishmen, all Catholics or future Royalists.

Milton arrived in Naples by coach in late November or December. Naples was then under Spanish rule, and Milton may have learned some Spanish to add to his several other languages. He there met one of the greatest of literary patrons, Giovanni Battista Manso, Marquis of Villa. Manso had entertained Tasso during the 1590s and had also been a sponsor of the younger poet Marino, to whom he erected a fine tomb and monument. He was, like Galileo, in his seventies when he met Milton and guided him around the city and the Spanish court. Milton paid him tribute in an elegant, unforced Latin poem, *Mansus*, written before he left Naples, a poem in which he mentions both Tasso and Marino (and also for the first time mentions his ambition to write an epic on an Arthurian theme, 78-84). Manso gave Milton books, and probably wrote in one of them the verse epigram that Milton later published at the head of his Italian and Latin poems:

> Ut mens, forma, décor, facies, mos, si pietas sic,
> Non Anglus, verum hercle Angelus ipse fores
>
> ('If to your mind, form, elegance, features and manners your
> religion were matched, you would I swear be not an Anglo-Saxon
> but a very angel').

When Milton left, Manso apologized for not having shown him more attention: he would have been a better host, he said, if Milton had been less explicit about his religious views. Milton was likely as proud of the rebuke as of the compliment.

He had planned to go on to Sicily and Greece, but now decided to return to Rome. He later attributed this decision to 'the sad news of civil war from England'. He thought it base, he claimed, that he should be travelling abroad to cultivate his mind while his fellow citizens were fighting for their liberty. Perhaps the news reached Milton through the English merchants in Naples. He was warned that the Jesuits in Rome were plotting against him but took pride in facing down the threat: 'in the very stronghold of the pope, if anyone attacked the right religion, I openly, as before, defended it' (*YP* IV.1 619). Probably on this occasion he visited the Barberini Library, and met Lukas Holste (Holstenius), a German scholar who had studied in Oxford.

Holste was a convert to Catholicism, and was now secretary to Cardinal Barberini and his librarian. He showed Milton round the library, including some Greek codices, and gave him a copy of a book he had just published, an edition of the sayings of the Pythagoreans. He also asked Milton to copy parts of a Medici manuscript for him when he returned to Florence.

A few days later Milton attended 'a public Musical entertainment', a comic opera entitled *Chi soffrem speri* by Giulio Rospigliosi, at the new Palazzo Barberini, and was impressed by the attention paid to him by the cardinal, who greeted him at the door and invited him for a private audience the next day. Milton attributed this to Holste's influence, but Barberini, as well as being chief adviser to his uncle, Pope Urban VIII, was responsible for taking care of English visitors. The set designs for Rospigliosi's opera were by the same Bernini who was embellishing and remodelling St Peter's. It was common at the time for famous architects to design ephemeral settings for important occasions; a parallel would be the designs for court masques by Inigo Jones at the Stuart court in England.

Milton also attended at least one recital by Leonora Baroni, rumoured to be mistress both of Cardinal Mazarin and of Rospigliosi, and wrote three epigrams in her honour. Milton already had considerable musical experience, partly through his father's encouragement and partly from having produced *Comus*. The Lady and Sabrina both have fine voices, as does the Emilia of Milton's early Italian sonnets for his boyhood friend, Charles Diodati. Yet Leonora Baroni must have been a new experience. She was a remarkable talent, both as performer and composer, and was widely praised by many contemporaries. She was sometimes accompanied on the lyre by her mother, also a professional musician, or on the harp by her sister. Milton's praise of her reworks the theme familiar from his earlier poetry, that music has the power to restore the mystic harmony of earth and heaven. Indeed 'the music of your voice', he writes, 'pours forth the presence of God'. In another epigram he recalls that other Leonora for whom Tasso went mad with love, and wishes he, Tasso, had been able to listen to this Leonora, 'whose voice could have composed his wandering wits'. Hyperbole is common in poems of praise, but something about this woman's performance certainly moved the young man.

When he returned to Florence in March 1639, he recited more of his Latin poems and renewed contact with his friends; they now wrote for him the tributes he later included in his 1645 *Poems*. The language of Carlo Dati echoes Milton's theme for Leonora: he hears the harmonious strains of the heavenly spheres, but with an important difference. The guide to those heavenly spheres is not now music, at least not explicitly, but astronomy. Evidently Milton's scientific interests were already being developed and discussed, perhaps through the presence of Galileo in the city. Dati, who had studied with Galileo, goes even further in his encomium, and addresses Milton as 'one in whose memory the whole world is lodged, in whose intellect is wisdom'. While in Florence, Milton went to the Laurentian Library and tried unsuccessfully to get permission to copy the manuscript Holste had asked for. Looking back on his experience of Florence and his friends there, Milton later wrote in 1642 that their praises, as well as his own 'inward prompting', now began to propel him towards his destiny as a poet: 'by labour and intent study (which I take to be my portion in this life), joyn'd with the strong propensity of nature, I might perhaps leave something so written to aftertimes, as they should not willingly let it die' (*YP* I 810).

Milton now went on for a month to the Republic of Venice, probably in May 1639. From here, his nephew Edward Phillips later reported, he shipped home cases of books picked up on his travels, including music by Monteverdi, then living in Venice, as well as many books later cited in his Commonplace Book (Dante, Ariosto, Tasso, as well as classical authors and church fathers). He could observe here the form of government he came to consider as the best for promoting human rights and liberty, an aristocratic republic, which Grotius had also praised. Building work was going on, he must have noticed, including the completion of the glorious Santa Maria della Salute, which celebrates the city's survival from the plague of 1631 and dominates the entrance to the Grand Canal. Though Venice was in decline, it was seen at the time as embodying the ancient ideal of Greek and Roman republics. It had resisted a papal bull of excommunication in 1606, and had even expelled the Jesuits.

Finally, Milton left Italy for the contrasting environment of Calvinist Geneva, another republic, but one which was labouring under a theocratic regime. This time he crossed the Alps, either via the Simplon or the Grand St Bernard (both still snowed up but passable in May). Here in Geneva his chief contact was the eminent biblical scholar Giovanni (Jean) Diodati, Charles's uncle, and it may have been here that Milton learned of the death of his great friend. He had taken a side trip from Florence to Lucca, the place of origin of the Diodati family, so may already have heard the sad news. Charles had been buried in London, at St Anne's in Blackfriars, on 27 August 1638, some nine months before, while Milton had been in Florence.

Milton probably stayed with the Diodatis in Geneva but visited other distinguished Protestants too, including the Neapolitan aristocrat and refugee Camillo Cerdogni. In his visitor's book, Milton wrote two characteristic epigrams: one was the last lines of his *A Maske*:'if vertue feeble were/ Heaven it selfe would stoope to her'; the other a line borrowed from Horace:'Coelum non animam muto dum trans mare curro' ('I change my sky but not my mind when

I cross the sea'). Evidently there was a certain amount of relief at being back among Protestants, and he was proud to be able to say he had not changed.

Crossing now into France and retracing his steps from more than a year before, Milton arrived back in England in July or early August 1639. He had to set up a new home in London and adjust to the changed political and financial situation. But he also had a sad task to be fulfilled from his voyage, the necessary tribute to his dead friend.

The poem he wrote, probably in the autumn of 1639/40, 'Epitaphium Damonis', is his finest Latin poem and also one of his most revealingly autobiographical. Latin was the appropriate language for Diodati, since Milton's letters to him were in Latin, and perhaps even some of their conversation (though Diodati wrote to Milton in Greek). Of the separate editions of this poem Milton then published only one copy seems to have survived, in the British Library. When he republished it in his 1645 collection, it formed a deliberate pair with 'Lycidas', also a pastoral elegy written for a dead friend. Each poem comes last, the one in the English section, the other in the Latin part of the book. But the poetic problem posed is different. In 'Lycidas', the poet wonders how he is to devote himself to poetry or any other task in God's service when the death of a young man is apparently so meaningless. But in the Latin poem, he expresses his anguish, grief and loneliness in a far more intense and personal way. There is no procession of mourners or weeping shepherds: now the only mourner is Thyrsis/ Milton. As in 'Lycidas' there is an outside narrator, this time in a proem which explains why the poem is belated in its expression of grief: Thyrsis was enjoying the delights of Florence, but now his return home has increased his sense of loss. 'To whom shall I open my heart? Who will teach me to soften the cares that eat me away? Who will beguile the long night with sweet conversation?' (46-7). The poem gives the impression that the writing of it has reawakened his love for his friend in all its intensity. He recalls Damon's charms, his laughter, his flashes of Attic wit, his cultured jokes (55-6). Diodati was fun to be with. At the end, he is received, like Lycidas, into heaven. But whereas for Edward King the saints gather and sing hymns, for Diodati there is dancing. And in an oddly suggestive conclusion his modesty is mentioned, but a blushing modesty ('purpureus pudor'): and the 'virginal young man who never tasted the pleasures of the marriage bed' (212-13) is caught up in an eternal celebration of divine marriage, raving in Bacchic frenzy under the thyrsus (staff) of Zion ('Festa Sionaeo bacchantur et orgia thyrso').[4] That is line 219, the last. It is a bizarre combination of Ovid and the Book of Revelation. And it is a lot sexier than the end imagined for King.

A refrain echoes throughout the poem: 'Go home unfed, for your master has no time for you, my lambs.' The contrast is surely deliberate with the bad pastors of 'Lycidas' to whom 'the hungry sheep look up and are not fed'. Here the poet himself is the one who, for grief, cannot feed his flock. The refrain is repeated seventeen times with no variation. But as it rings through the poem its meaning subtly changes, till it becomes a renunciation of the pastoral genre, perhaps also of Latin, in favour of the new projects Milton imagines for his poetic future, chiefly the British historical epic on Arthur and his knights that he expected one day to accomplish. He spells out these plans in greater detail now, and with even more excitement, than in the previous sketch he had made in *Mansus*. So an epic after the manner of Tasso (but also Spenser, not yet clearly distinguished) is to be the major task that God sets him. The figure of Sabrina in *Comus* was daughter of Locrine and therefore related to myths of Trojan British and also Welsh or Arthurian ancestry. Milton's thinking had clearly advanced since then. But now contemporary politics pushed aside poetic prospects. By the time Milton was free to return to large-scale poetic conceptions, Arthur had given way to Adam.

7

No Bishop, No King

Milton had decided not to take the holy orders for which his education had prepared him. But he remained committed to what he regarded as the true church throughout his life, and struggled at various times to make the actual Church of England conform to his ideal. Since governance of the church was controlled by the competing authorities of Parliament and the king, efforts to reform the church were directly and often damagingly political. And differences over how the church was to be governed were the instigating cause of the civil wars that spanned the middle years of the seventeenth century. Indeed, the first of these wars, between the English court and Scottish Presbyterians, are known as the First and Second Bishops Wars (January–June 1639, August–October 1640). The word *bishop* derives from the Greek word *episkopos*, whence English 'Episcopal', and in all discussions of these struggles, the two terms are interchangeable. It is for this reason that the Anglican church in North America is known as 'Episcopalian'.

Charles I tried to impose the high-church Episcopal structure and liturgy on the Scots Kirk, and was humiliatingly resisted. Between the two wars Charles had to call a parliament, the first since 1629, to raise money. Parliament was recalcitrant, and after three weeks, Charles dissolved what became known as the Short Parliament. Charles's second defeat left Scots troops on English soil, occupying Newcastle, Durham and all of Northumberland. A preliminary treaty signed on 27 October 1640 required Charles once again to summon Parliament, and this time it lasted for the rest of his life – and longer. Quickly, this newly assembled body acted to compensate the puritan victims of Archbishop Laud's persecution (William Prynne and John Lilburne among them), and began impeachment proceedings against Laud for 'subversion of the laws… and of religion' – he was sent to the Tower – and also against the earl of Strafford, for having tried to use the Irish army 'to reduce this kingdom'. He too was in the Tower by 25 November. After a long trial for treason, and London mobs screaming for his blood, Strafford was eventually executed on 12 May 1641. The new Parliament passed an Act prohibiting its dissolution without its own consent, thus constituting itself as what became 'the Long Parliament'. These events had broken open the power structure of England. It would never be the same again. Charles had lost control and shown his weakness. Rebellion had succeeded: armed resistance to tyranny now became a possible course of action, both for the English and even more dangerously, for the Irish.

Milton returned to England between the two Bishops Wars. At first he was occupied with finding a place to live and deciding what he should do. His father was still living in Horton with Christopher Milton and his wife, though they would soon move to Reading now that Christopher had been called to the bar. John Milton decided not to return to the family home but to live in London. He found temporary lodging in St Bride's churchyard, just near St Paul's where he had grown up, and soon moved to a bigger house in Aldersgate, just outside the city walls. Milton's sister Anne had died and so his nephews John and Edward Phillips, aged eight and nine, came to live with him as boarding pupils. He also engaged a servant, Jane Yates, about this time, presumably to help with the boys. Milton mapped out a plan of study for them 'far above the Pedantry of common publick Schooles (where such Authors are scarce heard of)', says Edward (in his first-hand account of his uncle's life). Here is a part of the extraordinary list he gives of this reading: 'Of the Latin, De Re Rustica, Cato, Varro, Columella, and Palladius; Cornelius Celsus, an Ancient Physician of the Romans; a great part of Pliny's Natural History, Vitruvius his Architecture, Frontinus his Stratagems, with the two Egregious Poets, Lucretius and Manilius'. There is an equally long list for the Greek. Not only did they read well beyond the main authors in Greek and Latin, but they learned enough Hebrew, Aramaic and even Syriac 'to go through the Pentateuch' and other versions of scripture. On Sundays they would read a chapter of the Greek New Testament and discuss it (or listen while Milton expounded it). Milton summarizes a typical day like this. His mornings he spent

> up and stirring, in Winter often ere the sound of any bell awake men to labour… in Summer as oft with the Bird that first rouses, or not much tardier, to reade good Authors, or cause them to be read, till the attention bee weary, or memory have his full fraught. Then with usefull and generous labours preserving the bodies health, and hardinesse, to render lightsome, cleare, and not lumpish obedience to the minde, to the cause of religion, and our Countries liberty, when it shall require firme hearts in sound bodies to stand and cover their stations. (*YP* I 885)

Nothing gives as good a sense of the difference between Milton's discipline and ours as this apparently quite realistic programme.

During this time, Milton also made several entries in the Trinity manuscript for projects he had in mind, including mostly tragedies and even an epic poem on a historical subject such as King Alfred ('especially at his issuing out of Edelingsey on the Danes, whose actions are wel like those of Ulysses'). The topics include several Old Testament stories ('Dinah', 'Elias in the mount', 'Gideon Idoloklastes'), even a brief sketch under the title 'Paradise Lost', and a fuller version of the story called 'Adam unparadiz'd'. There is also a 'Christus patiens' ('Christ suffering', perhaps a reaction to the meeting with Grotius in Paris). Eventually these ideas, with various shifts of focus, turned into the three great poems of his final years: *Paradise Lost, Paradise Regained* and *Samson Agonistes.* He was also writing in his Commonplace Book, making notes from Chaucer and Gower (his *Confessio Amantis*), but chiefly from English history. Citing the way Alfred turned the old laws into English, he adds 'I would he liv'd now to rid us of this Norman gibbrish' (*YP* I 424) – a sign of how sensitive Milton always was to the ways officialdom hides itself behind wooden and obscure styles. He also cites several instances of abuses of royal power, such as those of Richard II, Edward II and King John. And he makes a summary of Macchiavelli on why a republic is preferable to a monarchy.

These peaceable months spent in reading and teaching could not last. Milton soon found himself drawn into the struggle to reform the church and get rid of the bishops, not only from the ecclesiastical hierarchy but from the House of Lords. He wrote five anti-prelatical tracts over the next two years in favour of the 'Root and Branch' petition, signed by 15,000 Londoners and handed in to Parliament on 11 December 1640. According to the petition, there had been a 'great increase of idle, lewd and dissolute, ignorant and erroneous men in the ministry, which swarm like locusts of Egypt over the whole kingdom'.[1] The text goes on to denounce the 'growth of popery and increase of papists, priests, and Jesuits in sundry places, but especially about London since the Reformation; the frequent venting of crucifixes and popish pictures both engraven and printed, and the placing of such in Bibles'. The main fear, it seems, is of

> the great conformity and likeness both continued and increased of our
> Church to the Church of Rome, in vestures, postures, ceremonies, and
> administrations, namely as the bishop's rochets and the lawn-sleeves,
> the four-cornered cap, the cope and surplice, the tippet, the hood, and
> the canonical coat; the pulpits clothed, especially now of late, with the
> Jesuits' badge upon them every way.

Further signs of this problem are 'the standing up at Gloria Patri and at the reading of the Gospel, praying towards the East, the bowing at the name of Jesus, the bowing to the altar towards the East, cross in baptism, the kneeling at the Communion'. There is a good deal more in the same vein. The tone was set.

Milton was not yet as radical either in politics or in theology as he soon became: like most Englishmen, he still recognized the king and thought of his power as shared with the Lords and the Commons. But Parliament, he argued, should be the sole agent of church reform. If not, the king would impose his own high-church ceremonial and doctrine through his control of the appointment of bishops. Milton's pamphlets helped to generate an extraordinary explosion of tract and counter-tract, a war of words such as no modern European country had ever seen (though the Rome of Cicero and Cato may have been some sort of precedent).[2] His friend, the bookseller George Thomason, collected some 22,000 pamphlets in the next twenty years on everything from the imminence of the apocalypse, to the renewed power of Satan, to how the people could take power from their rulers. The rhyme that had been popular during the Peasant's Revolt of 1381 was now again on many lips: 'When Adam delved and Eve span, who was then the gentleman?'[3]

Milton's first step into these polemical waters was probably his brief contribution to a pamphlet published in March 1641 under the name SMECTYMNUUS, an acronym formed from the initials of the five authors, Stephen Marshall, Edmund Calamy, Thomas Young, Matthew Newcomen and William Sperstow. This was a response to two treatises written at Laud's instigation by Bishop Joseph Hall. Underestimating the strength of feeling in Parliament, Hall had argued in *A Humble Remonstrance* for the maintenance of bishops. Making use of his readings in history, Milton wrote the anonymous nine-page postscript to SMECTYMNUUS that reviews the history of prelacy in England and shows what a danger all these priests have been.

Then, a few days after Strafford's execution in May, *Of Reformation Touching Church-Discipline in England* appeared. It was published anonymously, though Milton soon acknowledged it as his. It is an extraordinarily direct and rhetorically powerful document, unlike anything that preceded it in these tract wars. It cites 'our Chaucer' as a satirical model against the Popish ecclesiastics such as the Friar in the General Prologue to *The Canterbury Tales*. But its real affinities are elsewhere. It is comparable rather to Swift in its vitriolic, even physical, vehemence (*saeva indignatio* or 'savage indignation' are the words Swift used for the inscription on his tomb in Dublin) than the reasonable-sounding Smectymnuans. It seeks to excite disgust – it still does – at these prelates who for centuries have served their bellies rather than the peoples' souls, 'belching the soure Crudities of yesterdayes *Poperie*', enough to make God himself vomit. And not only God but also time vomits. England had once been in the vanguard of reform, but now it is betraying the cause.

The anonymous (but unmistakable) author, supposedly writing a letter to 'a Freind', traces the decline of the church, as it 'backslides one way into the Jewish beggary, of old cast rudiments, and stumbles forward another way into the new-vomited Paganisme of sensual Idolatry' (*YP* I 520). He goes on to imagine these bishops as 'a huge and monstrous Wen' or a 'swolne Tumor' in the head. He addresses them as 'a bottle of vitious and harden'd excrements', as all men will see, 'when I have cut thee off, and open'd thee'. He implores the '*Tri-personall* GODHEAD! Looke upon this thy poore and almost spent, and expiring *Church*, leave her not thus a prey to these importunate *Wolves*'. The echo of his own poem 'Lycidas' is unmistakable, and the same biblical references are resonant: John 10:12, about hirelings as wolves; Matthew 7:15 about 'false prophets, which come to you in sheep's clothing, but inwardly they are ravening wolves'; Matthew 10:16, 'Behold, I send you out as sheep in the midst of wolves. Therefore be wise as serpents and harmless as doves'; and Acts 20:29, about the savage wolves who will come in among the faithful flock after Christ's departure. With this fiercely eloquent treatise, Milton announces himself as one of the great writers of English prose. He is to be 'violent, undeferential, and implacable'.[4] As for the bishops, 'those vassals of perdition', they should be executed, and will in any case spend eternity being tortured in Hell.

This tract was representative of the new print culture. The Company of Stationers, which controlled all aspects of the printing trade, including copyright and the prevention of piracy, had been in turn controlled by the Star Chamber. But in 1641 Parliament abolished the hated Star Chamber. One effect was to remove licence controls. *Of Reformation* was not registered for publication, nor was its author identified. Only the bookseller is named, Thomas Underhill, with his address 'At the Sign of the Bible, near the Compter in Great Wood Street'. Perhaps five hundred or a thousand copies were printed (the normal number), but would soon be yesterday's news. Or at least they would be if they had not been by John Milton. Ephemeral they might be, but Milton nonetheless sent a copy to the Bodleian Library in Oxford. It was not only the memories of Edward King or Charles Diodati who would be thus preserved, as his poems had promised. Even the spitting, cat-like fury of the momentary prose would make a bid for immortality. In June 1641 the 'Root and Branch' Bill to abolish the bishops and everything that went with them was passed by Parliament. Spitting worked and Milton now had a taste for it.

In his next pamphlet, published very soon, entitled *Of Prelatical Episcopacy*,

Milton addressed by name one of the bishops responsible for the earlier pro-episcopacy pamphlets, Ussher, bishop of Armagh (famous in another context as the man who showed the universe was created in 4004 BC), and, incidentally, Bishop Hall. The tone this time is more respectful. Like a seasoned debater, Milton leaps on a concession of his opponents and claims the fight is over: the terms 'bishop' and 'presbyter' were used interchangeably in the New Testament. For his opponents, this signifies the antiquity and divine authority of the bishops. For Milton it means they are indeed the same as 'presbyters', and should therefore be subject to the same 'humane priviledge, that all men have ever since Adam, being borne free', should have the power to retain or remove episcopacy, 'consulting with our owne occasions, and conveniences' (*YP* I 624). Still he continues the arguments and tries to show how all the non-scriptural authorities, such as the fathers of the church, cited by his opponents, are insufficient and indeed seriously unreliable. Only the Bible will do as an authority, a doctrine that most Protestants share, and that was known as *sola scriptura*.

While this tract was being absorbed by the public, Milton was already working on yet another reply to Hall (whom the Smectymnuus also denounced in a separate tract) – *Animadversions upon the Remonstrants Defence Against Smectymnuus*. It came out in July, anonymously, a few days after the Smectymnuus's own pamphlet, but is very far from following their own moderate tone. Instead, Milton works up a defense of vehement satire, and places himself, not for the first or last time, in the line of prophets 'transported with the zeale of truth to a well-heated fervencie' (*YP* I 663) – he is thinking, he later says, of Daniel against Nebuchadnezzar and Elijah against Baal (700). The pamphlet is even more scurrilous than *Of Reformation*. He attacks this hireling clergy and urges them: 'Wipe your fat corpulencies out of our light' (732). He also imagines God coming down among us again: 'When thou hast settl'd peace in the Church, and righteous judgement in the Kingdome, then shall all thy Saints addresse their voices of joy, and triumph to thee, standing on the shoare of that red Sea into which our enemies has almost driven us' (706). Clearly the language allows for little compromise. Nevertheless, in a reversal of the previous policy, on 29 December 1641, the bishops were allowed to return to the House of Lords. Milton was incensed and sat down again to denounce this backsliding.

Meanwhile, Charles made one of his major errors, one that has resonated down the ages. His prerogative, he felt, had been attacked by the demands that Parliament approve ministers, reform the church, and even oversee the military expedition to Ireland to put down the rebels there. On 3 January 1642 Charles sent an sergeant-at-arms to the House of Commons to arrest five of the leaders for treason. The Commons refused, on the grounds that any such attempt was a breach of its privilege. The next day, the king himself, with a small guard, went to Westminster Hall. Word quickly got round and by the time he arrived he had an entourage of some four-hundred, many of them officers. No king of England had ever interrupted a session of the Commons, and at first the members were stunned as Charles swept down the centre aisle. Then, remembering their duty, they rose and stood bare-headed as the king demanded the speaker, William Lenthall, identify the five members he had come to arrest. Lenthall answered, 'I have neither eyes to see, nor tongue to speak but as this House is pleased to direct me'. Rebuffed, Charles looked along the ranks of the members. 'Well', he now famously said, 'I see all the birds are flown. I cannot do what I came for'[5]. As he strode out of the house, cries of 'Privilege, privilege' followed him. The five escaped and went into hiding. A riot ensued in the City of London, King and court left town for Windsor, and the five were triumphantly reinstated a week after the violation of the Commons' privilege. The people were marching: that was what politics had become. Some 4,000 or 5,000 from Buckinghamshire alone presented a petition in support of Parliament. London was becoming an exciting and even dangerous place.

Milton's tract, which he wrote rapidly during this tense period, was published in January or February. *The Reason of Church Government* takes a different approach from the vitriolic satire of the earlier tracts. Milton here makes a broad argument against episcopacy based on an ideal church order that includes the equality of clergy and laity that he takes to be anticipated in the gospel. The degree of his advancing radicalism may be judged by the way he here defends the sects called by their enemies 'Puritans and Brownists'. He claims that 'the Primitive Christians in their times were accounted such as are now call'd Familists and Adamites' (*YP* I 841–4). Familists, members of the Family of Love, had spread widely through England in the Elizabethan period: they believed that men and women might recapture on earth the state of prelapsarian innocence; they held property in common; and they thought the spirit of god within was the only guide to understanding the Bible. The Adamites, at least according to their enemies, went naked whenever they could, and especially were baptised as adults, nakedness being a sign of their regained purity and simplicity. Milton clearly feels no need to distinguish his own views from those of these extreme sects, who have much in common with such groups as the Ranters, some of whom, like Lawrence Clarkson, argued for complete sexual freedom (*YP* I 788). But for now Milton's target is the priesthood. To oppose the claim of the bishops that episcopacy had developed over time in order to counter schism during the early years of the church, he argues that the priesthood itself is the chief promoter of schism, labelling sects and denouncing heretics instead of encouraging controversy as a way to truth. The 'reason' of the title means something like that 'spiritual power or purpose' that will emerge from disciplined exchange of views. Unlike the civil magistrate, the church has power over only the inner man, and so must plead and cajole and reprove, perhaps even excommunicate if necessary, but always reason. Like Calvin, he speaks of 'a company of Saints'. Any Christian, not just a speciously sanctified priesthood, should be able to teach and expound scripture 'though never so laick, if his capacity, his faith, and prudent demeanour commend him'. In Milton's view 'the congregation of the Lord' needs to recover 'its true likenesse' as of a 'holy generation, a royall Priesthood, a Saintly communion'.[6]

The tract also includes an extended use of the biblical story of Samson as an allegory. The king grows up healthy 'with those illustrious and sunny locks the laws waving and curling about his godlike shoulders'. But along comes Delilah, that is, he lays 'down his head among the strumpet flatteries of Prelats, while he sleeps and thinks no harme, they wickedly… deliver him over to… those Philistines', that is, violent counsels, who deprive him of his sight, his 'natural discerning' (*YP* I 858). Only with great difficulty can he recover his strength. The tract ends by invoking divine vengeance 'on this godlesse and oppressing government', like that which fell upon Sodom.

Unlike the earlier tracts, this one bore Milton's full name on the title-page. And in the second of its two books, he presents himself to its reader in a long autobiographical statement. Why? Partly because in the books of ancient rhetoric he had been studying for so long, it was said that one way to convince your audience is to show yourself to be worth following, what is known as an 'ethical proof'. Yet Milton goes much further. He engages in a public dialogue with himself, imagining what he would say if he did not write this tract. All that study, and yet you could not turn your eloquence to defend the true church when it needed it?

> Thou hadst the diligence, the parts, the language of a man, if a vain subject were to be adorn'd or beautifi'd, but when the cause of God and his Church was to be pleaded, for which purpose that tongue was given thee which thou hast, God listen'd if he could heare thy voice among his zealous servants, but thou wert domb as a beast; from hence forward be that which thine own brutish silence hath made thee. (805)

Indeed he *was* supposed to be doing something else, not writing all this prose.

> I should not choose this manner of writing wherein knowing myself inferior to my self, led by the genial power of nature to another task, I have the use, as I may account it, of my left hand.

The contrast of self and self, of 'I' and 'I', of right and left, is curious here, as if Milton can at any time withdraw from his own image, and then step back into the picture. Prose, he says, may be what only his left hand produces, but now that he has started, he'll go on to tell you more about himself, and more. The 'I' who has use of the left hand can be discussed by yet another 'I', another step removed, as at the end of 'Lycidas'. One of these selves would prefer still to be writing poetry, because among other things he could more readily write about himself (it gets dizzying), but 'let that not stop me'.

> For although a Poet soaring in the high region of his fancies with his garland and singing robes about him might without apology speak more of himself then I mean to doe, yet for me sitting here below in the cool element of prose, a mortall thing among many readers of no Empyreall conceit, to venture and divulge unusual things of my selfe, I shall petition to the gentler sort, it may not be envy to me. (808)

And so he goes on, putting aside the whole attack on the bishops, to 'a leisurely contemplation of his own merits'.[7] Having been encouraged by his father to learn 'tongues, and some sciences', his teachers praised him and the Italians offered 'written Encomiums'. Friends offered further encouragement, but the final confirmation (and thus perhaps the decision not to pursue the ecclesiastical career) came from within. 'An inward prompting... now grew daily upon me, that by labour and intent study (which I take to be my portion in this life) joyn'd with the strong propensity of nature, I might perhaps leave something so written to aftertimes, as they should not willingly let it die' (810).

He then gets down to detail. He wonders whether any subject for a historical epic is left, since Arthur, he had previously admitted, was not sufficiently historical. As in the Trinity manuscript, he wonders about tragedy, whether Sophocles or Euripides might perhaps be 'more doctrinal and exemplary to a Nation' than the epic of Homer, Virgil or Tasso (815). Even the Apocalypse of St John, he thinks, offers 'the majestick image of a high and stately Tragedy'. He is attracted to high lyric, following Pindar and Callimachus but using the Psalms as the chief model, while hymns (like his own 'Nativity Ode') may celebrate God and his works. Or he might 'sing the victorious agonies of Martyrs and Saints, the deeds and triumphs of just and pious Nations doing valiantly through faith against the enemies of Christ.' Clearly, in spite of the jottings in the Trinity manuscript, he had no serious notions yet of *Paradise Lost*. We may be glad that he did not now get started on the project for the epic: it might have been about historical heroes like Alfred – or, in a year or two, Oliver Cromwell.

He now makes an important claim. The abilities of a poet are the gift of God, rarely bestowed, yet given to some in every nation: they are 'of power beside the office of the pulpit, to inbreed and cherish in a great people the seeds of vertu, and publick civility, to allay the perturbations of the mind, and set the affections in right tune' (815). He has now evidently resolved the conflict about his career, not exactly by abandoning the church, but by adopting a profession that would duplicate its effects ('*beside* the office of the pulpit').

Milton's recent *Animadversions* was soon answered by someone unknown who identifies himself as 'a young scholar'. He accuses the author (not identified as Milton) of spending his spare time in bordellos and playhouses. He 'blasphemes God and the King' as before 'he drank Sack and swore'. Milton could not take this. He replied, again anonymously, though apparently knowing he would be recognized, in *An Apology Against a Pamphlet* (usually called *Apology for Smectymnuus*), defending his studious and healthy life, as if he were preparing for military service, as indeed he may have thought he was. He is not a fornicator, but does not deny visiting playhouses. And he is moved (how wonderfully uncomplicated!) to launch a defense of the chastity he has acquired from his reading of poetry and philosophy, where he has learned to love and honour women without being 'defil'd' by them. Unchastity in a man is indeed 'much more deflouring and dishonourable' than in a woman (892). Marriage, he insists, is not a defilement – and one wonders if already he is considering marriage. Edward Phillips also tells us that at this time Milton allowed himself some relaxation with two Gray's Inn friends, 'Young Sparks of his Acquaintance... the *Beau's* of those times'. But we must not imagine a John Milton haunting the local pubs: he permitted himself what Phillips calls a 'Gawdy-day' like this once every three or four weeks.[8]

Milton also attacks his anonymous opponent (whom he must have thought he could identify) with insults, sarcasm and personal attacks. 'This tormentor of semi-colons is as good at dismembering and slitting sentences as his grave Fathers the prelates have bin at stigmatizing and slitting noses' (894). There is a great deal more in the same vein, attacking the style as if it were the man. His own style, on the other hand, is unstudied, and yet somehow, since he is 'possest of a fervent desire to know good things', the words 'like so many nimble and airy servitors trip about him at command, and in well order'd files, as he would wish, fall aptly into their own places'. What a wonderful description of how good it feels to write! The good writer, he also claims (less admirably, but with charming naivety), 'ought him selfe to bee a true Poem, that is, a composition, and patterne of the best and honourablest things; not presuming to sing high praises of heroick men, or famous Cities, unless he have in himselfe the experience and the practice of all that which is praiseworthy' (890). And he returns to the image of the soaring poet left behind temporarily for cool prose; he now imagines that he 'ascends his fiery Chariot drawn with two blazing Meteors figur'd like beasts', the one a 'Lion to express power, high autority and indignation, the other of count'nance like a man to cast derision and scorne upon perverse and fraudulent seducers and then 'drives over the heads of Scarlet Prelats... Thus did the true Prophets of old combat with the false' (900).

There is something heroic but deeply unsettling about the way Milton presents himself in this tract. Granted that he is replying to unjustified charges that he spent his time in brothels, the length and tone of his defense of his chastity are troubling. He wants to write something great, and in order to do so he must himself be above reproach. Both are a 'composition'. So he admits to no flaw. He claims to have conducted an 'unfained and diligent inquiry of mine owne conscience at home', and found no sins. He even claims that 'a certain reserv'dnesse of naturall disposition, and morall disciplines learnt out of the noblest Philosophy' (892) are enough to keep him out of the bordello, 'though Christianity had bin but slightly taught me'. He then turns round and attacks his opponent for writing as if 'he only were exempted out of the corrupt masse of Adam, borne without sinne originall' (909). In the heat of his argument, Milton has lost sight of the fact that he is open to the same charge. And yet the claim to be somehow above the rest of us, exempt, is a recurring characteristic of Milton's prose.[9] And it is not always easy to breathe up there. In this respect he is very unlike other religious writers of a puritan bent: for them, confession of sin, if not humbled prayer and hope, were the main reasons to 'compose'.

In the five years since he wrote 'Lycidas', where he attacks the greed of the clergy but still allows for a national church hierarchy (though we must remember the repressive force of Laud's censorship at the time), Milton had progressed rapidly toward the radical positions he would now be identified with. In the first of his anti-prelatical tracts, he writes still as a Presbyterian, or at least expects the established Presbyterians to be on his side in the struggle for reform. But in the space of a few months he had moved beyond the idea of an established and centrally controlled church to become an Independent. In practice, this meant that he was prepared to tolerate almost any of the sects that were now springing up, even if he belonged to none himself.

In July 1642 Parliament voted to raise an army. On 22 August the king and the prince of Wales unfurled the royal standard in front of 2,000 men, on horse and on foot. Civil War in England had officially begun. Since rebellion had already broken out in Ireland, historians nowadays refer to the Wars of the Three Kingdoms. First Scotland (the Bishops' Wars), then Ireland, now England.

8

Mary Powell

Marriage and separation were to be major themes of the next years. In February 1642 Charles I sent his wife, Henrietta Maria, and daughter Mary to the Netherlands. At Dover all were in tears, and when the *Lion* stood out to sea, Charles galloped along the cliff till the ship was out of sight. Ostensibly, the reason for their departure was to bring the fifteen-year-old Princess Mary to her husband, William of Orange, whom she had officially married in May 1641. But the real reason for the separation was fear of the incipient Civil War. Charles's French queen was a Catholic, and contemporaries, not always hostile ones, often blamed her intransigence and her influence over her husband for the war and would in the future blame her for his eventual death. Nevertheless, by an odd quirk of fate, the departure shaped the longer future of the English monarchy, once the turbulent years of the Civil War were over. William III of Orange was the son of this Princess Mary, the first to be known as Princess Royal, and it was his marriage to his cousin, James II's Protestant daughter, that allowed the couple to come to the throne in 1689 as William III and Mary II.

In May 1642, just before the war began, Milton set out for Oxford. With the fine weather approaching, Milton may have felt the need for a break from his teaching duties. And perhaps he would visit the Bodleian Library, which had not acknowledged receipt of the pamphlets Milton had sent. On the way, he could visit his father and his brother Christopher, now a practising barrister and the father of two little girls, in Reading. Christopher was already a Royalist and we do not know which way their father leaned, but in spite of political differences, the family stayed in touch through the war years. In this respect they were typical of many families throughout the realm.

While in Oxford, Milton went over to Forest Hill to visit a man called Richard Powell. Since 1627 Powell had been paying semi-annual interest of £12 on a loan of £300 from Milton's father (who came from the neighbouring village of Stanton St John), but he was falling behind and in danger of losing his estate.

What followed is extraordinary, though the evidence we have for it is mainly the account of Edward Phillips, Milton's nephew, written fifty-two years later. 'After a Month's stay, home he returns a Married-man, that went out a Bachelor; his Wife being *Mary*, the eldest daughter of Mr *Richard Powell*, then a Justice of Peace.' What had happened? Milton was thirty-three, and, in the course of protesting a few months before that he did not spend time in bordellos or had need to marry a rich widow, had hinted that he would rather choose a virgin 'of mean fortunes honestly bred'.[1] And here she was. Mary Powell was seventeen. She was one of five daughters – there were nine children altogether – and Powell would be glad to have found a prospective son-in-law who might be tractable over the marriage portion. In the event, Powell paid the interest he owed, and promised a dowry of £1,000 that Milton must have known would never be paid. (The normal dowry for a comparable family would be something between £250 to £400.) Before the month was out, they were married. Bride and groom returned to Aldersgate.

Along with them came at least three of Mary's siblings. The Powell household was a noisy, boisterous one, and they brought their habits to Milton's quiet bachelor household in London. Phillips, who was twelve at the time, tells us that 'the feasting held for some days in Celebration of the Nuptials, and for entertainment of the Bride's Friends. At length they took their leave, and returning to *Forrest hill*, left the Sister behind; probably not much to her satisfaction, as appeared by the sequel.'

It is not hard to imagine how problems developed. All Milton's biographers do so in their own way, with varying degrees of imaginative or sympathetic engagement with one or both members of the couple. Mary was young, but she had grown up in a noisy careless home, a country estate, not a city household. At first Milton must have seemed attractively different, clever, deeply interesting, musical, as well as good-looking. A man in the prime of life. But when did they have a chance to be alone together, to explore each other's difference, or sexuality? In this household full of vibrant youngsters, did they manage even to have sex? If so, what was it like? Milton admired women, but his only really close relationship had been with a young man, Charles Diodati, and he was dead. Milton had read a lot about sex and its effects in the course of his intense and wide reading, but he had no personal experience. Mary, so much younger as she was, was also likely to have been inexperienced. When her friends and family went back to Oxford, Milton returned to his studies and teaching duties, and the house was suddenly quiet.

Tempted as she might have been, like Dorothea Brooke in *Middlemarch* (the analogy that perhaps approaches as closely – and explicitly – as any to the sense of good intentions gone wrong, the idealism of a young intelligent woman who marries an older man), what Mary felt was an unpleasant shock.

> She had for a Month or thereabout led a Philosophical Life (after having been used to a great House, and much Company and Joviality). Her Friends, possibly incited by her own desire, made earnest suit by Letter, to have her Company the remaining part of the Summer, which was granted, on condition of her return at the time appointed, *Michaelmas* [September 29], or thereabout.

On the basis of this, Edward Phillips's account, others built or invented theirs. Anthony à Wood tells us that 'she, who was very young, had been bred in a family of plenty and freedom, being not well pleased with her husband's retired manner of life, did shortly after leave him and went back to the country with her mother.' John Aubrey, another early biographer, tells us that in his view Mary 'found it very solitary: no company came to her, she often-times heard his nephews beaten, and cry'. So she went back to her old home and that was the last Milton saw of her for three years.

What happened? The evidence, as always in these intimate stories, is unreliable and must be treated with care and sensitivity. There may well have been something wrong with the Miltons' sexual connection. Milton felt that the prime end of marriage was 'meet and happy conversation', not bodily comfort, as he was soon eager, perhaps over-eager, to argue. But unlike George Eliot's Casaubon, Milton, we know for sure, was not impotent.[2]

The overriding impulse to separation lay in the wider political situation. The Powell family may have sensed that war was coming, and wanted Mary home. Phillips adds a significant 'possibly' to his suggestion that Mary herself wanted home. But the Powells were Royalists, and obviously knew where Milton's sympathies lay. Events were moving quickly. In the warm summer it may have been possible to ignore politics, or to assume that war, if it broke out, would soon be over – almost every war begins that way: 'it'll be over by Christmas'. But now things were getting serious, and London was in the thick of it. And Oxford was where the king eventually made his base. Once she returned home, Mary was trapped. Or, in effect, kidnapped. Whether she wanted to be kidnapped, we do not and cannot know.

Milton expected her back by the end of September. She did not come. Had he done something she objected to, or had he not done enough? We cannot know. Plenty of young brides are disturbed by their first weeks of marriage, and go home to complain or gossip with their mothers. This will have been seriously irritating, to say the least, to Milton, who expected that his young virgin bride would settle down and learn from him, and above all obey him. That is what men, especially older men who knew little of real young women, looked for at that period in a wife. He hoped, almost unconsciously, that she would shape her needs and desires to his – and she was gone.

Milton returned to his books. We know that he read Harington's translation of *Orlando Furioso* now, while he was waiting for his wife to come back, because he dates the book: 'Questo libro due volte io letto, Sept 21, 1642'. ('I have read this book twice.') Was he more likely to identify with Bradamante pining for her absent lover Ruggiero, or with Renaldo, who has fallen out of love with Angelica? Both are in the forty-second book of the poem. Perhaps he felt both emotions. Meanwhile, Mary's mother was probably forbidding her to return to London and her husband: it was too dangerous. As indeed it was. Michaelmas came and went. No Mary.

Milton turned to his friends and neighbours, the Hobsons, John and his wife Margaret. To the wife, Lady Margaret Ley, who was the daughter of James Ley, earl of Marlborough, he wrote Sonnet X, one of only three poems he seems to have written in these years. Politically, these people were sympathetic. Phillips describes the relationship as close:

> Our Author, now as it were a single man again, made it his chief
> diversion now and then in an Evening to visit the Lady… being a
> Woman of great Wit and Ingenuity, had a particular Honour for him,
> and took much delight in his company, as likewise her Husband Captain
> *Hobson.*

If this were not John Milton, we would begin to suspect more than a passing, neighbourly friendship. Instead, in the sonnet, Milton evokes, for comparison with Margaret's father, the great Athenian orator Isocrates, who is said to have dropped dead when Philip of Macedon, father of Alexander, conquered Athens at the battle of Chaeronea in 338 BC.[3] The poem reads like a compliment to the accomplished earl until suddenly it shifts from father to daughter in line 10: 'yet by you/ Madam, me thinks I see him living yet'. One may wonder, though, how much the praise of the father extends to and includes the daughter, who is praised for praising him! Probably no irony is intended (unless there is some private allusion lost to us). Indeed the form of the poem, beginning with 'Daughter' and ending with 'Margaret', suggests that the daughter rather includes the father.

The other sonnet Milton wrote to a woman, probably at this time, is even stranger. 'Lady that in the prime of earliest youth' (Sonnet IX) is addressed to an unknown woman: she may be Mary Powell as she was when they first met when she was seventeen; she may be an idealized woman who compensates for what Mary lacks; or perhaps she is a Mary as Milton still imagined she might be. She is a young virgin who has shunned 'the broad way and the green' to struggle with the faithful few 'up the Hill of heav'nly Truth'. He continues that 'the better part with Mary and with Ruth / Chosen thou hast', suggesting both the spiritual uplift he wants to find in this woman and the loyalty; but then he ends, in the sestet, with an allusion to the parable of the wise and foolish virgins, twisted into an indirectly erotic proposal, that she will one day share the bliss of 'the Bridegroom with his feastfull friends... at the mid-hour of night', though still a 'virgin wise and pure'. It is not very surprising that Milton should be indulging in such fantasies: it is only surprising there were not more such efforts to write out what he was feeling.

When Mary did not come, Milton sent messengers to her with letters. Not only did they receive no answer, but the last came back to report 'that he was dismissed with some sort of Contempt'. Evidently the Powells expected an imminent Royalist victory. 'They began to repent them of having Matched the Eldest Daughter of the Family to a Person so contrary to them in Opinion.' The indecisive battle of Edgehill was fought in October: the parliamentary leader, the earl of Essex, claimed it as a victory, but the dashing and brutal Prince Rupert had overwhelmed his cavalry. Soon the road to Oxford became impassible as the war intensified, and Charles pressed on towards London. How seriously did the participants take these actions? Most of them surely still hoped that Charles would come to his senses and grant the perfectly reasonable demands of Parliament. The Royalists, however, expected that he would soon crush these half-hearted rebels, establish his power to levy taxes and impose his will on church and country.

In this climate Milton wrote a third sonnet, which he published under the title 'When the assault was intended to ye Citty'. It appears with the other two sonnets in the Trinity manuscript, but it is a radical departure in English literature, initiating the sonnet as a political rather than amorous means of expression. The hand of the amanuensis in the manuscript headed it 'On his door when the City expected an assault'. Even though Milton has crossed this out, the words explain the situation the poem evokes. It was pinned to the door of Milton's house, since it begins as an address to whoever reads it, 'Captain or Colonel, or Knight in Arms'. It invites potential marauders to remember that Alexander had spared Pindar's house in the sack of Thebes, and the Spartan Lysander, hearing a recitation from Euripides' *Electra*, refused to destroy Athens. Is the sonnet lightly ironic? Is Milton really comparing himself to Pindar and Euripides? London to ancient Athens? We recall that his copies of both poets are very heavily annotated. What was he imagining? That this relatively unknown poet, and his poem, could actually save the cultural heritage from extinction? In any case, the troops did not get as far as Milton's house. Able briefly to ignore the war, Milton took on more students, including one, Cyriack Skinner (grandson of the great Elizabethan lawyer, Sir Edward Coke), who soon got to know him well, and was later to write the so-called 'anonymous' biography of Milton.

The Royalist forces, having advanced from Banbury to Oxford (Charles's headquarters for the rest of the war), pushed on down the Thames valley to Reading (a route along which close members of Milton's family were now living, his wife near Oxford, his brother in Reading). Charles prepared to lead his troops on London in November. If he had taken it, the war would have been over. He paused while Prince Rupert laid siege to Brentford, hardly a major prize but an important location north of the river, on 12 November, and sacked the town. The earl of Essex had been chasing the Royalists and caught up, with reinforcements from London known as 'trained bands'. The armies squared off the next day at Turnham Green. This became a great non-event, the battle that never was. Charles's forces turned and retreated, having apparently decided the Parliamentary troops were too strong (according to the earl of Clarendon's history they were five times larger). Also, the king had been advised that to engage such an oddly assorted army, containing what was obviously a large contingent of armed civilians, would not endear him to London, and it was too early in the war for the Royalists to contemplate taking London without the support of a sizeable part of London's population. With the end of the campaigning season close at hand, Charles decided not to press the issue and withdrew. Thus the Parliamentarians secured a victory without engaging in a battle, which was perhaps fortunate for them, as many of their number had never seen a battle before and were not used to army discipline, formations and deployments. They allowed Charles to retreat. In Lucy Hutchinson's memoir of her puritan husband, this was a mistake: they had the king surrounded and 'the war had been ended'.[4] Charles could return with his troops to Oxford. With all this going on, it is hardly surprising that, whatever her personal inclinations, Mary Powell stayed there.

9

Civil War

Milton's father was still in Reading, along with Christopher and Thomasine, who was far advanced in another pregnancy, when Reading was besieged by Essex on 15 April 1643 and surrendered twelve days later. Royalist propaganda said that Essex tried to hide the extent of the carnage by hastily burying the slain in mass graves outside the town. Christopher, serving in the Royalist army, survived the slaughter but did not stay to be taken prisoner. He fled. He was to stay separated from his family for three years. Thomasine took the children back to London, to her mother's, and old Mr Milton, as Edward Phillips recalls with affection for his grandfather, came to live in Aldersgate, 'wholly retired to his Rest and Devotion, without the least trouble imaginable'. Surely it was with his son John's encouragement that the old man, now nearly eighty, published some of his own psalm music in William Slater's *Psalms of David*. And possibly Harry Lawes would come over to play music with his old friend, whom he had known since before the peaceful days of *Comus*.

The political activity became more intense as the military manoeuvres increased. Prompted by threats of conspiracies, Parliament enacted a strict Licensing Order on 14 June 1643 to control the enormous proliferation of printing presses, largely unregulated since the Star Chamber had been abolished on 5 July 1641. The Stationers Company, who usually owned copyright and had a monopoly over the book trade, was complaining about the many pirated, unlicensed works. Small presses everywhere had been taking advantage of the lack of supervision to publish their views on the end of the world, the latest comet, or the necessity of going naked to recover the innocence of Adam. The new ordnance required the licensing and regulation of all publications, copyright guarantees and the imprisonment of offenders.

During the same period religious affairs also came to a head. The Westminster Assembly of Divines was established to advise Parliament. It was stacked with Presbyterians, many from Scotland (a sign of dependence on Scots troops), and it pressed the authorities to establish a national church and eliminate heresies, sects and schisms. It insisted on the Scots Presbyterian model of church governance, highly centralized and dominated by the clergy. Independents, who were becoming stronger, argued for broad-based toleration of all Protestant sects, and some even for all Christians, including Roman Catholics. These differences gave rise to some of the sharpest and most unforgiving polemics of the period. Intolerance (in its Roman Catholic form at least, and for some even in its Presbyterian form) could not be tolerated. In September 1643, Parliament adopted the *Solemn League and Covenant*, which attempted to establish a unified Reformed Church throughout the realm, and yet allowed for the king's authority 'in the preservation and defence of the true Religion and liberties of the Kingdoms'.[1] Milton soon contributed major publications to all of these burning issues.

He quickly published four tracts relating to marriage and divorce, apparently expecting that most of the Presbyterian divines from whom he was now feeling considerable distance would nonetheless rally to his cause. He was very wrong. In spite of Henry VIII, or perhaps because of him, divorce was virtually impossible in England. In exceptional cases it might be granted by Parliament, but it was mostly a matter for the ecclesiastical courts. Canon law had stipulated six grounds for divorce: sexual offences (adultery, sodomy and bestiality), impotence, physical cruelty, apostasy, entry into holy orders and the discovery of consanguinity. Milton characteristically set out to bypass all this precedent and addressed, in the first edition of *The Doctrine and Discipline of Divorce*, the Westminster Assembly, and in the second, Parliament directly, proposing that divorce be allowed merely for incompatibility. Since this would mean a change in the most fundamental unit of society, the family, he convinced himself this was not merely a personal need but a contribution to the national struggle for reform. He met fierce hostility even from former supporters and he was soon reviled as a libertine.

The grounds for his argument were that the main purpose of marriage is a fellowship of mind and spirit, what he calls a 'fit conversation', rather than procreation or relief of lust. Thus

indisposition, unfitness, or contrariety of mind, arising from a cause
in nature unchangeable, hindring and ever likely to hinder the main
benefits of conjugal society, which are solace and peace, is a greater
reason of divorce than natural frigidity, especially if there be no children,
and that there be mutual consent.[2]

Milton appeals to the Protestant idea that marriage is a covenant, not a sacrament, and he tries to shift the focus away from those who think of marriage or divorce in purely physical terms. As usual, he is obliged to argue from scripture, but he faces a major problem: at Matthew 19:3–9, Christ appears to forbid divorce except for adultery. Even more problematically, Christ appears to argue that the law of Moses, which was less rigid, has been surpassed: a man who remarries is now said to have committed adultery himself. How is Milton to get round this prohibition?

His strategy is to put the text in what he regards as its context. If one reads it in the light of Christ's overriding principle of charity, it can't mean what it says.

> There is scarce any one saying in the Gospel, but must be read with limitation and distinction, to be rightly understood; for Christ gives no full comments or continu'd discourses, but scatters the heavenly grain of his doctrin like pearle heer and there, which requires a skilful and laborious gatherer. (*DDD 1*, 182)

So Jesus cannot have meant to rescind the Mosaic permission to divorce and remarry, which is 'a grave and prudent Law, full of moral equity, full of due consideration toward nature'. The word 'nature' is the clue that Milton is arguing in part from natural law theory, which he found worked out both in Jewish sources brought together in a book by a current member of Parliament, John Selden, and also in the work of his acquaintance from Paris, Hugo Grotius. However unusual are Milton's views and his way of reading scripture, the words 'grave and prudent' are obviously designed to appeal to his puritan readers.

No court should have rights in the matter, he says. It is up to the husband to decide, as in Jewish law, since he is

> the head of the other sex which was made for him: whom therefore he ought not to injure, yet neither should he be forc't to retain in society to his own overthrow, nor to hear any judge therein above himself. (186)

Later Milton would allow that the logic of his argument would also permit women to initiate proceedings.

This first edition of the tract was published anonymously on 1 August 1643, and without licence, contrary to the recent law. Perhaps Milton was trying to avoid the charge that he was merely writing for personal reasons, and no doubt he knew he would never have been granted a licence. But he was recognized as the author anyway, and so the second edition, much enlarged, appeared in his name in February 1644. The preface makes clear that he was both worried and excited by the response to the first edition, which had sold out in six months. Some had shown such enthusiasm that one woman, a sectarian preacher named Mrs Attaway immediately left her husband and hooked up with another enthusiast, declaring they were both as free from sin as Christ when he was in the flesh. A Ranter, John Robins, authorized his disciples to change spouses, and set the example by changing his own wife. On the other hand, Milton's old tutor, Thomas Young, the TY of Smectymnuus, disapproved. Still a Presbyterian, and now master of Jesus College, Cambridge (having long returned from Hamburg), he prepared a sermon to the Commons that denounced the cause of legalizing bigamy. For the first time in his life, Milton faced a serious split between his respect for another and his respect for himself. He also realized that, in his earlier life, he had been able to present himself as more or less spotless (the self-righteousness that irritates many of his readers): now he was making an argument based on human weakness, our propensity to make mistakes.

The argument of Milton's second edition is more restrained. 'Honest Liberty is the greatest Foe to dishonest Licence', he maintains. And he makes a new and important move. Parliament, he reminds his audience, has also suffered from being unjustly misinterpreted. The larger reform of society cannot succeed without first changing the marriage laws. Similarly, if the people have a right to forswear their allegiance to a monarch who proves a tyrant, so can a man save himself 'from unworthy bondage... For no effect of tyranny can sit more heavy on the Common-wealth, than this houshold unhappiness on the family' (*DDD 2*, 229). This imagery extends also to the body, as is usual in Milton's treatises. Loveless sex, he memorably says (and as I noted in the Introduction), is a grinding 'in the mill of an undelighted and servil copulation' (258). No one endowed with reason ought 'to be made to pay out the best substance of his body, and of his soul too, as some think' (271). These tracts are shot through with revealing passages such as these, as when Milton constructs a story about inexperienced and chaste young men persuaded too rapidly into marriage and not realizing that 'the bashful muteness of a virgin may oft-times hide all the unlivelines and naturall sloth which is really unfit for conversation'.

Mary Powell, lively and sociable in Phillips's description, does not sound much like this dull creature, but the language may register Milton's resentment at her unwillingness or inability to share the high intellectual pleasures he so prized. Other kinds of men, he imagines,

who have lived most loosely... prove most successful in their matches, because their wild affections unsettling at will, have been as so many divorces to teach them experience. (*DDD 1*, 150)

There is perhaps a certain wistfulness in that thought, since it would have allowed him, he can see, to avoid knowing that 'not to be belov'd, and yet retain'd, is the greatest injury to a gentle spirit' (*DDD 1*, 152). That special pain no one can rightly understand, he added later, 'unless he have a soul gentle anough, and spacious anough to contemplate what is true love' (*DDD 2*, 333). In the midst of such strong feelings, even though they reveal themselves only intermittently, it is surprising, surely, that Milton never argues for desertion as a reason for divorce (admitted as legitimate grounds in England only in 1857[3]). Clearly he is constructing a general case, not simply his own.

In this second edition, the Mosaic law from Deuteronomy 24:1, far from being abrogated by Christ, becomes the central focus. And he has begun to move beyond the Calvinism of his contemporaries towards conceiving of a God who reveals himself thus in his laws, and who 'enters into a cov'nant with us, swears to keep it, binds himself like a just lawgiver to his own prescriptions... and is commensurat to right reason' (*DDD 2*, 292). God even becomes a precedent for Milton's argument, in that his method of Creation was to make the world rise out of Chaos 'by a divorcing command' (*DDD 2*, 272), a method he uses again in *Paradise Lost*.

The divorce issue was proving immensely controversial. In order to shore up his position, Milton was delighted to find a precedent in one of the leaders of the Reformation in the previous century, Martin Bucer. Bucer had been a professor at Cambridge, and had written a work which Milton partly translated and partly summarized in *The Judgement of Martin Bucer Concerning Divorce*, published on 6 August 1644. On the title page he adds a motto from John 3:10: 'Art thou a teacher of Israel, and know'st not these things', and in the preface he complains about the responses of his erstwhile Presbyterian colleagues to the first treatise, but also constructs a long story about how he had worked out all these ideas for himself before he came across Bucer. (There are indeed a few entries in his Commonplace Book about divorce that appear to predate the meeting with Mary Powell.) Like Milton, Bucer thought marriage a civil rather than an ecclesiastical matter, entered into for love and by consent, and so Christ's apparent prohibition applied only to those Pharisees whose reasons for divorce were too slight. Marriage, a point he had also made before, was instituted in Eden for solace and affection, and this should now be the basis for the whole of our social relations, not only the family.

But the quarrel over the divorce tracts intensified, as did the war. The key battle of Marston Moor was fought on 2 July 1644 just outside York. The king's forces lost some 4,000 men, and surrendered on 5 July. Much credit went to the newly emerging military leader, Oliver Cromwell. The

Presbyterians in the Jerusalem Chamber at Westminster continued to insist on the establishment of their own form of church. On 13 August one of them, Herbert Palmer, preached a rabid sermon to the two houses of Parliament against 'ungodly Toleration pleaded for under the pretence of Liberty of Conscience', and included among those threats to religion and civil order 'a *wicked booke*' that was 'abroad and *uncensored*, though *deserving to be burnt*'[4] – Milton on divorce. Eleven days later the Stationers petitioned Parliament to enforce the laws against unlicensed books, including Milton's, and then William Prynne, formidable and earless, denounced the tendency toward toleration of Independents (who were supported by Cromwell) and pamphlets advocating '*Atheistical opinions, as of the soules mortalities, divorce at pleasure, &.*' During these months Milton met most or all of those linked with him in these calls for suppression of heresy, the mortalist Richard Overton, the radical John Goodwin, and Roger Williams, recently returned from New England, where he had founded the Rhode Island colony. Williams published a tract in favour of general toleration in 1644, entitled *Bloudy Tenent, of Persecution, for Cause of Conscience*, and opponents lumped him in with Milton. Ephraim Pagitt declared that extremists 'preach, print, and practice their hereticall opinions openly; for books, *vide* the bloody Tenet, witness a tractate of divorce in which the bonds are let loose to inordinate lust'.[5]

To these and similar attacks, Milton constructed a much broader defense, one of the greatest of all works of English prose, *Areopagitica*. Published about 23 November 1644, it is constructed as an oration to Parliament, and alludes portentously to the discourse of the Greek orator Isocrates who had written 'from his private house' to the popular assembly in Athens (Milton calls it too a 'Parliament'), the same Isocrates to whom Milton compared Margaret Ley's father in Sonnet X. Milton's advice to his state thus has serious political precedent, and he hopes his readers see the link that now the most important of all political rights is the right to read. The tract defends the right to publish any tract without prior censorship (which the law had required since June 1643). Every man needs to think for himself in order to choose between good and evil. Evil we need to know about, even if only in books.

Contemporaries such as the Leveller, William Walwyn, had read enough Montaigne to have learned the importance of toleration from his religious scepticism. Milton now went even further in *Areopagitica*. 'A man may be a heretic in the truth' is the startling paradox he there formulates; 'and if he believe things only because his Pastor says so… though his belief be true, yet the truth he holds becomes his heresie.' He challenges his readers to exert their own judgment, and goes even further than Paul, who in 1 Corinthians 11:18 argued that 'there must be heresies among you'. Milton refers to the heresy hunters of the early church, who 'discover more heresies than they well confute, and that oft for heresy which is the truer opinion'. This last phrase gives the essence of Milton's reason for allowing a wide variety of opinion to flourish.

> I cannot praise a fugitive and cloister'd vertue, unexercis'd & unbreath'd, that never sallies out and sees her adversary, but slinks out of the race, where that immortal garland is to be run for, not without dust and heat. Assuredly we bring not innocence into the world, we bring impuritie much rather: that which purifies us is triall, and triall is by what is contrary. (*YP* II 514)

What is needed is open and free debate in the new public sphere being created in revolutionary England through the deluge of pamphlets and books. 'How can a man teach with autority, which is the life of teaching, how can he be a Doctor in his book as he ought to be, or else had better be silent, whenas all he teaches, all he delivers, is but under the tuition, under the correction of his patriarchal licenser to blot or alter' (532).

In this passage we glimpse briefly not the beleaguered polemicist nor the new and abandoned husband but the benevolent if stern tutor of the Phillips boys and others. In fact he had just written at about this time a brief eight-page tract, *Of Education*, published in June 1644 and framed as a letter to the well-known educational reformer, Samuel Hartlib. It was the first of Milton's writings to be officially registered with the Stationer and licensed. The two tracts are related in that they both set out how to prepare citizens, or members of the governing class at least, for the new world that is even now in the making.

> I call therefore a compleate and generous Education that which fits a man to perform justly, skilfully and magnanimously all the offices both private and publick of peace and war. (*YP* II 379)

In a more visionary mode he claims that 'The end then of learning is to repair the ruin of our first parents by learning to know God aright' (366). And in *Areopagitica*, he seems to don the prophet's mantle in a sentence to which we shall return: 'Methinks I see in my mind a noble and puissant Nation rousing herself like a strong man after sleep, and shaking her invincible locks' (557).

And yet there are many uncertainties and contradictions within the often inspiring language of *Areopagitica*, especially its exclusion from toleration of 'Popery and open superstition'. That phrase seems to contradict what Milton writes earlier, where he insists on toleration because 'it will be hard to instance where any ignorant man hath bin seduc't by Papistical book in

English'. He tries to distinguish the books of the Jesuits and others, which the 'ignorant' are unlikely to read, from the practices and rituals of Roman Catholics, which he would still be denouncing after the Restoration in *Of True Religion* in 1673: 'Popery, as being Idolatrous, is not to be tolerated either in Public or in Private' (*YP* VIII 430). In a further phrase in *Areopagitica*, Milton also excludes what is 'impious or evil absolutely either against faith or maners'. This latter phrase may refer to those Ranters or Quakers who were disrupting church meetings (as Thomas Corns suggests[6]), but surely 'evil absolutely' must have a stronger reference: more likely he is thinking of those 'sons of Belial' (later denounced in *Paradise Lost*, I 503–5) who wandered the streets of Sodom, and those who, one night in Gibeah (Judges 19), provoked a Levite to give them his concubine to avoid 'worse rape'.

The violence of Milton's language reproduces the Bible's, and asserts Milton's need to struggle for his identity within the idealized community. But it also reproduces his own vibrant energy.

> Books… are as lively, and as vigorously productive, as those fabulous Dragons teeth; and being sown up and down, may chance to spring up armed men. And yet, on the other hand unlesse warinesse be us'd, as good almost kill a Man as kill a good Book; who kills a Man kills a reasonable creature, Gods Image; but hee who destroyes a good Booke, kills reason it selfe, kills the Image of God, as it were in the eye. Many a man lives a burden to the Earth; but a good Booke is the pretious life-blood of a master-spirit, imbalm'd and treasur'd up on purpose to a life beyond life.
> (*Areopagitica, YP* II 492–3)

In a more or less contemporary poem by a poet who declared briefly for the Royalist cause, Henry Vaughn, we find him addressing his books in a memorable phrase as 'the dead alive and busy'. Milton's overwhelming poetic prose is easily as memorable, and far more influential.

Reacting to this tract as well as the divorce pamphlets, the Stationers protested to the Lords on 28 December 1644 of the 'frequent printing of scandalous Books by divers as Hezekiah Woodward and Jo. Milton'. Both were summoned by the Westminster Assembly to be examined by Justices Reeve and Bacon, appointed by the House of Lords, on the charge of unlicensed printing. Woodward was indeed examined and released on 31 December, but there is no record of Milton's appearance. Another attack, echoing Pagitt, referred to 'the bonds of marriage let loose to inordinate lust'. Clearly such language reflects little in Milton's own texts and a lot in the fantasies of the attackers. Yet Milton could not let it go. He published two more divorce tracts together in March 1645, unlicensed of course but with the author clearly identified.

Colasterion (Greek for a place or instrument of punishment) is a contemptuous attack on the anonymous 'cock-brained sollicitor' who had dared answer the earlier tract. 'I mean not to dispute Philosophy with this Pork, who never read any.' On the title page is a citation from Proverbs 26:5 which justifies the insults and abuse: 'Answer a Fool according to his folly, lest hee bee wise in his own conceit.' *Tetrachordon* is very different. The word refers to a four-stringed Greek instrument like a lyre. The tract takes up and analyses carefully and at length the four main scriptural passages which seem to contradict each other but which Milton again makes to harmonize ('Gen. 1.27, 28. compar'd and explain'd by Gen. 2.18, 23, 24; Deut. 24.1, 2.; Matth. 5.31, 32. with Matth.19. from the 3^d v to the 11th ; 1 Cor.7. from the 10th to the 16th', as the title-page lists them). And the examples of marital unhappiness here, unlike the ones he invented in the earlier tracts, bear some resemblance to what Milton may actually have experienced. He speaks of marriage as a 'divine blessing', but goes on:

> if we do but erre in our choice the most unblamable error that can be, erre but one minute, one moment after those mighty syllables pronounc't which take upon them to joyn heavn and hell together unpardnably till death pardon, this divine blessing which lookt but now with such a human smile upon us, and spoke such gentle reason, strait vanishes like a fair skie and brings on such a scene of cloud and tempest, as turns all to shipwrack without havn or shoar but to a ransomles captivity. (*YP* II 600-1)

Did Milton know he had erred 'but one minute' as soon as the vow was spoken, 'one moment after those mighty syllables pronounc't'? It sounds personal, though he had now had almost three years to reflect on it.

Although *Tetrachordon* often maintains a neutral tone, since it is expounding the Bible, there are other moments when a standard kind of misogyny intervenes: it was Eve's fault first (read Mary Powell's), so why should an innocent man suffer? No longer is a difficult marriage simply a matter of incompatibility. Blameless error is occasionally transmuted into the woman's 'most unnatural fraud' (*YP* II 626). On the other hand, this tract recognises clearly a woman's right to divorce her husband (691). It even allows for the possible inversion of the gender hierarchy: 'if the wife exceed her husband in prudence and dexterity, and he contentedly yield...the wiser should govern the lesse wise, whether male or female' (589). In the course of his meditations, and because of his chosen method of exposition, Milton turns back again and again to the story of Adam and Eve, as if he is using it to think through everything that happens in a marriage. Commenting on Genesis 2:18, 'I will make a help meet for him', he writes that God was not satisfied with the naming of a help, but 'goes on describing *another self, a second self, a very self it self* (600).The seeds of *Paradise Lost* were being sown.

According to Edward Phillips, there was now some talk of making Milton an adjutant-general in the army of Sir Hardress Waller. We do not hear of this again, although it may be significant that this is the time when, Milton tells us later, he began to notice his failing sight. And indeed the war was going well for the Parliament under its lieutenant-general, Cromwell (still subordinate to General Fairfax), with his New Model Army. William Laud, still archbishop of Canterbury, was executed for treason in January 1645 (the office of bishop was eventually abolished a year later). In February Cromwell forced the Self-Denying Ordinance through Parliament, making it impossible for members of either house to hold commissions. The bill was eventually also passed by the Lords in April. Peers like the earls of Manchester and Essex, who had been losing battles, and were in any case somewhat ambivalent about the war, were thus removed from command.

Essex was the son of a man who had been executed for rebellion against Elizabeth and it is not hard to imagine his ambivalence. His father had not wanted to overthrow the monarchy but to become king himself. Manchester is quoted thus in the State Papers Domestic for 1644: 'If we beat the king 99 times he would be king still, and his posterity, and we subjects still; but if he beat us but once we should be hang'd, and our posterity be undone' (503.56.10). Obviously the idea of a republic was beyond his, or their, conceiving – but this remark shows why it began to seem necessary. How soon it seemed so to Milton is unclear, but he would soon be one of the staunchest republicans. The change of command soon had its effect. In June 1645 the Battle of Naseby was a crippling defeat for Charles, and indeed the First Civil War was almost over.

Milton took a larger house in the Barbican near London with a view to expanding the school, and perhaps because he hoped to marry again. He was not of course divorced as yet, though he may have intended simply to declare himself single, as he implies in *Tetrachordon* a man might legally do. The young woman he had in mind was a Miss Davis, according to Phillips 'a very Handsome and Witty woman'. She, however, was 'averse… to this Motion', though Phillips does not explain what that might mean. In any case, something else now happened to impede any new alliance. Mary Powell came back.

In the wake of the king's defeats, the Powells felt vulnerable again. Hearing rumours of the proposed new marriage, they set to work with Milton's relatives the Blackboroughs, whom he used to visit from time to time. On one such visit, 'the Wife was ready in another Room, and on a sudden he was surprised to see one whom he thought to have never seen more, making Submission and begging Pardon on her Knees before him'. Phillips admits he is reconstructing the story, but this part at least sounds circumstantial enough to be true. He goes on: 'he might probably at first make some shew of aversion and rejection; but partly his own generous nature, more inclinable to Reconciliation than to Perseverance in Anger and Revenge; and partly the strong intercession of friends on both sides, soon brought him to an act of Oblivion, and a firm League of Peace for the future.' So Mary came back to London and, perhaps to make the transition back to wedded life more palatable, stayed with Mrs Isabelle Webber, Christopher Milton's mother-in-law, until the new house in the Barbican was ready.

10

New Houses, and a Family

The new house was ready in October, and the family moved in: Milton, his wife, his father, now eighty-two, and the pupils – his nephews and Cyriack Skinner. Others, including members of the minor aristocracy such as Richard Jones, son of Lady Ranelagh, a widely admired woman whom Milton described as standing to him 'in the place of all kith and kin', and the fifteen-year-old Richard Barry, second earl of Barrymore, came soon now that Milton's reputation had been established with the publication of his treatise *Of Education*. He had proposed a simplified way of learning Greek and Latin grammar so the boys could get quickly to reading actual texts. And he modified previous grammars by deleting examples which might reinforce regal or ecclesiastical authority, including expressions of loyalty and almost all instances of the word 'rex' (king).

Education began with topics based on the senses: ancient texts about agriculture and geography (Varro, Pausanias); then the natural sciences, such as astronomy and physics (some Aristotle and Pliny); then the practical sciences of architecture, engineering, zoology, anatomy and medicine. Gradually the students would also be reading the poetry of nature, such as Virgil's *Georgics* and Lucretius. Soon their studies introduced them to moral philosophy – Plato, Cicero, Plutarch – but mingled with readings of scripture. They read choice comedies and tragedies too, for relaxation, and learned 'at any odde hour the *Italian* tongue'. After some politics and law, they moved on to the climax of logic, rhetoric and poetics. The programme sounds extraordinary, perhaps, and indeed has little to do with modern systems, but there is at least one institution known to me, Bard College in the USA, which tries to follow a pale variant of such a curriculum, introducing (somewhat older) students via Latin and Greek to everything from mathematics to poetry. Milton's educational system is, like most of his work, based on an ideal – but that does not mean it is entirely out of reach. Edward Phillips, as we saw, confirms that this was more or less how the programme actually went.

It also included some physical exercise before lunch, music with and after the meal, plus two hours of riding and military activity – swordsmanship or fencing – before supper. Young men so prepared should be ready to govern, to fight and to farm.

The house in the Barbican did not survive the extension of the Metropolitan Railway, the world's first 'underground', from Farringdon to Moorgate in 1865. An engraving from the invaluable *Illustrated London News* gives an impression of how it looked in 1864, when it bore a large sign reading 'Milton House'. At the same time as they moved to this house, in fact on 6 October 1645, Milton registered a new work for publication, not a pamphlet this time but his collected poetry to date, *Poems of Mr John Milton, both English and Latin.* The publisher, Humphrey Moseley, had brought out the Cavalier Edmund Waller's poems with great success, and was looking for another project. Milton was no doubt happy to find a publisher committed to poetry, whatever his politics. But Moseley's preface and the frontispiece are at odds with the reformed politics that are occasionally evident in the poems themselves, or in their organization.

The frontispiece became notorious. Moseley wanted a portrait of Milton, and proposed William Marshall, an experienced engraver, as the artist. But Milton did not want to waste time sitting for the portrait, so he offered Marshall the beautiful painting known as the Onslow portrait (the original is lost, but a copy is now in the National Portrait Gallery in London). Of course Milton now looked older than that lovely, probably twenty-one-year-old man with his bright eyes, sensual mouth and auburn hair. So perhaps there was a touch of vanity in his decision to offer the painting instead of his thirty-eight-year-old presence. In any case, the result of Marshall's labours is ludicrous. To begin with, the collar is asymmetrical and does not clasp properly, but then as you look closely at this hideous and rather stupid face you realize the whole thing is a travesty: one half is a youngish man, the other is much older and distorted, resulting in a double chin and a twisted frown.

Milton was displeased. But he had his revenge. Moseley would not change or withdraw the picture, so Milton composed some Greek verses to be engraved beneath the portrait, knowing full well that Marshall could not read Greek.

> You would say, perhaps, that this portrait was drawn by an ignorant hand, once you look at the living face; so friends since you do not see the likeness, laugh at the botched effort of this incompetent artist.

What matters is not the portrait but the poetry. Milton had explained earlier to his father that his destiny was devoted to becoming a poet: that was how he had presented himself the previous year in *Areopagitica*, and in a less serious context in the sonnet 'Captain or colonel' nailed to the door of his house to keep the military vandals at bay. Here in one volume were the most perfect pastoral elegy written since the tradition began with Theocritus, the greatest masque in English, including Lawes' laudatory preface, unrivalled odes, and sonnets which shifted the very definition of the word. And in the second part were Latin poems that had captivated Florence, had charmed the ears of Manso, of Barberini, of Galileo. He even included some failures – surely a sign of his great confidence – the unfinished 'Passion', written, he admits, when he was too young, as a subject 'above his years', and the Ovidian elegies presented as youthful indiscretions long abandoned for the conversion to 'the Socratic streams' (as he says in verses attached to Elegy VII). What is more, there are even poems to dead bishops, including Launcelot Andrewes, imagined on his way to heaven. But Milton did not allow his readers entirely to ignore the connection with the writer of all those recent pamphlets, including *Of Reformation*, which sent all bishops to hell. He added a distinctive headnote to 'Lycidas' pointing to the poem's prophecy of 'the ruine of our corrupted Clergy, then in their height'. Milton perhaps hoped the volume would make a very different statement from the Cavalier. It did. Unlike Waller's book, which went through three editions in 1645, Milton's excited less interest than the pamphlets, and it took another fifteen years to sell out.

Milton sent out copies of the book. One went to George Thomason, his bookseller friend, and is now in the British Library, dated 2 January 1646. Another he sent to Henry Lawes, with a covering sonnet praising his friend for his musical settings of Milton's and others' poems. He ends with typical modesty by comparing himself to Dante meeting his composer friend on the edge of Purgatory. He also sent a copy to the Bodleian Library, but it never arrived, unlike the various pamphlets. The librarian, John Rouse, wrote to tell him so, and Milton eventually sent another copy, with a covering letter which was to be his last serious Latin poem. 'Ad Joannem Rousium' (dated 23 January 1647) begins playfully by addressing the lost book, and feeling sorry for it, 'taken and thumbed by a block-headed bookseller with calloused grimy hands'. Fortunately Rouse will provide this new copy with a safe home, which 'the insolent clamourings of the rabble will never penetrate, far away from the vulgar mob of readers'. No sentimental democrat, Milton!

Allowing for the linguistic inflation characteristic of Milton's Latin poetry, the words of 'Ad Joannem Rousium' still register a strong loathing for this 'damnable civil war', *nefandos civium tumultus*. He contrasts the present with the innocence of his youth, wandering about the English or Italian countryside. But he soon rises to the role of an inspired Pindaric poet divinely appointed to rid the land of evils, promote a new social order, honour heroes and serve the Muses. He imagines the book taking its place in the great Oxford library alongside the names that were once the lights of and are now the true glory of the Greek and Latin races. The verse is experimental, as he somewhat pretentiously announces in an appended note: it mixes forms and metres for convenience of reading rather than conforming to classical rules. This little book, *libellum*, will go to a liberated Oxford, now free from accursed tumults among the people and from the degenerate Cavaliers, who are like the Harpies that fouled the river while the king was there. Oxford is now a happy sanctuary of the Muses.

It didn't last. Mary was pregnant when in May 1646 the news reached Milton's household that Oxford was once again under siege. Parliamentary forces had once again surrounded the city and taken possession of Royalist lands, including Richard Powell's estate in Forest Hill. The king had been intriguing with the Irish and the French to land troops in England, and with the pope to urge English Catholics to rebel. But seeing that these intrigues had been exposed and would come to nothing, the king had his hair cut short and escaped from Oxford disguised as a servant. He tried to get the Scots to protect him. They withdrew together to Newcastle, but soon the king told his forces to surrender. By August the First Civil War was over.

To judge from their position in the Trinity manuscript, as well as their topics, it was during this time that Milton composed three sonnets in response to the various attacks on him and his divorce pamphlets. 'On the detraction which follow'd upon my writing certain treatises' is the general heading, and the first sonnet uses colloquialism and comic rhymes to express his contempt. It begins

> I did but prompt the age to quit their clogs
> By the known rules of ancient liberty,
> When straight a barbarous noise environs me,
> Of owls and cuckoos, asses, apes and dogs.

We also get some frogs and hogs to extend the rhyme. The wretched opponents 'bawl for freedom in their senseles mood', but that is not what they really want: 'Licence they mean when they cry Liberty'. The second of these sonnets has a different kind of satirical fun, and makes even more burlesque rhymes. 'A Book was writ of late call'd *Tetrachordon*' amuses itself at the expense of that Greek title, the booksellers who did not understand it, and even the book itself: 'what a word on/ A title page is this.' Beneath the humour and rhyming wordplay (the rhymes with *Tetrachordon* are 'pored on', 'word on' and 'Gordon'), one can hear Milton's irritation at his former Scots allies and disappointment that his most closely argued divorce tract has been ignored. The third sonnet speaks up for the tolerationist or independent cause against the Presbyterian 'Forcers of Conscience'.

The winding down of the war had immediate consequences for Milton. Christopher Milton, his Royalist brother, came back to London in April. He retrieved his wife and children, whom he had not seen for three years, agreed to swear to the new Covenant (allegiance to Parliament, not the king), and got back his sequestered property on 25 August, probably with John Milton's help. There was also a further domestic crisis. The Powells had been dispossessed of Forest Hill and the rest of the property. Richard Powell's finances were in such a mess that the lawyers never really sorted it all out. As a delinquent Royalist he was responsible for unpayable debts through his heavily mortgaged property. The Powell family descended en masse on the Barbican in early July, mother-in-law, father-in-law and at least five of the underage children, perhaps older children as well.

Imagine how Milton felt. The house could barely accommodate all its residents in any case. He was hard at work on his newly recovered calling of poet. These noisy Powells had taken his wife away, written him abusive letters when he tried to get her back, never paid the dowry, and had even stopped paying interest on the loan. Yet Milton took them all in. Perhaps his hand was forced, but he was not obliged to accept them. One could say that, at the moment of crisis, he came through. It was an act of simple Christian charity.

Perhaps too it was renewed love, for, almost immediately, according to the family Bible, on 29 July 1646 his first child was born, named Anne. 'A brave girl', says Edward Phillips, but soon the symptoms began to appear of her lameness and other handicaps, including defective speech – 'whether by ill Constitution, or want of Care, she grew more and more decrepit'. That 'want of Care' is chilling. Doctors, wet-nurse, servants, parents, an overcrowded house? We have no way of knowing.

Clearly Milton was now the only responsible member of the household, in legal terms at least. He witnessed his father-in-law's will on 13 December, and Richard Powell died a few days later. He may have been buried in St Giles Cripplegate, since he died 'at the Howse of Mr John Milton, Scituate in Barbican', as his widow testified, and St Giles was the local parish church. If so, the record is missing. Now began a complicated series of legal manoeuvres on Milton's part. They lasted several years but eventually Milton's efforts to establish a claim on the Powells's Wheatley estate both enabled him to receive payment of the debt Richard Powell owed him and also allowed his in-laws to retain some rights in the property. His immediate interest was to see that his mother-in-law and dependants could move back there, and he seems to have achieved this, for she was already resident there on 20 November 1647, when the Oxfordshire court allowed her to receive her 'widow's third' from the income of the estate. Milton paid this regularly.

St Giles Cripplegate, as the local parish church, was the obvious place for the burial and it is probable that the Powell family would have approved of it. It had been Ben Jonson's parish church, Launcelot Andrewes had once been its vicar, a nephew of Shakespeare's had been christened there, with William himself in attendance, and several Elizabethan celebrities were buried in its grounds, including John Foxe, author of the *Book of Martyrs*, John Speed, historian and cartographer, and Martin Frobisher, explorer and privateer. The Powells might not have been so happy if they had known that Oliver Cromwell had married Elizabeth Bouchard at its altar.

Milton returned to the same church on 15 March 1647 to bury his own much-loved father, who had died at the age of eighty-four. He had been able to read to the last without glasses, and had continued to play the small organ that Milton had moved with him from house to house. Part of the 'modest patrimony' Milton inherited from his father was the house on Bread Street where he had been born. John and Mary Milton now both faced the world fatherless, but with a baby, and soon another on the way.

Unusually, we do have some direct evidence as to how Milton felt during all these events. A letter arrived unexpectedly from Milton's Italian friend, Carlo Dati, and Milton soon answered it (though in general, as he had admitted to Diodati, he was not a good correspondent). He complains in direct terms about the Powell entourage ('daily sit beside me, exhaust me, torment me as often as they please'), the recent deaths (Diodati, his father, his old friends Alexander Gil and Catherine Thomason), and the general chaos of revolutionary London. And yet, in the midst of all that, 'I am forced to live in almost perpetual solitude', an unusually revealing remark. He misses his Italian friends and especially the carefree life he had led there. It had been a tumultuous time, but he had still, he proudly tells his friend, been able to publish his poems.

11

Rudest Violence

The political turmoil continued. In January 1647 the Scots surrendered the king to the English Parliament in return for the £400,000 owed in back-pay to their soldiers. The king was settled at Holmby House in Northamptonshire, but he kept trying to negotiate with the various factions, and to Milton's displeasure the Presbyterians often supported his demands and continued to attack the divorce tracts. The rift was growing wider between the army, now controlled by Cromwell and the Independents, and the Presbyterians, who were still insisting on their own form of worship and resisting any toleration of others. Even within the army, the senior officers were increasingly at odds with the rank and file, who understandably insisted on their arrears of pay.

A measure of the increasing instability was that the Levellers (as their opponents called them) were more and more influential, especially in the army. They made very clear their dissatisfaction with Parliament, which had failed to bring about a godly reformation. 'Thousands of men and women', wrote William Walwyn in June 1647,

> are still (as formerly) permitted to live in beggary and wickedness all their life long and to breed their children to the same idle and vicious course of life, and no effectual means used to reclaim either or to reduce them to any virtue or industry permitted to live in beggary and wickedness all their life long.[1]

The Levellers called for extension of suffrage, abolition of church tithes and commercial monopolies and reform of the constitution. What that meant was a republican government, and thus abolition of both the House of Lords and the monarchy. On 5 June at Newmarket the army swore to a *Solemn Engagement* not to disband until their demands were met, and then made a *Declaration* on June 14 that they had taken up arms for 'the peoples just rights and liberties, and not as mercenary Souldiers'.

They acted 'upon the principles of right and freedom, and upon the law of nature and of Nations'.[2]

On 4 July 1647 Colonel Holmby abducted the king, and the army officers now began negotiating with him directly. There were riots soon in the City of London, fomented by Presbyterians, and many moderates fled to the army for protection. On 4 August 1647 the army marched back into London and quelled the riots. While the king was installed at Hampton Court, and continued vainly to hope for a solution, the soldiers, stationed nearby at Putney, debated in the local church on the basis of radical documents like *The Case of the Armie Truly Stated*, a manifesto signed on 15 October, and then a new *Agreement of the People*: 'all power is originally and essentially in the whole body of the people'; the laws of reason and nature take precedence over civil and common law; the Civil War had returned the country to a state of nature; a new constitution is required, subscribed by the whole people. As one participant in the debates put it: 'every man that is to live under a government ought first by his own consent to put himself under that government'.[3] The *Agreement* was inspired by the writings of John Lilburne, around whom the Levellers movement had formed. For the first time in English history, something like a modern democracy was genuinely imagined.

Cromwell and his son-in-law, Henry Ireton, still held out for some property qualification for suffrage, and even sought a role for the king and the Lords. But when the king again escaped, this time to the Isle of Wight, on 11 November, the various factions in the army pulled together in a compromise. In January 1648 Parliament passed a resolution of 'No Further Addresses' to the king. But he had concluded a secret pact with the Scots, agreeing to establish a Presbyterian church if an invasion would restore him to the throne. Royalist uprisings in the remoter areas of Wales, Cornwall and Devon, and the North in April, launched the Second Civil War.

Soon after the City riots, early in 1648, Milton moved house again, this time to a smaller house in High Holborn (and thus away from the City), backing onto Lincoln's Inn Fields. He had given up the school, his noisy in-laws had left, and so he had no reason to stay at the larger Barbican house. He profited from the relative calm, however brief, to work on a projected *History of Britain*, to which his friend Samuel Hartlib refers at this time, and also, oddly enough, a *Brief History of Muscovy*. Not published until much later, these works nonetheless show some contemporary concerns. He writes eloquently of Russia's tyrants, of her salvation from the chaos of civil war by one strong man and of the Russian husband's right to put away his wife 'upon utter dislike'. At this time he may also have written what we know as the 'Digression', inserted into the *History of Britain*, but later excluded, denouncing the Presbyterian Long Parliament and its corruption through parallels with Britain after the Romans left. It is redolent of fresh political turmoil: these 'late commotions' make it look as if it were written during 1648 and the Second Civil War.[4]

In April 1648, as the political struggle intensified, Milton made a further significant choice of what he would write. He translated some more Psalms, this time numbers 80–88, and clearly mingles his own voice with that of the psalmist. He cries out to God to guide and save the nation and its new prophet from treacherous friends. Israel becomes rather English:

> Why hast thou laid her Hedges low
> And brok'n down her Fence,
> That all may pluck her as they go,
> *With rudest violence?* (Psalm 80:12)

(the italics are Milton's, scrupulously admitting, as Bible translators do, that these words are not in the Hebrew). He also looks towards the new millennium, a common theme at the time, when the Kingdom of God shall be established in a repentant Israel.

> Surely to such as do him fear
> Salvation is at hand,
> And glory shall *ere long appear*
> *To* dwell within our Land. (Psalm 85:9)

In July or August 1648, Milton addressed another of his political sonnets to the General Thomas Fairfax as he was besieging Colchester. Fairfax is cast as Hercules lopping off the Hydra heads of new rebellions amid Scottish perfidy. But the poem's sestet adds thoughts about peace:

> For what can Warr, but endlesse war still breed,
> Till Truth & Right from Violence be freed
> ...In vain doth Valour bleed
> While Avarice & Rapine share the land.

The Second Civil War ended now quickly. In August 1648 Fairfax accepted the surrender of Colchester, and Cromwell won a victory over the Scots at Preston. While the king continued to intrigue and hope for an invasion, word arrived of the end of the immensely destructive Thirty Years War (1618–48) on the continent with the Treaty of Westphalia in October. In the midst of these momentous events, Milton's second daughter, Mary, was born and baptized at St Giles-in-the-Fields on 7 November.

On 20 November Ireton and the army presented the 'Grand Remonstrance' to Parliament. It contained the familiar terms of the Levellers' programme, but also demanded that the king be brought to justice for 'treason, blood and mischief'. Parliament was reluctant to accede, but then events took over. Charles, living in some fantasy world, insisted on preserving the bishops. He was seized by the army on 1 December and locked up in Hurst Castle on the Hampshire coast across from the Isle of Wight. Parliament denounced the army's action, but the army was entirely out of patience. Soldiers under Colonel Pride arrested over two-hundred members of Parliament. Pride's Purge, as it was known, was a clear affront to Parliament's legal authority even greater than that of Charles' efforts earlier to arrest five leaders. But now it was not legality that mattered, only power. Other members withdrew in fear or disgust, leaving the so-called Rump Parliament of some eighty members of the Commons and five or six peers.

On 4 January 1649 this Rump declared its own supremacy without king or lords – a de facto republic. A commission of 135 men was appointed to bring the king to trial. Upon reflection, Fairfax withdrew from the commission, and was followed by many others. But the remainder pressed on. It is hard to imagine that Milton would not have attended the trial, which opened on 20 January in the Great Hall at Westminster. His own lawyer in those tangled financial affairs in Chancery, John Bradshaw, presided over the court. It was Bradshaw who read out the charge of high treason, specifying Charles' efforts to 'overthrow the rights and liberties of the people' and that he 'hath traitorously and maliciously levied War against the present parliament and the people therein represented'. Every day, Charles kept his hat on in defiance of the court's authority and refused to answer any charges. He was sentenced on 27 January as a public enemy 'to the good people of this nation'. His head was to be severed from his body.

During the trial the Presbyterian presses and pulpits poured out execrations on this parliamentary Rump, and Milton could not resist entering the fray. He began writing *The Tenure of Kings and Magistrates* to defend the acts of the army and justify the existing government, such as it was, and to rally the people towards the trial of the king and a republican constitution. He ridicules recent tracts by men like the still formidable William Prynne but saves his real fury for the 'dancing divines' of the Westminster Assembly and Sion College. They had been foremost in stirring up the revolt against Charles: they 'devested him, disanointed him, nay curs'd him all over in thir Pulpits and their Pamphlets'. But now they have turned their coats, and are worthy only of contempt. Milton derives his argument both from classical sources and the Bible and appeals to 'the Law of nature and right reason'. The people have a god-given right to execute their king: 'be he King, or

Tyrant, or Emperour, the Sword of justice is above him… to avenge the effusion and so great a deluge of innocent blood'. He appeals in particular to the Roman political thought of a Cicero or a Sallust or a Livy, which distinguishes between a slave, who is subject to someone else's power, and a citizen, who is not. Several recent theorists had argued for the right of the people to resist tyranny, basing legitimacy on the consent of the governed, and Milton comes close to at least some Leveller ideas in arguing the power and right of the people themselves, not simply their representatives or inferior magistrates, to choose their governors, both the king and the Parliament.

Milton offers a kind of historical summary of these political ideas, and the end of the story, as he sees it happening now is that the people may depose a king or magistrate, 'though no Tyrant, merely by the liberty and right of free born Men, to be govern'd as seems best to them' (*YP* III 206). There is, however, a characteristic Miltonic twist. In the present circumstances, even this patently unrepresentative Parliament may act for the people, partly from the widely recognized principle of '*salus populi*', the safety of the people and realm, but chiefly because these men have established their worth by staying the course amid so much backsliding. They are a kind of natural aristocracy, and so fit to rule. This is something like the ancient government of Israel under the Judges, before God finally if angrily agreed to the clamour of the people for a king (I Samuel 8). And it is a matter for national pride, 'wherein we have the honour to precede other Nations who are now labouring to be our followers' (236). Before Milton could finish this treatise, events outran his pen.

The king was executed on January 30, 1649. An eyewitness records a 'dismal Universal Groan' as the axe fell. Charles met his final moments with dignity as he knelt on the black-draped scaffold with outstretched arms. Milton's young friend Andrew Marvell described the scene in famous lines:

> While round the armed Bands
> Did clap their bloody hands,
> He nothing common did, or mean
> Upon the memorable Scene:
> But with his keener Eye
> The Axes edge did try:
> Nor call'd the Gods with vulgar spight
> To vindicate his helpless Right,
> But bow'd his comely Head
> Down as upon a Bed.

Bravely though the king faced his end, England had abolished its monarchy and started the first modern revolution.

Milton quickly finished the *Tenure* and it was published on or about 13 February 1649. On the title-page, probably written after the event, he claims that 'it is lawful… for any who have the power, to call to account a Tyrant or a wicked King and after due conviction, to depose, and put him to death' (190). Milton was the first person of any standing to defend the regicide in print. But the new republic was instantly vilified throughout Europe, and a new book, supposedly written by the king himself, dominated the public space.

12

Image Breaking

The English Civil War had been fought as much on fields of rhetoric as on the muddy countryside. In those battles of rhetoric no text was more important than Charles I's personal testament, *Eikon Basilike* ('The King's Image'), apparently written in prison before his execution. It was published on or soon after 30 January 1649, the day he was beheaded outside the Banqueting House in Whitehall, London, and it quickly became an international bestseller. The regicides did what they could to stop the act of beheading the king becoming a royal martyrdom: the platform was low, it was surrounded with troops of soldiers to stop the people from seeing or hearing the king's dying speech, and the people had to leave as soon as the severed head was raised high. But these efforts could not prevent the rapid spread of public sympathy. The book itself was seized and most copies in London were destroyed, but a Royalist publisher moved his press outside the city, and some thirty-five editions appeared before the end of the year, some adding Charles's final speech and private correspondence. A further twenty-five editions were published on the Continent, where the execution of the English king was held to be a great scandal.

Formally, the book consists of a series of chapters reviewing the public events that led the king to prison. Each chapter protests his innocence in relation to some particular event, and even if he admits a fault, as when he had yielded to the demands of Parliament to execute Thomas Wentworth, earl of Strafford, the effect is rather to expose the cruelty of his opponents. Each section is complemented by a longish prayer printed in italic type to mark it off from the rest of the text and highlight its piety. Both political apologia and spiritual autobiography, the book gives a cloying and at times self-pitying portrait of the king as heroic victim of those wicked rebels. Charles read Foxe's *Acts and Monuments* during his imprisonment, and casts himself in the same mould as those Protestant martyrs. And just as Foxe had written one of the most widely read books of the previous century, so now the popularity of *Eikon Basilike* affected the rest of English political history in the seventeenth century.

Even at the time many suspected the work was not really by Charles, and eventually John Gauden, a minor cleric who later rose in the ranks of the church to become bishop of Exeter and then Worcester, was revealed to have been the ghostwriter. Probably it was a collaboration. Charles's papers and notes were organized and given shape by Gauden, then submitted to Charles for his approval and final edit. It was not unusual then, any more than it is now, for a monarch to have help with his public discourse, but in this case the pretence at spiritual inwardness made the actual authorship a vital matter. When a later edition recycled the language of Pamela's prayer from Sidney's *Arcadia* as if it were the king's own, Milton had some pointed fun exposing the plagiarism. In turn Samuel Johnson was so incensed by Milton's charge that in his notoriously prejudiced *Life of Milton* he repeated the accusation that Milton himself had forged the text to discredit the king's piety.

The frontispiece to the first edition of *Eikon Basilike* is another engraving by William Marshall. In later editions the image came complete with a versified 'Explanation of the Emblem'. What it boils down to is that the engraving sets up the book's representation of Charles as suffering saint and martyr and turns him into an object to be revered. The portrait shows him kneeling, perhaps in prayer, and grasping a crown of thorns (inscribed *Gratia*), with his regal crown at his feet (*Vanitas*) and another crown awaiting him in the heavens (inscribed *Gloria*). He looks upwards to that heavenly crown, with a look on his face that is supposed to remind you of Christ as he faces his crucifixion, though it could also be due to the painful contorted position Marshall has depicted. The image deliberately recalls what Charles said at the moment of his death, that 'I go from a corruptible to an incorruptible Crown, where no disturbance can be, no disturbance in the world.' In the landscape beside the image of the king, emblems of a palm tree hung with weights and a rock blasted by tempest apparently represent the king's virtue strengthened by trial.

All this elaborate canonization of the king was hard to answer. Milton's response, a task laid upon him by the Council of State, the new governing body 'for the first time established by the authority of Parliament', as Milton describes it (*YP* IV.1 627), was boldly called *Eikonoklastes*, a title which gains extra resonance in relation to the frontispiece since it means 'The Image-Breaker'. He scorns 'the conceited portraiture before this Book, drawn out to the full measure of a Masquing Scene, and set there to catch fools and silly gazers'. Indeed, Charles had appeared several times in court masques and drawn puritan disapproval. His courageous appearance on the scaffold could thus be seen as a performance. But that approach had little hope of countering the powerful sentimental appeal of the king's own book, a more powerful weapon in death than he had ever wielded alive.

It was the publication of *The Tenure of Kings and Magistrates* on 13 February 1649 that had called the attention of the Council to Milton's value as a polemicist and produced the invitation to write *Eikonoklastes*. And it was also his mastery of Latin that led to his appointment two day's later as 'Secretary for Foreign Languages', or in his alternative title 'Latin Secretary'. The salary was £288 15s 6½ d. For the first time Milton had a real job. Within a week, Parliament abolished the House of Lords and the monarchy. Milton became the first contractual employee of the new republic. His job was to communicate with the rest of Europe in the midst of the crisis provoked by the death of the king and the new state of England as a Commonwealth. He had to protest the attacks of exiled Royalists, including the murder of the Parliament's envoy to the Hague (a man who had taught history at Cambridge) and also the murder of the ambassador to Spain. These tasks gave Milton membership of the circle of secretaries around the council. Already blind in one eye, he did not have to accept every commission, and indeed his personal views now agreed more with the Levellers than the government would have found comfortable. He was asked for his 'observations' on Leveller pamphlets, but never responded.

Milton's writings had often been denounced during the wars alongside those of John Lilburne, William Walwyn, and Richard Overton, the Leveller leaders. But there was no apparent or direct contact. At the moment, indeed, the Leveller leaders were back in the Tower of London. Though he would later speak highly of Milton for his honesty about the shortcomings of Parliament,[1] Lilburne opposed the execution of the king on the grounds that the Rump that voted for it was not representative of the popular view. While in the Tower, the Levellers composed the third and extended version of their famous and widely influential 'An Agreement Of The Free People of England. Tendered as a Peace-Offering to this distressed Nation'.[2] They were eventually acquitted of treason and released on 8 November 1649. The city celebrated.

The king had tried to get the Irish Catholics to invade England, and Ireland still posed a problem. The Presbyterians in the North also denounced the regicide. Milton replied in an appendix (*Observations*) to *Articles of Peace*, published at the request of the Council on 16 May, playing skilfully on common English disdain for the savage Irish, revulsion at the massacres of English residents in 1641 and general Protestant hatred of Popery. If we want an explanation for Milton's vehement anti-Catholic rhetoric, other than the heritage of the Gunpowder plot and Milton's poem about it, we may look to the legacy of Charles's Queen Henrietta Maria, always intriguing for her cause while she remained in England. No doubt widespread paranoia in a time of civil war increased the ever-present danger of rebellions in a largely

Catholic Ireland. The terrible history of Ireland, which has continued to our own time, runs like a scar through this period. In retrospect, we may well assess the proposals to 'pacify' Ireland as unreasonable, tyrannical even, but in the context of the time, Milton felt that Ireland should belong to England by conquest and by feudal suffrage. He could not allow for a parallel between Irish calls for independence and English desires for toleration and religious freedom. He did not see Roman Catholicism as a religion, so much as a rival political system. The papist antichrist is at work. He would soon argue explicitly that Popery cannot

> be acknowledged a religion; but a Roman principalitie rather, endeavouring to keep up her old universal dominion under a new name and meer shadow of a catholic religion... supported mainly by a civil, and, except in Rome, by a forein power. (*YP* VII 254)

This is the atmosphere that may explain, if not excuse, Cromwell's butchery, in a series of bloody battles, of native Irish at Dublin, Drogheda, Wexford and Kilkenny. Milton may not have encouraged the slaughter, but he showed he understood it.

Milton had moved house yet again, to Charing Cross, next to the Bull-Head tavern. He was now closer to the Council meeting place in Whitehall, where he would go on foot from time to time to get his instructions. At home he worked on those assignments, like *Eikonoklastes*, probably with scribal help from his young nephew John Phillips. In June he was asked to become a kind of censor or spy-catcher. So the author of *Areopagitica*, by an odd twist of fate, found himself in the strange position of having to approve a book prior to publication. But he did it. The House of Commons Journal for 10 August 1650 records a note 'under the hand of John Milton' to authorize publication of the Socinian *Racovian Catechism*, including a denial of Christ's divinity. He was also given the task of licensing the weekly publication of *Mercurius Politicus*, one of the many weekly newsbooks being published in London. This particular 'Mercury' was Marchamont Nedham, a witty and prolific writer, who had started out as a republican but had switched to the king's side, becoming the pro-Royalist *Mercurius Pragmaticus*, and had been arrested and imprisoned in Newgate. He escaped and was recaptured, but soon agreed to change sides again, perhaps with some prompting from Milton, as they now became friends. He continued for a long time to write as *Mercurius Politicus*. This newsbook, which was one of the first publications to include regular advertising, was immensely popular and widely read throughout Europe. And Milton continued to license it.

Only when he was almost completely blind, in January 1652, was he relieved of this duty. The fact that he did it at all may have made him uncomfortable. Apparently he would approve the newsbooks in batches, sometimes after publication. So apparently neither he nor the Council took the task very seriously. Quite probably regular meetings with Nedham to discuss the contents and avoid embarrassment led to their developing friendship.

Soon after the publication of *Eikonoklastes*, on 19 November 1649, the Council granted Milton lodgings at the Scotland Yard end of Whitehall itself. He took over an apartment formerly occupied by the elegant and fashionable Sir John Hippersley. A few months later, when the magnificent art collection of Charles I was put on sale at Somerset House, Milton was invited to choose some hangings from the royal collection 'for the furnishing of his lodging at Whitehall'.

He was also asked to write diplomatic letters in support of the Council's decisions. One such involved a letter to Hamburg on 4 January 1650 explaining and defending the controversial Engagement Act, which required everyone to declare allegiance to the Commonwealth. It was not an oath, so no one had actually to swear, but many demurred, and one intelligent commentator, Algernon Sidney, protested that 'such a test would prove a snare to many an honest man, but every knave would slip through it'. But Milton's letter calls it a legitimate demand of allegiance from those who hold office or enjoy the benefits of government.

He now began a much bigger task. An eminent professor, a Protestant and humanist scholar at the University of Leyden, Claude de Saumaise, or Salmasius, now resident at Queen Christina's court in Sweden, had written an elaborate treatise to summon the kings of Europe and all Royalists to unite against the new illegal republic and place Charles II (as he was now known in Scotland and elsewhere) on his father's throne. Milton was asked by the Council to frame a reply. According to his own account, he was warned by the doctors that if he undertook the task he would lose the sight of both eyes. He was faced with a solemn choice: 'I resolved therefore that I must employ this brief use of my eyes while yet I could for the greatest possible benefit to the state' (*YP* IV.1, 588). The resulting text, *Joannis Miltonii Angli Defensio pro populo Anglicano*, had to be written piecemeal with a break every hour, due to Milton's failing health, especially the pain in his right eye, but it satisfied both his patriotism and his desire for eminence in Europe. In often scurrilous Latin, the *Defensio* (or *First Defence*, as it is often known) attacks Salmasius personally (a hen-pecked husband, slavish at home and in his politics) and takes up again the arguments of *The Tenure*: Charles was executed after due process of law, and for tyranny and high treason. The tract quotes liberally from the Bible in support of Christian liberty.

Edward Phillips likened it to David's accurate stone thrown at Goliath's forehead, and many agreed that it had put paid to Salmasius, who died soon after its publication. It was widely read in European editions, France, Germany, Holland (a Dutch translation) and Sweden, and was burned publicly in Toulouse and Paris. According to one correspondent this made it even more eagerly sought after. Soon there was a second edition published as an elegant folio on heavy paper, several of which Milton gave to friends or official contacts. One copy (now in the Huntington Library, California) was bought by the second earl of Bridgewater, who as a boy of eleven had played the elder brother in *Comus*. He wrote in the margin: 'liber igne, auctor furca, dignissimi' ('the book deserves the fire, the author the gallows').

In the midst of all this, Milton's mother-in-law was proving troublesome. The legal wrangle over the Oxford property continued, and on 11 July 1651 she petitioned for payments from her husband's estate 'to preserve her and her children from starvation'. She did indeed have a large family, the youngest of her children being now eleven. The whole issue was complicated by the rules governing what happened to the property of former Royalists, and at first the Commissioners denied her the widow's third Milton had been paying her. Her petition notes that 'Mr Milton is a harsh and Chollericke man, & married to Mrs. Powells daughter, he having turned away his wife heretofore for a long space upon some other occasion.' Milton's reply is attached, urging that she be allotted her income, but saying nothing about her effort to rewrite family history. The documents were considered by the Commissioners, many more papers were filed, and eventually, three years later, the dispute was resolved and Anne Powell was granted her redress at Milton's urging.

Among the many tasks Milton performed for the Council were a series of letters to Spain and Portugal, at war since Portugal's declaration of independence from Spain in 1640. Portugal supported the Royalist forces and Spain, somewhat half-heartedly, the Commonwealth. Prince Rupert of the Rhine, the nephew of Charles I, led a fleet to Lisbon, but was blocked and eventually defeated by Admiral Blake. Milton wrote urging the Portuguese king to drive out these 'pirates', or permit the English fleet to attack them. In Spain the newly appointed ambassador, Anthony Ascham, was murdered as soon as he arrived, and the ambassador to Portugal, Henry Vane, had to flee for his life. Milton sent letters in his formal Latin to give the ambassadors' credentials, then to protest their treatment. The assassins had taken sanctuary in a church. Negotiations were protracted. Milton also had to write protesting injuries to English merchants in areas controlled by Spain, such as the Canary Islands. Since the letter about the Canaries survives in both the Council's English and Milton's Latin we can see that he often improved upon the drafts he was given.

A contemporary witness, Herman Mylius, a representative of a German principality, for whom Milton had been negotiating a treaty with the Council, recorded in his diary entry for 6 March 1652 his thanks for Milton's efforts and his farewell. Milton, he wrote, was 'wholly deprived of his sight in his forty-second year and so in the flower and prime of his age'. When Milton tried to sign a Swiss visitor's autograph album, he misjudged the size of the space available and had to spill over onto the next line – Johannis Milto/-nius. (The album is now in the Stadtbibliothek in St Gall.)

Nonetheless, in the family Bible, Milton now proudly inscribed the birth of a son, John, 'born on Sunday March the 16th about half an hower past nine at night'. Milton was still able to see him, if only just. He could also write in a visitor's autograph book his new motto in Greek, from 2 Corinthians 12:9: 'I am perfected in weakness.' Such visitors were becoming plentiful now that his fame was spreading throughout Europe as a 'strenuous defender' of the republic.

Later, in 1654, he wrote in Latin to the eminent Athenian scholar Leonard Philaras describing the loss of his sight.

> Everything which I distinguished when I myself was still seemed to swim, now to the right, now to the left. Certain permanent vapours… oppress my eyes with a sort of sleepy heaviness, especially from mealtime to evening… When considerable sight still remained, when I would first go to bed and lie on one side or the other, abundant light would dart from my closed eyes; then, as sight daily diminished, colours proportionately darker would burst forth with violence and a sort of crash from within. But now, pure black, marked as if with extinguished or ashy light, and as if interwoven with it, pours forth. (*YP* IV.2 869)

The treatments he sought out must have been torture. One involved piercing the skin below the hairline and passing through the holes a red-hot cautery with a diamond point and a needle with thread dipped in egg white and rose oil.[3] So detailed is the account he gives of his failing sight that one feels one might reach into the past and help him correct it. Certainly a modern medical investigation would be able to identify the problem. There have been many such attempts, not all agreeing with each other. Glaucoma is the general and most common diagnosis. One theory states that it was a cyst on the pituitary gland that gave the painful headaches Milton suffered, also the gastric disturbances, and that would eventually cause total blindness if not treated, though the eyes, as he reported, would be clear 'to outward view of blemish or of spot'. The intense pain would have subsided once blindness became complete.

In the same letter, Milton courageously tells his friend that, if indeed his case is incurable as he fears, he is prepared. 'Many days of darkness, the wise man warns us, are everyone's destiny', and his own have been eased, through the kindness of Providence, by 'the voices and visits of friends'. Sight is not in the eyes alone. 'Indeed while he himself looks out for me and provides for me, which he does, and takes me as if by the hand and leads me through life, surely, since it has pleased him, I shall be pleased to grant my eyes a holiday.'

In the days when he was finally losing his sight, he waited for his appointment to be renewed. Finally it came through on 29 December 1651. Perhaps because of his blindness (though there was much competition among the saints for the choice apartments), he was also obliged to move from Whitehall to what Phillips described as 'A pretty Garden-house in Petty France (York Street) in Westminster, next door to the Lord Scudamore's, and opening into St James's Park.' The house was later owned by Jeremy Bentham, and both William Hazlitt and J. S. Mill lived there. An engraving of it was published in the *Illustrated London News* for 9 January 1874, but this did not stop the Metropolitan Railway Company from demolishing it in 1877.

By a bizarre irony, just as Milton had been finally and permanently thrown into the eerie darkness of his blindness, 'pure black, marked as if with extinguished or ashy light', as he explained in the letter to Phalaras, there was a total eclipse of the sun on 29 March 1652.

13

Blindness

A few weeks later, in spite of his blindness, Milton struggled to write a note in the family Bible: the first words are in his hand, but the entry had to be completed by another.

> My daughter Deborah was born the 2nd of May, being Sunday somewhat before 3 of the clock in the morning 1652, my wife hir mother dyed about 3 days after.

The entry continues: 'my son about 6 weeks after his mother'. Edward Phillips thought the boy's death might have been due to 'ill-usage or bad Constitution of an ill-chosen Nurse' – which, if anything, would have made it harder to bear. Perhaps because Milton was already refusing to attend the established church, there is no record of John's death and burial or of Deborah's baptism in the churches of Milton's local parish of Westminster. Of course we must allow for the fact that many documents were destroyed in the 'late commotions' or in the Great Fire of London in 1666. In any case Milton was now almost totally blind, his wife had died and then his only son. He now he had three young children to care for, including a new baby who would have been with a wet-nurse.

Some men might have blamed themselves for these misfortunes. One contemporary father mourned the death of a baby boy and saw the reason in his 'unseasonable playing at chess', or else his lusts. Such was a common belief of the time. But Milton was incapable of any such reaction. Far from retreating into self-reproach, he continued for several more years to fulfil his duties for the government. Various helpers were assigned to him, but it was his phenomenal memory that allowed him to keep working, listening to the texts he had to translate and then producing his elegant Latin or English. Hearing someone read was not uncommon: Pepys often had a boy or a literate servant read to him. From now on, though, as we follow Milton through his life, we need to be more conscious of the aural-oral means by which he received and produced language. He is no longer a defender of 'books promiscuously read' so much as he is a judge of the swell and fade of sound.

England was heading toward a war with the Dutch republic that nobody really seemed to want. Milton was in close and respectful touch with the two new Dutch ambassadors, and in July he had to translate with no enthusiasm whatsoever Parliament's official *Declaration* of the causes of war. Intense diplomatic activity failed to head off the war, in spite of a general admiration for the way the Protestant United Provinces had thrown off the Spanish yoke. Soon the Council was writing to the grand duke of Tuscany, who had proclaimed his neutrality, thanking him in Milton's Latin for allowing English ships into the protection of Livorno harbour. But then, when the English seized a captured warship within sight of the Livorno lighthouse and pursued an escaped prisoner onto the shore, Milton had to write and apologize for violating Tuscan neutrality. Milton was also translating correspondence and treaty proposals with other European states, including a letter to Spain complaining that the murderers of the ambassador, Anthony Ascham, were still unpunished, and another to the Danes, traditional allies of the Dutch, about an alliance. This letter produced no result. The Danes were soon allied with the Dutch and closed the Baltic to English shipping. The war was to last two years.

During the negotiations over the Dutch war, Milton was learning the language from his friend Roger Williams, and practising other languages with him as well (Hebrew, Greek, Latin and French). Williams was back from America for a couple of years to negotiate terms for his new settlements in Narragansett Bay, and also to continue the fight for complete Toleration. In one pamphlet he quoted Cromwell's famous declaration to the committee: 'That he had rather that Mahumetanism were permitted among us than that one of God's children should be persecuted.' Milton was also friendly with Henry Vane at this time. Though Vane was soon to fall out with Cromwell, all of these men were working against the Presbyterian efforts to suppress what they regarded as heresy. 'What formerly was accounted errour, is now esteemed truth', as the Leveller William Walwyn put it,[1] or, as Milton himself had written in *Areopagitica*,

> who finds not that *Irenaeus, Epiphanius, Jerome* and others discover more heresies than they well confute, and that oft for heresie which is the truer opinion. (*YP* II 518)

There were, nonetheless, alarming signs even for someone as used to religious and political strife as Milton. Radical religious activity was rapidly increasing – Ranters, Quakers, Levellers, Muggletonians, Fifth Monarchists, even the proto-communist Diggers, were holding meetings in private houses or disrupting public services. Not only Presbyterians in the Rump and beyond were still clamouring for a state church and the repression of heresy, but now some Independents joined them, at least in so far as the need for tithes to support an impoverished clergy seemed obvious. Cromwell felt more and more need to assert himself in order to achieve any of what he and the army commanders wanted, back pay for the troops and a loose coalition of various moderate or established churches and tendencies, tolerant of all. On 10 February a 'Committee for the Propagation of the Gospel' was appointed, including Cromwell, to attempt to settle the state of religion. Immediately a group of Independents, flushed with their new sense of power, proposed an established church with a paid clergy and restrictions on liberty of worship. The Socinian *Racovian Catechism*, publication of which Milton had approved himself two years previously, was also now under attack. The committee declared it 'Blasphemous, Erroneous and Scandalous' and ordered it burned. Both the publisher and Milton were examined, but no action taken: Milton admitted having licensed the book, and told the committee 'that men should refrain from forbidding books; that in approving of that book he had done no more than what his opinion was'[2]

Milton had apparently written almost no poetry for four years – not since the sonnet to Fairfax – during all the turmoil of the revolution. He now determined that he should revive his skills at the same time as he continued his other duties, and wrote two powerful sonnets. One he sent to Cromwell in May, perhaps just a few days after the death of his wife, praising him, 'our chief of men', for victories. In the Trinity manuscript the sonnet carries a title that links it to a protest against a new threat to freedom of speech: 'On the Proposals of Certain Ministers of the Committee for Propagation of the Gospel'. What especially annoyed Milton was the proposition that no one should be permitted to speak on any religious question unless two divines at least had certified his orthodoxy. The octave spills over into the sestet, as often, with words added with difficulty in Milton's own hand in the manuscript: 'Worcesters laureat wreath'. This is a reference to the decisive battle of Worcester of 3 September 1651, in which Cromwell had defeated the Scotch Covenanters led by Charles *fils* (temporarily returned and not yet Charles II). The battle put paid to any Royalist hopes. As in the Fairfax sonnet Milton changes his tone and reminds his heroic reader that it is time to think about peace as well as war:

                    yet much remaines
To conquer still; peace hath her victories
No less renownd then warr.

Milton then urges Cromwell to defend religious liberty and to make no provision for a stipendiary clergy. The enemies of these positions are identified with the hireling wolves of Matthew 7:15 (familiar to all of us as the wolves who wear sheep's clothing). The final couplet – unique in Milton's English sonnets – rhyming 'paw' and 'maw' contemptuously aligns the enemies with those denounced in Philippians 3:19 'whose God is their belly'. These are among the biblical texts Milton had in mind when he wrote, years earlier, the famous passage about the clergy's bellies in 'Lycidas'.

A few weeks later Milton wrote another political sonnet, this time to Henry Vane, praising him for his military career (as treasurer of the navy he had helped prepare for victory over the Dutch fleet) and also for his defense of religious liberty. Magistrates should have nothing to do with religion, and Vane is exemplary in that respect. Unlike the sonnet to Cromwell, this poem does not turn into a veiled warning. It is tempting to read into the contrast Milton's growing disillusionment with the course of the revolution. These are also the first poems he wrote in his full blindness, and they show his need to use another more pointed kind of language than prose or diplomatic Latin.

Milton's sympathy with the Tolerationist cause and the disestablishment of religion is clear in this poem. The cause was enhanced by the publication in July 1652 of Brian Walton's *Polyglot Bible*. Milton had known Walton since 1624 at All Hallows Church in Bread Sreet, and he helped him gain permission for publication. The *Polyglot Bible* is a remarkable tour de force, scholarly and enormously broad in scope, printing Old Testament texts in its various languages spread across double pages. Besides the usual Hebrew and Greek, it prints the Samaritan Pentateuch and Aramaic, Latin, Ethiopian, Syrian, Arabic and Persian biblical texts. Milton may even have contributed to it, making use of his extensive knowledge of the languages he had taught his pupils, or learned himself.

A new use for his best language, Latin, now came to preoccupy him. In August 1652 an anonymous document appeared, *Regii Sanguinis Clamor*, or 'The Cry of the Royal Blood to Heaven Against the English Parricides'. It was not the expected response of Salmasius himself, but it was one of several answers to Milton's *Defensio*. It stirred Milton to set about writing one of his most powerful tracts, the *Defensio Secunda*, though the task would take him over a year. The author of the *Clamor* was an English Royalist called Pierre Du Moulin, who for obvious reasons did not want his identity known. He had sent his manuscript to Salmasius, who was too ill by now to take on this new polemic but passed it to Alexander More, a Protestant pastor who had been removed from his post as professor of Greek in Geneva for a sexual scandal, and who was a house-guest of Salmasius in Leyden at the time. More composed a letter to Charles II, to be prefixed to the document of Du Moulin, and which was signed by the printer, Adriaan Vlacq. Eager to profit from the controversy, Vlacq rapidly produced and sent the unbound sheets to Milton's friend Samuel Hartlib to pass on to Milton, with an offer to publish his reply. Milton received the sheets in the Council, he later claimed, and was indeed asked by the Council to reply. He began work on his reply, mistakenly assuming that the *Clamor* was written by More. Even when he heard to the contrary, Milton kept insisting the author was Alexander More. Du Moulin was not identified until years later, at which point he recorded his pleasure, 'a soft chuckle, at seeing my bantling laid at another man's door, and the blind and furious Milton fighting and slashing the air'.

The *Clamor* attacks the parricides, as it calls the regicides, vigorously, but it was no doubt the personal and vicious attack on Milton himself that actually prompted his reply. The prefatory epistle refers to him, quoting Virgil, as a sort of Cyclops, '"a monster horrible, deformed, huge and sightless". Though to be sure he is not huge: nothing is more weak, more bloodless, more shrivelled than little animals such as he.' There is a lot more in this vein of schoolboy insult ('a great stinking pestilence', a 'dung-heap'), accusing Milton of having been expelled from Cambridge for some homosexual scandal and thus fleeing to Italy in shame. While there, said another calumny, he had 'sold his buttocks for a few pence'. Milton was especially stung, it seems, by the attack on his looks. When he replied, he wrote:

> Ugly I have never been thought by anyone… I admit that I am not tall, but my stature is closer to the medium than the small, as is the case with so many men of the greatest worth. (*YP* IV.1 582)

One can almost hear his sensitivity about his height ('closer to the medium than the small'). He also claimed that most people thought he looked ten years younger than his forty-four years. Evidently his vanity was wounded. He took some time over his reply.

Meanwhile political events became even more heated, and Milton was involved directly or indirectly from day to day. He did not attend Parliament, and went less to the buildings of government in Whitehall since his blindness, but he was in regular contact with all the prime movers in these affairs. And he would be anxious to know what was happening. Parliament and the army clashed over the regulation of elections (how to exclude those too dangerous to be allowed a vote) and the state of the churches. Parliament wanted control over the church and the army, while the army leaders felt they had as good a right as any, having shed their blood for the Commonwealth, to decide who would govern and how, certainly as good a right as this poor Rump of a parliament. The crisis came in April 1653.

Cromwell proposed the Rump dissolve itself and that a new council of forty members drawn from both camps should put in place reforms and govern. The Rump seemed to agree but then the next day acted to vote itself an extension and the right to co-opt new members, or to judge their qualifications. Just as the vote was called, Cromwell put on his hat and began to denounce his fellow members of Parliament as corrupt and interested only in their own power, not the public good. In one account by an outraged republican (Ludlow), he furiously told them that

the Lord had done with them, and had chosen other instruments for carrying on his work that were more worthy… Then walking up and down the House like a mad-man, and kicking the ground with his feet, he cried out, 'You are no Parliament, I say you are no Parliament; I will put an end to your sitting.'

Many protested, including Henry Vane. Cromwell called them whoremasters and drunkards, and ended by saying: 'you have been sat here too long for any good you have been doing. Depart, I say, and let us have done with you. In the name of God, go!' Cromwell then had the speaker's mace carried away, saying 'What shall we do with this bauble? Here take it away.' He dismissed the Council of State, and provoked Milton's friend Bradshaw to attack him: 'Sir, you are mistaken to think that Parliament is dissolved; for no power under heaven can dissolve them but themselves; therefore take you notice of that.'[3]

Probably Milton had already denounced the corruption and reactionary politics of the Long Parliament in the 'Digression' to his *History of Britain*, but he had, after all, defended the rights of this republican Parliament forcefully in his *Defensio*. He will have been disturbed by these events, though we have no specific evidence till a year or so later when he supported Cromwell's action in his reply to the *Clamor*. Many others supported Cromwell's act, though Vane, Bradshaw and Fairfax refused to recognize the new government Cromwell quickly set up. It was to be an interim council, rooted in what was pejoratively called the 'Barebones Parliament' after one of its prominent members, an Anabaptist leather merchant with the splendidly ridiculous puritan name of Praisegod Barebones.

While all this was going on just outside his door, Milton composed some versions of Psalms 1–8. This may seem strange to those of us who would not go home of an evening and translate a psalm. But Milton was different: he had frequently turned to the psalms as a source of poetic and even political ideas. The typical theme of these psalms is pertinent to the moment: the cry for God's protection against enemies and confidence of God's deliverance. The psalms suggest a millenarian hope, reinforced by the interpretive tradition that applied the adoption of an heir in Psalm 2 to the begetting of the Son. Milton will later re-use this idea, in a highly original way, for the Satanic rebellion in *Paradise Lost*[4], but here he simply adds God's promise to the rebels that I 'anointed have my King (though ye rebel)'. He also adds, in his English of another psalm, the word 'dark', with obvious reference to his blindness. Psalm 6:7, a description of grief, becomes in Milton's lines

>   mine Eie
> Through grief consumes, is waxen old and dark
> I'the midst of all mine enemies.

These psalm translations are all experimental, unlike the translations of 1648, which had been in straightforward common metre. Now Milton plays with *terza rima*, elaborate stanzaic patterns and rhymed iambic pentameter couplets. It is tempting to see Milton as playing with these verse forms in order to escape momentarily from the intensity of affairs of state. At the same time one can read them as Milton's effort to recall his spiritual and poetic focus in the midst of all this political confusion.

He also composed a playful little poem in Latin as he was working on his reply to the *Clamor*. 'Gaudete scombri' it begins ('Rejoice mackerel'). The point is that now these fish who live in freezing waters will, when they end up in fish stalls, be able to wear the paper livery of the great Claude Saumaise, that is, the publications of Milton's opponent and his minions. So worthless are those writings that they will serve to wrap dead fish, valued indeed by the fishmongers who fill boxes and would otherwise wipe their noses on their sleeves. The witty little poem was soon published in the midst of his great reply to the *Clamor*.

Meanwhile, Cromwell is said to have rejected the crown offered to him by Major-General John Lambert, and most informed observers will have noticed the allusion to Julius Caesar, even to Shakespeare's play. The alignment of Caesar and Cromwell did not reassure either side. Eventually, Cromwell was sworn in as Protector on 16 December 1653. He was to govern with a permanent Council of State whenever Parliament was not in session. Of this, one minor result was the reappointment of Milton to his post in February 1654 – and this in spite of the withdrawal from the Council of his friend and supporter, John Bradshaw. Cromwell's surviving writings never mention Milton, rather surprisingly. But we may allow ourselves to see in this reappointment a sign of his recognition.

In his blindness, Milton needed help with his duties. In spite of his explicitly announced preference for his fellow poet Andrew Marvell, Milton's new assistant was the young Philip Meadows. He was aided by John Thurloe, the general secretary to the Council, whose network of spies was immensely useful for drafting diplomatic documents, not to mention for the decisions behind them. In any case Milton was well placed within the new political power elite, and was probably given time away from his regular duties to finish his reply to the *Clamor*. Milton continued to ignore the increasing number of messages from friends and acquaintances that the author of the *Clamor* was not in fact Alexander More. He preferred to publish all the scurrilous anecdotes he had already amassed against More: he had in fact checked with the Diodatis and others in Geneva and confirmed a story about More's affair with a servant girl. Many of his friends would have preferred that he not attack More so directly or so fiercely, since it had been established by now that More was not the father of Salmasius's maidservant's child. John Dury wrote as much to Hartlib from the Hague, but it was already too late. The immense power of Milton's invective had been unleashed and could not be called back.

Discreetly but insistently, the treatise that Milton published on 30 May 1654 at Thomas Newcomb's in London finally established him as the foremost Latin controversialist in Europe: *Joannis Miltonii Angli pro populo Anglicano defensio secunda, contra infamem libellum anonymum cui titulus, 'Regii sanguinis clamor ad coelum adversos parricidas Anglicanos'*. The book, usually known as the *Second Defence,* or *Defensio Secunda*, attacks with superb eloquence the arguments of the *Clamor* as well as the private lives of its supposed author and the Royalists concerned. Milton picks out five main points for extensive rebuttal: the attack on his own appearance, the greatness of Salmasius (who had died in the interim), the unlawfulness of the judgment against the king and the attack on Cromwell; above all, and this has proved its most important ingredient for subsequent generations, the insulting attack on Milton's sexual habits. He responds to this with an account of his own life.

The whole work is imagined as being orally delivered – he refers to it as 'my speech' – and indeed the work he is answering, the *Clamor*, he would have heard read to him. Perhaps the attacks on him were that much more painful for being read aloud rather than absorbed by silent and private reading. The response pairs a devastating attack on Alexander More with a defense of his own rectitude. Once again, he is using the method of ethical proof, presenting the speaker's character as blameless. But for Milton this is not simply standard rhetorical practise. He believed always that only a good man could write good poetry – or speeches. His model is Cicero, defending liberty against the wretches, like Catiline, who would impose tyranny. Just as Cicero's opponents (most notably Clodius) could be tarred with any insult, and the sexual ones are the most damning, so Milton feels free to name the women his opponent has slept with and to tell the stories of his adulteries. He is lecherous, priapic, 'the rankest goat of all' and also a hermaphrodite who both begets and conceives. In a very different key, Milton is replaying the Lady's response to Comus. Now Milton has to explain, or explain away, his nickname as 'the Lady of Christ's'. Milton turns back the homosexual ('Lady') charges made against him by suggesting More and Salmasius (or 'Salmasia') together produced that 'empty wind-egg', the *Clamor*.

Soon Milton's book was causing a scandal. More seems to have tried to buy up 500 imported copies of the book, but he could not prevent the Dutch publisher of his own *Clamor*, Vlacq, from publishing a pirated edition. All this invective contrasts with the heroic mode in which Milton defends both Cromwell and himself. Indeed he imagines the work as a kind of epic in defense of the new English nation. Just as Homer or Virgil focus on one particular event in the hero's life, so Milton claims 'to have celebrated at least one heroic achievement of my countrymen' (*YP* IV.1 685). As at Troy, there are many heroes: officers of the state such as Fleetwood Overton and Lambert; Queen Christina of Sweden – she had praised Milton's first *Defensio*; even Fairfax and Bradshaw – they had both been opposing Cromwell's coup, and Milton thus quietly appeals to Cromwell to try to bring them back into the fold. And the main hero is Cromwell himself, a great victor in war and in politics because he is 'victor over himself'. He is therefore the man most fit to rule, the *pater patriae*; he showed his magnanimity by refusing the crown. In the background of this portrait is Plato, whom Milton admired, imagining and then addressing his philosopher-king. But there is a big difference. Unlike Plato, Milton warns Cromwell to take good care of the liberty that has been temporarily committed to his care. If he were to be seduced by the title of king, he would succumb to the worst temptations of power: 'to refuse no toil, to yield to no allurements of pleasure, to flee from the pomp of wealth and power, these are arduous tasks compared to which war is a mere game' (674). Milton makes a set of political proposals to Cromwell about how he is to do this, principally by sharing power with other good men (the aristocratic republic Milton had always admired), by separating church and state and by removing all power from the church. This the republic had achieved earlier by abolishing the bishops and their place in the Lords, but now the danger is money, 'the poison of the church': the clergy must not be paid. Cromwell should also repeal all the laws that inhibit free expression.

In spite of all the attention devoted to Cromwell, the hero praised at greatest length is Milton himself. He tells us a lot here, both directly and indirectly. He came of a good family and had a rigorous education. The *Clamor* had charged that he was sent down from Cambridge for sexual scandal, so he is able to rebut this charge: he left university with an MA, much respected and loved, and a virgin. He travelled abroad and met such great men as Grotius and Galileo, and yet he defended Protestantism boldly in the face of Jesuits in Rome. Even in Geneva, renowned for its licence, 'I lived free and untouched by the slightest sin or reproach.' Anyone who knows Geneva will blink here, until we recall that More had been guilty of sexual scandal there. Milton goes on that he cut short the journey in order to return home and join his fellow citizens fighting for liberty. The various tracts he wrote were designed to promote virtue and inner liberty, even the divorce tracts. And he tells at some length about his decision to continue writing the first *Defensio* even though the doctors told him he would entirely lose the sight of his one remaining good eye. He chose to do his duty. This might all be rather sickening in anyone else, and at times it is so. But his Royalist enemies had charged that God had punished his radical politics or his libertinism with blindness. So he needs to tell his version: he has examined his inmost soul, he claims, and found no wickedness that could call down this 'supreme misfortune'. He is sure that everything he has done and written was 'right and true and pleasing to God'. And now he has accepted his blindness as God's will. He feels he is following the road that leads through weakness to greatest strength (a reference to Hebrews 11:34, a text that Augustine cites to powerful effect in the *Confessions*: it explains his spiritual career as modelled on that of Christ). In Milton's own life, he trusts, 'divine favour not infrequently is wont to lighten these shadows again, once made, by an inner and far more enduring light'. The 'speech' ends with a moving appeal to his fellow citizens to become inwardly free in that way and so be wise, just and temperate, capable of rule by being capable of self-rule.

Some time during these years of his first blindness (perhaps in the second half of 1655), Milton wrote one of his finest sonnets, one which encapsulates the personal point of view explored at much greater length in the tracts. 'When I consider how my light is spent / Ere half my days, in this dark world and wide' is how the poem begins. These lines introduce an almost bitter reflection on his blindness and on his literary 'Talent / Lodg'd with me useless'. The pun on the biblical Talents implies fear of sharing the fate of him who hid his one talent under a bushel and was cast into 'outer darkness'.

'Doth God exact day-labour, light deny'd, / I fondly ask'. In the poem's sestet, however, the impatience of the first part is dispelled and he realizes he must trust God's will: 'who best / Bear his milde yoak, they serve him best'. The resolution of the problem is characteristic. It opposes frenetic activity to quiet inwardness:

> Thousands at his bidding speed
> And post o'er Land and Ocean without rest:
> They also serve who only stand and waite.

14

Cromwell Protector

The next chapter in Milton's life was both politically and emotionally intense. And yet there is one episode that his admirers find the most difficult to understand. It is not so much his continued support of Cromwell's role as England's strongman that one finds distasteful, since the tangled and chaotic politics of the mid-century required someone to give it order and direction – and besides one can sense, as one works through the various documents from which Milton's biography must be constructed, a growing distance. No, it is the continued quarrel with Alexander More that is at times frankly offensive.

More wrote a reply to Milton's *Defensio Secunda* but went to Paris, and thence to a new position as pastor in Charenton, before he could finish it. Vlacq published it anyway in October 1654. More denies any part in the *Clamor* which occasioned the *Defensio Secunda*, and insists Milton knew as much by the time he finally finished the tract. He just wanted to keep in all the clever wordplay on More's name, since in Latin *morus* means cock, mulberry tree and, above all, fool. It also allows some play with words meaning black (*maurus*, from Greek *mauros*, which became *moro* in Italian and Spanish, cf. 'blackamoor'). More's charge rings true. He also points to the high-toned moral stance Milton adopted toward Cromwell, warning and even threatening him if he did not follow Milton's advice. He makes fun of the Marshall engaving that Milton so disliked as an 'elegant picture', and claims he referred to mental rather than physical blindness in *Clamor*, or else Milton's blind self-love. Perhaps Milton's eyes were removable, like those of witches.

Milton was stung to a response, entitled *Pro Se Defensio*. It was written by February (with an addition on More's *Supplementum* in May) but not published till August 1655. Meticulous as ever, Milton had received further information from Geneva about More's conduct, including material from the archives and library about his heretical views and his adulteries. He also had heard the story of one woman's assault on More for breach of promise. All this information, obtained partly from direct correspondence with Geneva and partly from Thurloe's spy network (anonymously presented in either case) he turns to his advantage, making fun of the assault as a mock-epic battle (leaving More's face scarred with her nails, and so 'engraved', as Milton's had been), and representing More and his adultery with the serving-woman as if it took place in a sordid Garden of Eden. He defends the sometimes obscene language of his own 'most just vituperation' by quoting the classical rhetoricians as well as Christian precedents like Thomas More or Erasmus, and even the Bible, where 'words unchaste and plain… signify not obscenity but the vehemence of gravest censure' (*YP* IV.2 744). Yes, the attack might have risen to that level, but it doesn't. It is merely self-serving and vulgar. And the 'comedy' is not at all funny.

Milton also had to defend himself against More's claim that he knew More was not the author of the *Clamor*. He wriggles but cannot get off this hook. He tries to assume an idea of authorship in which everyone involved in the production of a book can be identified as its author, publisher (true in law), compiler, adapter, even someone who contributes 'just one versicle' (712). But he admits it was not More who wrote the tract itself.

Geneva, in the course of the tract, is presented no longer as a place of sexual scandal but as an implicit model of what England might be.

Though hemmed in by narrow boundaries and by threatening and powerful neighbours on both sides, she has for so many years preserved and defended herself in the height of liberty and peace. (785)

England has not attained this level. We begin to hear in Milton's prose, idealist that he was, a yearning for something greater and more inspiring than the messy world over which Cromwell presided.

Messy it certainly was, with radical sects and ecstatic experiences proliferating, and Parliament unable to decide how to control or react. One revealing case was that of a young woman called Anna Trapnel. She was 'seized by the Lord' in January 1654 and began praying, prophesying and singing hymns she made up herself, all in Whitehall. She went without food or drink while in her ecstatic states. Many people, including some members of Parliament, came to see her and hear her rambling verses, which included threats to 'Protectors' who shall 'expire and die'. The Council of State eventually took action, making it treasonable to 'imagine the death of the Lord Protector' – exactly as if he were the king. Nedham warned Cromwell that some radical sectarians planned to publish Trapnel's 'discourses and hymns', and offered to move in swiftly and seize them. In the end poor ecstatic Anna Trapnel was sent to Bridewell prison to languish amid sewage and rats.[1] Trapnel's case was perhaps not a serious challenge in itself, but it was symptomatic of the problem: in the absence of external checks, could anyone know for sure which side was God's? Some men, like Cromwell and Milton, certainly felt they could.

Cromwell eventually dismissed the obstructive Parliament in January 1656 following often chaotic instability throughout 1655. Apart from a Leveller revolt, Royalist plots were uncovered by Thurloe's spy network. A consistent orderly government was desperately needed. Parliament had consumed its energies in trying to revise the *Instrument of Government*, by which Cromwell ruled and Parliament 'co-operated', and in prosecuting heretics like John Biddle. He was an anti-Trinitarian, a view with which Milton by now certainly sympathized; more specifically, he was a Socinian and argued Jesus was a mere human, not an aspect of God – a position Milton never reached. Cromwell intervened to have Biddle released and exiled to the Scilly Isles, but with an annual pension. He also had the Quaker leader George Fox released, with some of his followers.

Cromwell also called a conference to discuss the re-opening of immigration to Jews, banished since the reign of Edward I. He wanted official toleration of their forms of worship in a London synagogue that had in fact existed – illegally and unofficially – for several years. As Latin Secretary, Milton may have been involved in negotiations with Rabbi Menasseh ben Israel. Cromwell promoted the cause for political reasons (to split the Dutch), but there was an apocalyptic expectation behind the move as well. Before the final Redemption could happen, the Jews needed to be scattered from one end of the earth to the other, including the 'end of the earth' itself (England). And they had to be converted, as Christian millenarians like Cromwell imagined. Marvell's Coy Mistress 'could refuse/ till the conversion of the Jews' – which was some way off, a way of saying 'till the end of time'. But still if it was ever to happen, England needed Jews to convert.

It is tempting to see in these tolerationist policies of Cromwell an attitude with which Milton had long sympathized, and a reason for his continuing support. No doubt that is true. But I think it is more likely that it was the almost daily involvement in affairs of state that kept him close to Cromwell. It was Milton's Latin that continued to represent Cromwell abroad, and he obviously agreed with most, if not all, of the policies he wrote to defend. Whether it was his praise for the king of Sweden, his efforts to keep an international Protestant community peaceful and flourishing, or his support for the Waldensian victims of a horrendous and murderous attack, Milton was not simply the mouthpiece but also at times the silent architect of Cromwell's foreign policy. It has been thought odd that Cromwell never mentions Milton, and perhaps it is. But it may also be a sign of his ability to delegate to a trusted adviser matters that really did not interest him as much as home affairs.

Milton's salary was briefly reduced but then restored to £200 in the spring of 1655. Philip Meadows had been recently designated secretary for the Latin Tongue, but Milton continued to share the work, and when Meadows was appointed an ambassador for Cromwell, first to Portugal (where he was brutally attacked) and then to Sweden, Milton's workload increased and he often worked alone. It was above all the sudden need to reconstruct Protestant unity across Europe in the face of the attack on the Waldensians by the Savoyards that propelled the blind Milton back into the turmoil of government propaganda.

The background for this attack, which resulted in one of Milton's most powerful sonnets, was as follows. The duke of Savoy nourished a longstanding hostility for the Protestants who surrounded his territory. In 1602 he had launched a surprise night attack on Geneva, and the successful defense of the republic, in part by the pouring of hot soup down onto the soldiers attempting to scale the walls, is still celebrated every 11 December as 'Escalade', and has become the defining event of Geneva's historical identity. Now, in April 1655, that duke's successor, Charles Emmanuel II, ordered his army to attack the Waldensians, a sect founded in the twelfth century who had lived in the mountainous region of Piedmont in Northern Italy and who had been officially tolerated by Savoy since an edict of 1561. The stated reason for the attack was that some of these quasi-Protestants were living outside the designated area, but in fact the army set out to massacre the whole group. Women were raped and impaled on spikes, old men burned in their beds, younger men nailed to trees upside down, children burned and thrown down into ravines. It was a shocking atrocity. Milton's eloquent Latin was called on to frame the official letters to the duke, as well as appeals to other European Protestants to come to the relief of the Waldensians. He also wrote to Louis XIV and his chief minister Mazarin to protect Protestant refugees throughout France and to exert pressure on Savoy. And indeed the Swiss, with Mazarin, did broker a treaty by which Savoy restored the Waldensians to their property and guaranteed their liberty. Above all Milton wrote, in his angry and native English, one of the most remarkable political sonnets ever written, readily comparable with Petrarch's: 'Avenge O Lord, thy slaughter'd Saints, whose bones/ Lie scatter'd on the Alpine mountains cold.'

Milton's reputation was now bringing him visitors from home and abroad. Henry Oldenburg, released from gaol after his efforts to oppose Cromwell; Andrew Marvell, his young friend and fellow poet; Marchamont Nedham, still politically active; Edward Lawrence, son of the president of Cromwell's

Council of State, and probably a former student of Milton's; Samuel Hartlib himself, who was now living at Charing Cross; Theodore Haak, a member of Hartlib's influential circle (and later one of the first translators of *Paradise Lost* into German); John Dury, a roving ambassador for Cromwell and translator of *Eikonoklastes* into French; and above all Lady Ranelagh, together with her son, Richard Jones, and her brother, the famous Oxford scientist Robert Boyle. Jones, along with Cyriack Skinner, both of them former pupils, were now regular readers and writers (amanuenses) for the blind Milton. Edward Phillips was also back in London from July 1655 onwards, and acted as another scribe. Milton needed them all.

Milton wrote two sonnets for Skinner and one for Lawrence during the winter of 1655–56. Milton obviously enjoyed the constant companionship of these lively and intelligent young men, and two of the sonnets express this delight, with echoes of Horace. They celebrate the pleasures of hospitality and relaxation, belying the received image of a puritan. We may infer that Milton was not in favour of Cromwell's new system of official major-generals scattered in various localities around the country and enforcing repressive rules against drunkenness, swearing, 'and prophaning of the Lord's day and such like wickedness and abominations'. Indeed one of the books soon repressed under those rules was a poetic miscellany full of sportive wit, or what the Council called 'scandalous, lascivious, scurrilous, and prophane matter', which had been edited by John Phillips, Milton's younger nephew.

The other sonnet to Skinner gives an upbeat assessment, perhaps a little strained, of his first three years of blindness. He needs still to reply indirectly to the charge, which had evidently hurt, that his blindness was inflicted by God. He answers Skinner's question about what supports him with the insistence that he lost his sight because it was 'overplied/ In liberty's defence, my noble task,/ Of which all Europe talks from side to side'. John Aubrey in fact reported that foreigners came to England chiefly to see Cromwell and Milton, indeed 'he was much more admired abrode then at home'.[2]

In the wake of the Waldensian affair, Milton's workload increased. He wrote many letters to further Cromwell's efforts to create a united Protestant front in Europe. He congratulated Charles X of Sweden on the birth of his son, but warned against conflict with the Danes or the Dutch. Negotiations continued in the next years to extend England's 1654 treaty with Sweden (including English efforts to restrict sale of Swedish timber and hemp to Spain), and at one point Milton's blindness seems to have been used as an excuse for the dilatory conduct of the Cromwell government.

Opposition to Cromwell's dictatorship was growing, and treatises by friends of Milton were in the forefront of the movement. Henry Vane, Marchamont Nedham and James Harrington all wrote treatises or essays to assert the right of Parliament, as the people's representative, to exert sovereign power, usually laden with wit and classical references. Nedham's *The Excellencie of a Free-State*, for example, revised from earlier 1651–52 *Mercurius Politicus* pieces licensed by Milton, seems to defend the Protectorate against Royalist advice to govern merely by force of arms, without recourse to Parliament, but in fact attacks Cromwell for doing just that. All the classical republics, as well as Venice and the newly independent Netherlands, are reviewed and praised.

The argument over toleration was severely tested by more cases like that of Anna Trapnel. In the autumn of 1656, a Quaker, James Nayler, became the latest *cause célèbre* in the ongoing struggle. He enacted a symbolic performance of Christ's entry into Jerusalem on an ass, riding backwards. Arrested for blasphemy and sent to London, he submitted to a ten-day examination by Parliament and was eventually sentenced to 300 lashes. His forehead was then branded with the letter 'B' and his tongue burned and bored with a red-hot iron. Cromwell opposed these ways of treating people whose views differed. But he did not intervene this time. Nayler was eventually released from prison, but soon died: nonetheless he left his mark, indirectly, on Milton's future – as we shall see.

Matters important for the state now yielded briefly to the personal. On 12 November 1656 Milton was married again, this time to Katherine Woodcock. The banns were recorded in the Parish Register of St Mary the Virgin, Aldermanbury. The new law required that the ceremony take place before a magistrate, and so the couple were probably wed in the Guildhall with Alderman (now Sir) John Dethicke presiding. We are not told by the early biographers how they met. Her father had been a 'Captain Woodcock of Hackney', but he had died many years before leaving his wife and three daughters almost destitute. Her uncle, Sir Thomas Vyner, an alderman and goldsmith, was one of the treasurers for the funds rolling in to support the Waldensians, so that may be the connection. There was a difference of age: she was twenty-eight and he almost forty-eight. But Milton's three young daughters (Anne ten, Mary eight, Deborah four) needed a mother in the house. Years later Deborah said she was 'indulgent to her children-in-law'.

Within a few days of his wedding, Milton was back at work. He translated a letter to Cromwell from the king of Denmark warning about the effects of Sweden's war with Poland. In his reply Cromwell recalled the sufferings of the Waldensians in their Alpine valleys flowing with blood, and urges peace among Protestants. Nonetheless, Denmark declared war on Sweden in May 1657, and Milton framed a letter expressing Cromwell's regret. Some of the letters Milton was writing during these years are signed, which suggests how closely he identified with the government's foreign policy – trying to maintain Protestant unity throughout Europe.

Milton probably had less sympathy with the figure Cromwell was now cutting at home. Cromwell was invested as Lord Protector on 26 June 1657. He was sole ruler, a dictator, almost a king. Though he had refused the crown again in May, the ceremonies were now monarchic in their splendour. No more black velvet suit with a simple gold band around his hat, but purple robes, and he carried not a sword but a royal sceptre 'of massy gold'. His wife was now Her Highness the Lady Elizabeth and even his mother became the Dowager Mrs Cromwell. Cromwell immediately started reconstructing Parliament and setting up the 'other house', what was still popularly known as the House of Lords.

In spite of his politics, Milton was ready to help those of 'Wit and learning', as Cyriack Skinner put it: in March 1657 he played a role in helping Edmund Spenser's grandson recover land in Ireland. He also helped a French correspondent check a treatise about Saxon law, one he had himself cited in the *Defensio*, since it was often used in pro-republican arguments. He confirmed that there was no copy of this document in the Tower of London, but checked the relevant passages in copies owned by his scholarly friends John Bradshaw and John Cotton. His reputation was now solidly international: the famous geographer and astronomer, Nicolaus Mercator, who was employed as a tutor for the Percy family at Petworth (including the tenth earl of Northumberland, a friend and patron of Van Dyck), wrote to his friend Samuel Hartlib that he wished Milton's treatise *Of Education* could be a model for 'our method of teaching'. And finally, in September 1657, the assistant Milton had asked for earlier, Andrew Marvell, was granted him.

The time this allowed him Milton now invested again in his *History of Britain*. He wrote to his young correspondents that Sallust was the historian he most admired, clearly because of his account of how the Roman republic came into being by the overthrow of the kings and how it was threatened by corruption, avarice and military rule. During these months Milton probably completed his account of the wars among the Saxon kingdoms and the Danish invasions, down to the Norman Conquest in 1066. Milton comments that he found the research for this part tedious, reading through monkish chronicles, and he has deliberately omitted most ecclesiastical affairs, including (with an obvious pun on one of those sources, the venerable Bede) 'the long Bead-roll of Archbishops, Bishops, Abbots, Abesses' (*YP* V.1 269). Milton denounces the church leaders of the period for increasing subjection to Rome and 'mistaken Chastitie' (266).[3]

Alfred's reign was briefly heroic (Milton had, we recall, even considered an epic about him), but was followed by internal strife and by more Danish invasions. Milton retells the famous story of King Canute trying to send the sea back from his seat as if it were a deliberate demonstration for reluctant courtiers of the limits of royal power. Milton's ideas about the ancient constitution are revealing, as are some significant silences. He is scrupulous in recognizing that, in spite of a popular idea that the Saxon liberties were overthrown by an oppressive Norman invasion, some Saxon monarchs were tyrants who deserved to be put to death. Nonetheless, Edward the Confessor codified the common law to guarantee the liberties of the people, and even William the Conqueror swore at his coronation to maintain right law and prohibit unjust judgment. But Milton no longer insisted on what the *Defensio* had argued, that the king was subordinate to Parliament. It is tempting to find in this material clues to his thinking about Cromwell and even parallels to the warnings his friends Vane, Harrington and Nedham were addressing to Cromwell. Yet he did not write anything like their treatises and satires. And he seems, perhaps losing interest or finding no one to read these ancient materials to him, to have hurried to finish the work.

Cromwell was asserting his position even more strongly against a parliament increasingly unhappy with his dominance. Milton continued to write correspondence for him to European heads of state, including warnings about the renewed plight of the Waldensians. The duke of Savoy was not holding to the terms of the 1655 treaty. Milton wrote for Cromwell to the young Louis XIV, king of France, urging him to protect them or even make them his subjects, and to the Protestant Swiss cantons to urge them to defend the church against the madness of her enemies.

Katherine Milton gave birth to a girl in October but remained weak and died some three months later on 3 February 1658. The infant daughter also soon died. His wife's recent death is almost certainly, as I argued in the Introduction, the occasion for the beautiful sonnet on his 'late-espoused Saint'.[4] It presents a vision of the wife he had never seen in the flesh coming to him in a dream:

> Her face was vaild, yet to my fancied sight,
> Love, sweetness, goodness, in her person shin'd
> Soe clear, as in no face with more delight.
> But O as to embrace me she enclin'd
> I wak'd, she fled, and day brought back my night.

It is a moving and personal tribute to what sounds like an intense emotion, shared and now broken by death.

Katherine was buried on 10 February in the lovely little church of St Margaret's Westminster. The parish register records a quite expensive funeral with buckram escutcheons and an extra pound for the pall. We are told by one of the early biographers that Milton's coat of arms, the spread eagle (from the sign over the house where he was born), was hung over the coffin. Milton specified there should be twelve locks on the coffin, and the key for each be given to twelve friends at the funeral; 'he desired the coffin might not be opened till they all met together'.[5] The story is described as 'fantastic', but the source is a neighbour in Petty France and the detail is circumstantial enough to be true.

Life was extremely fragile in those days. Cromwell's favourite daughter Elizabeth died on 6 August from a bout of influenza, and Cromwell himself fell ill and was soon on his deathbed. There was barely time for him to pronounce that his son Richard should succeed him as Protector before he died on 3 September 1658. We have no record at all of how Milton reacted. That in itself is perhaps significant. His fellow poets Marvell and Dryden (both employees of Cromwell's bureaucracy at the time) came up with long and even effusive elegies for the funeral. Yet Milton was silent. Like the other secretaries for foreign tongues, he was allotted 9s 6d to buy mourning cloth, so presumably he attended. But he wrote nothing.

15

A Long Argument to Prove
That God is Not the Devil

Milton may not have written anything for Cromwell's funeral. He did, however, have a project. For years, at least since 1655, he had been working on a theological treatise that we know as the *De Doctrina Christiana*. He continued to work on it till near the end of his life, though it could not be published until the nineteenth century, as we shall see. During the sad days of his wife's illness and death and that of his infant daughter, the illustrious Samuel Hartlib, for whom Milton had written *Of Education*, sent him a 'secret treatise' and wrote to tell Robert Boyle, the Oxford scientist, about it on 2 February 1658. The treatise was Jean Bodin's *Colloquium Heptaplomeres*, a fictional discussion in the tradition of Plato's *Symposium*, an enormously popular genre in the Renaissance, by seven scholars of differing religious opinions. The 'treatise' circulated only in manuscript form and contained many heretical views, including arguments for Anti-Trinitarianism (by a Jew) and divorce (by a natural philosopher, i.e. scientist). It probably stimulated Milton to get back to work on the *De Doctrina Christiana*. We know that he did at least some work on it in 1658, because one of the scribes who helped him with the text, Jeremy Picard, was working with him from 1658 to 1660, and perhaps again in 1663. Picard wrote out a fair copy of the whole in these years. Milton kept working at it and changing things for the rest of his life, especially near the end. But now it became once again the focus of his attention, and while Picard worked on it he made revisions. In the revised edition of the *Defensio*, published in this same year, 1658, Milton promised a greater work, almost certainly the *De Doctrina*, that would benefit 'men of every land and particularly all Christian men'.

He called this treatise 'my dearest and best possession' ('quibus melius aut pretiosius nihil habeo'). Like its models among Reformation theologies it is in Latin, and thus addressed to a learned and European audience. Every argument is supported by scriptural citation, sometimes very many, though often slanted to fit Milton's own heterodox views. As a good Protestant he believed in the doctrine that for short we call *sola scriptura*, that is, that the Bible, and not church tradition or the early fathers, is the only authority. (This was important already, as we have seen, in his first treatise, *Of Reformation*.) He knew that there are differences among the innumerable manuscript and printed versions in which the text of the Bible comes down, and therefore that it is corruptible. He argues, for example, that I John 1:7, a verse used to justify the doctrine of the Trinity, is 'not found in the Syriac, Arabic or Ethiopic versions, nor in the majority of the ancient Greek codices' (*YP* VI 147). He could not know what was only discovered by much later scholars: that the Bible accumulated over centuries, and that there are even two different authors (at least) responsible for Genesis. Like any intelligent reader, he was aware of the apparent contradictions among versions of the same story, especially the gospels, such as the birthdate of Jesus or the order of the temptations in the desert. But he also thought that the Holy Spirit which illumines the believer is incorruptible. Where he thinks the Bible is clear, which it usually is, he strides forth confidently to make his argument. But he resists the scholastic tendency, which he had learned at Cambridge, to speculative reasoning, and about it he is often disparaging – except when he does it himself.

He refuses, where he can, to go beyond what the Bible says. Thus he finds no warrant for a Holy Trinity in the scriptures, and says so forcefully. God is one, and cannot be three. On the other hand, when God is said to have emotions, or to suffer, even to grieve or repent, he thinks we should take that seriously. God invites us to imagine him this way, at least, and so why not? This does not mean we should take the Bible literally: God accommodates himself to our understanding in such passages, and his indwelling Spirit must take precedence over a literal reading of the biblical text. On this basis, God can become a character, as he is, notoriously, in *Paradise Lost*. In fact we are told by his biographer John Aubrey, who had it from Edward Phillips, that Milton started work about this time – 1658 – on the great poem.

De Doctrina was composed in stages over many years. It began, he claims in the Epistle with which it opens, when he devoted himself as a boy to the 'earnest study of the Old and New Testaments in their original languages'. He reviewed many shorter treatises but soon saw that he had to 'puzzle out a religious creed for myself by my own exertions'. His method was, 'following the example of these writers, to list under general headings all passages from the scriptures which suggested themselves for quotation'. And that is also the form of the treatise in its final form. The effect is to disrupt the reading of the Bible, for citations are listed all together as having the same weight and are not usually referred to their context (except when it suits him, as in the part about divorce). Those 'general headings' give chapter titles such as 'Of God' or 'Of Predestination' or 'Of the Special Government of Angels'. As he gained confidence, he tells us in the Epistle, he read many longer works of theology and was seriously disappointed. Often they defended as truth what was manifestly false, and ignored the arguments of their opponents. So whenever Milton finds himself in disagreement with his models among the many Reformation theologians who wrote similar treatises, he produces elaborate arguments to persuade us (for he did intend to publish the book) that his heterodox views are correct. The longest section of all is Book I, Chapter V, 'Of the Son of God', for this is where he contests the Trinity. It even gets its own little 'Preface'. He takes far less space to defend polygamy, however unorthodox it may be, since it is much less important.

What are the key points of the treatise? Early on he argues (against the Calvinist position on predestination) that God allows genuine freedom of choice both to angels and to humans. The Fall has seriously diminished this, but Christ has atoned and won back our liberty, and not just for the few. But liberty also means that humankind can resist the grace that is freely offered. In effect Milton develops his own version of Arminianism. In his early works, the Calvinist Milton, like many Puritans, had identified Arminius closely with the Laudian church they so opposed, with its doctrines of grace through sacraments and good works, but he had come to see things differently now. The main point, as in so much of his writing, was the importance of freedom, asserted by Arminius, denied by Calvin. God certainly foreknew that Adam would fall, but of his own free will, not necessity ('novit Adamum sua sponte lapsurum; certo igitur lapsurus erat, non necessario'[1]). This mystery is restated clearly by the character 'God' in *Paradise Lost* (III 124-28).

Milton was an Arian, which means that he believed the Son to be a subordinate being.[2] He was produced ('generated or created') by God in time, not from all eternity. For evidence, see 'this day' in Psalm 2:7, quoted in Acts 13:33. God chose to produce the Son of his own will, and thus decrees the Son's priesthood, kingship and resurrection from the dead (all given proof texts). He was 'begotten, whatever that means'. He is of God's substance but not his essence, which cannot be shared (in this respect Milton goes beyond the Arian position).[3] He is sometimes called 'God' in scripture, but that should not be taken to imply he is one with the Father. He is the first of created beings, and responsible for the rest of creation. But he is also free and capable of change. Thus Milton can imagine him as offering to die to save humankind in Book III of *Paradise Lost*. And in *Paradise Regained*, as Jesus, in his human and distinct form, he can grow and learn and undergo a genuine temptation. Arianism is a blessing for the conception of a literary character.

The term 'spirit' is used in many different ways in the Bible, but when it does refer to the Holy Spirit it clearly means a being much inferior to the Son, a kind of minister of God. It descended at Christ's baptism in the form of a dove, not in its own right but as sent by the Father. It seems to be imagined as a little like Ariel in *The Tempest*, always constrained to do Prospero's will. And yet, unless perhaps we should make a strict separation between treatise and poem in this respect, it has some power to transmit the light of God, as the invocations to the Holy Spirit in *Paradise Lost* imply.

Creation, treated in Chapter Seven, is also conceived in a heterodox way. Nothing can come from nothing, as Lear's Fool wisely says, and Milton argues at some length that God made the universe (through the Son's agency) not *ex nihilo*, out of nothing, but out of his own substance, *ex Deo*. Matter is not, as in some philosophical systems like Manichaeism, intrinsically evil. It cannot be evil if it comes from God, but is nonetheless, when detached from him, capable of change and corruption. Once again Milton takes this doctrine to a further and logical conclusion, that spirit and matter differ only in degree of refinement. Spirit is thin matter, matter thick spirit. By degrees, as the angel Raphael explains to Adam and Eve in Book V of *Paradise Lost*, they could rise in the scale of being, 'if not deprav'd from good'. Raphael eats (he shares a meal, 'with keen despatch/ Of real hunger') and also explains, blushing, in answer to Adam's delicate but direct question, that angels have sex, described as 'Union of pure with pure desiring'. Behind it all, he says, 'one Almightie is, from whom/ All things proceed, and up to him return' (V 469-70). 'Your bodies may at last turn all to Spirit' (V 497). A corollary of this physical monism is the doctrine known as mortalism, that the whole person, soul included, dies when the body dies and is resurrected on the last day.

But the body's pleasure is not the main end of marriage, nor is procreation. Rather it is companionship, and if that is lacking, then there are grounds for divorce. Milton summarizes the argument of the divorce tracts, including the important argument, learned from John Selden's *Uxor Hebraica*, that the term 'fornication', with adultery the only grounds for divorce in the New Testament, means either any unclean thing or the lack of whatever is needful in a wife. Otherwise one is held in 'crushing slavery'.

On the practice of worship and the only two sacraments left to Protestants, baptism and communion, Milton takes a radical and sectarian view. Neither is important, he says, if they cannot conveniently take place – he is surely thinking of the difficulties of finding a church that would coincide with one's own doctrines. Like the Anabaptists, he opposes infant baptism – we should wait till capable of rational and free initiation. Similarly 'This is my body' is often taken literally, as by the Roman Catholics – a serious mistake.

This helps explain why for the last thirty years or more of his life there is no record of Milton's membership of a church or meeting house. There was none to suit him.

Of all these heterodox ideas and arguments, perhaps the most revealing of his method is the chapter, not a very long one, on God. Many readers have trouble accepting the God presented in *Paradise Lost*. Indeed the poem proposes 'to justify the ways of God to men' (I 26). So it is helpful to see how the treatise, on which he was probably working during the years he was composing the poem, copes with the problem of God. The chapter begins polemically, and stays on the offensive.

> That there is a God, many deny: *for the fool says in his heart, There is no God,* Psal. xiv. 1. But has left so many signs of himself in the human mind, so many traces of his presence through the whole of nature, that no sane person can fail to realize that he exists. Job xii. 9: *who does not know from all these things?*; Psal. xix. 2: *the heavens declare the glory of God,* Acts xiv. 17: *he did not allow himself to exist without evidence,* and xvi. 27, 28: *he is not far from every one of us;* Rom. i. 19, 20: *that which can be known about God is obvious,* and ii. 14, 15: *the Gentiles show the work of the law written in their hearts; their conscience is evidence of the same thing;* 1 Cor. i.21: *because, in accordance with God's wisdom, the world failed to know God by its wisdom, it pleased God to save those who believe by the foolishness of preaching.* It is indisputable that all the things which exist in the world, created in perfection of beauty and order for some definite purpose, and that a good one, provide proof that a supreme creative being existed before the world, and had a definite purpose of his own in all created things.

Not all of these quotations actually point in the same direction, and the final one from 1 Corinthians, where Paul is discussing salvation, might even be seen to undo all the rest. But Milton goes on as argumentatively as he began to assert the difference between the idea of God and the rival concept of nature or fate. Nature requires chance alongside, with the result that those who argue for this philosophical idea 'in place of one god, whom they find intolerable, they are forced to set up two universal goddesses who are almost always at odds with each other' (*YP* VI 131).

As if this is not enough, Milton actually goes on to say that 'visible proofs and the fulfillment of many prophecies and the narration of many marvels have driven every nation to the belief that either God or some supreme evil power of unknown name presides over the affairs of men. But it is intolerable and incredible that evil should be stronger than good and should prove the supreme power. Therefore God exists.' This extraordinarily weak argument stops there and does not go on to consider the possibility *Paradise Lost* seems to open up, that this God who exists is the same as that 'evil power of unknown name'. Milton knew nonetheless from his reading of Irenaeus or Epiphanius that such had been a widespread belief among those early Christians known as Gnostics. He also knew the Manichaeans had subscribed to the belief that the world was divided between good and evil powers, since Augustine, whom he follows closely at times, had been a Manichaean hearer for nine years.

Elsewhere in the treatise, Milton returns to the potential problems in his representation of God. His Anti-Trinitarianism, for example, like his Arminianism, both derive from his insistence on the omnipotence and benevolence of God. He cites a key passage from Isaiah 45:6–7 in both connections: 'I am the Lord, there is no other; I make the light, I create darkness, making peace and creating evil [Hebrew *ra*].' In discussing the creation, he quotes it (without the last verse) as evidence for his insistence on the supremacy of God, and then explains it in a way that supports his opposition to the idea of the Trinity, and to any suggestion that any power could equal God's, or that there could be any other God: 'If such things as common sense and accepted idiom exist at all, then these words preclude the possibility, not only of there being any other God, but also of there being any person, of any kind, equal to him' (300). And in the chapter on God's Providence, the same Isaiah passage reappears, though this time, since it imputes the creation of evil to God (the Latin Tremellius–Junius Bible Milton was using reads 'facientem pacem et creantem malum' *CM* XIV 66), the passage requires a different exegesis to fit the new context of Milton's argument: 'Isa. xlv. 7: *Making peace and creating evil* – that is, what afterwards became and is now evil, for whatever God created was originally good, as he himself testifies, Gen. i.' There is no ground whatever in the Hebrew or the Latin for Milton's interpretation: he merely needs to defend God's benevolence at the same time as he asserts his governance of all things, evil as well as good.

In his Commonplace Book Milton had already posed the question and admitted the answer to be unsatisfactory: 'Why does God permit evil? The account of Reason with Virtue may be correct. For virtue is attested by evil, is illuminated and trained. As Lactantius says: that Reason and Judgment may have a field in which they may exercise themselves by choosing the things that are good and shunning the things that are evil; although even these things are not satisfactory' (*YP* VIII 128–9). The idea of evil as a test of virtue is taken up again, but without the crucial concession, in both *Areopagitica* (*YP* II 527-28) and in Chapter VIII on God's Providence in the *De Doctrina*.

The key to the defense of God's providence is the experience of freedom, which Milton argues for throughout his prose as God's great gift. He often prefers heresy to orthodoxy, he says, and the Epistle which opens the treatise makes an impassioned defense of his freedom to find his own doctrine in the Bible (123). This argument leads him to denounce the Calvinist views he had previously held (without admitting his own complicity), since denial of man's freedom was tantamount to making God the cause of evil.

> It is sufficiently clear that neither God's decree nor his foreknowledge can shackle free causes with any kind of necessity. There are some people, however, who, struggling to oppose this doctrine through thick and thin, do not hesitate to assert that God is himself the cause and author of sin… If I should attempt to refute them, it would be like inventing a long argument to prove that God is not the devil. (166)

Witty or casual as that may sound, it is in fact deadly serious: it is what *Paradise Lost* sets out to do. Milton knew God may seem very like the devil.

16

Expiring Liberty

Cromwell's state funeral was magnificent, and few who attended could have sensed that the Commonwealth would survive for less than two years. An effigy was put on display and the London crowds duly came out to look. Eight silver candle-holders, five feet high, surrounded the bed on which lay the imitation corpse, a golden sceptre in its right hand, an orb in its left. On his head was a regal cap of purple trimmed with ermine. After three weeks of this, the procession marched on 23 November 1658 from Somerset House to Westminster Abbey. Milton's name appears on the order of march, paired with Marvell. At the abbey, there was an unseemly scuffle among ambassadors vying for precedence, and a loud quarrel erupted during the anthem between Swedish and Dutch representatives. So much for Protestant harmony. One participant wrote afterwards, 'Our solemnity is (God be praised) well over.'

Richard Cromwell, Oliver's son, was unsuited for rule, and seems not to have wanted it very much. He had not been trained to take over, it was a deathbed pronouncement of his father's that brought him to power, but once he had it, he seems to have clung to it as long as he could – which was not long. For the first few months Milton continued to write state letters for him, and when the Rump Parliament was restored, for them too. Yet Milton was increasingly concerned at what was happening to the 'Good Old Cause'. In the midst of a flurry of pamphlets and petitions urging all kinds of radical or conservative views, he published a new edition of his Latin *Defensio* and wrote new treatises in English urging his republican views. *A Treatise of Civil Power* was registered with the Stationers on 16 February 1659. It is a radical defense of Christian liberty, arguing that magistrates should have no authority over the church and that everyone should be free to follow his conscience. The principle follows from Paul's opposition of the old Law and the new Gospel, and is perhaps the most fundamental of all the ideas Milton defended. Unlike Milton's other polemical prose, the style of this treatise is notably straightforward and plain. Everyone has the duty 'to search, to try, to judge' of all aspects of belief. Milton presents himself, once again with a variant of the ethical proof, as someone who knows affairs of state from the inside and speaks with authority. For several years he has heard members of the Council defending the principle of liberty he here sets forth. The implied hope is that this will continue: otherwise we can look forward to 'the inward decay of true religion among ourselves, and the utter overthrow at last by a common enemy'.

In August Milton published the complementary *Considerations Touching the Likeliest Means to Remove Hirelings Out of the Church*, pressing his view that ministers should not be paid out of tithes or the public purse and that the church should be disestablished. Indeed, there should be no inherent difference between clergy and laity. Some training might be appropriate, but certainly not the kind he had endured at Cambridge; what counted was a sense of a calling and conviction. Pay them from the public purse and you risk simony and corruption: you let in the wolves with their 'Blind mouths' he had denounced in 'Lycidas' and would again in *Paradise Lost*. If a minister needed books, £60 should cover his personal library. Any more, 'for his own curiosity and delight in books further expensive', would not be necessary. We hear in these words the first intimations of the notorious rejection of wide reading in the classics that he puts into the mouth of Jesus in *Paradise Regained*. But here at least he allows for the possibility of ministers borrowing books from some publicly funded source like schools or libraries. The treatise again insists that marriage should be an entirely civil affair (as his own to Katherine Woodcock had been).

Milton restates in even more radical terms the broad principles of Christian liberty: there can really be no such thing as heresy if everyone is free to follow his conscience; only Christ can judge, not the magistrate, whether a man acts according to the guidance of the Spirit; and violence is never justified to enforce dogma. Yet once again, Roman Catholics have forfeited their claim to this liberty by following the pope's law. They do not deserve toleration, but on political, not religious, grounds. They seek to impose universal dominion. The closest analogy with this rather paranoid frame of mind would be the American fear of Communism during the Cold War. It was further provoked by the residual suspicion that the monarchy, in the person of the French queen mother, Henrietta Maria, had indeed been trying to restore Popery, and might still do so.

It is notable that these treatises ignore Richard Cromwell entirely, even though he did not formally abdicate his position as Protector until 25 May. The Rump Parliament was invited back by the Council of Officers on 6 May, and Milton's next, and last, letters of state announce its return to power. Foreign policy will not be interrupted or changed, and he reinforces the commission of his former assistant Philip Meadows to negotiate a settlement between Sweden and Denmark. Before it was published in August Milton added a preface to the *Hirelings* treatise challenging the Rump to endorse his case for the separation of church and state. But he also welcomes back the Rump which 'after a short but scandalous night of interruption, is now again by a new dawning of Gods miraculous providence among us'. This sounds like a repudiation of the protectorate for which he worked so loyally but with increasing uneasiness.

By now Milton was seriously disillusioned with Parliament. He had come to know it well, though unlike Marvell, he was never a member. The hellish dimension of *Paradise Lost*, which he was now composing, is not restricted to Satan or the place. It is represented with all its energy and corruptibility by the building of Pandemonium (as usual in fantasy it does not take long) and the debate within. Moloch, Belial, Mammon, Beelzebub, all make eloquent speeches, and are ultimately manipulated through a behind-the-scenes plan concocted by Satan and his first lieutenant. Hellish politics are not really democratic, though they sometimes seem so. They resemble, as in a bad dream or a distorting mirror, the aristocratic republic Milton admired and hoped to see installed in England. They are more like Homeric assemblies than anything Milton had known in person. Yet he had obviously itched to criticize and pillory the proceedings of Parliament, and in the poem he got his chance.

Very soon in the autumn of 1659 the army officers and the Rump were at odds over their respective powers, over the creation of the 'Other House', over the established church, over toleration. The army felt it had a special status as the true defender of the 'Good Old Cause' (the slogan was everywhere now). When the Rump tried to revoke the commissions of some leading officers, the army staged a coup on 13 October and General John Lambert dissolved the parliament. Republican defenders of the Rump now turned for help to General George Monck in Scotland, but insisted on maintaining the civilian authority over the military. Monck was an English soldier who had served with the Royalist forces in Ireland in the 1640s and Cromwell's occupying army in Scotland in the 1650s. He replied by calling the army coup a usurpation of the legal government, and threatened to march on England. He soon did. A new civil war looked possible.

Milton's response was to start writing, or dictating – not only the great poem, but more political prose. He no longer had any official capacity, and so felt free to recommend ways to settle the crisis in a letter to an unnamed friend, perhaps Henry Vane, perhaps John Bradshaw. He denounced the army for dissolving the parliament yet again and without just authority. Yet he proposed a compromise whereby a restricted Committee of Safety, with both army and parliamentary representatives, could take temporary charge of affairs. He probably knew from Vane that this was already under discussion. A larger more permanent body would then take over. In the first two weeks of November 1659 Milton also wrote up a new list of proposals for preventing civil war: legislators must support religious liberty and refuse to endorse 'a single person' as head of state; England should be governed by a 'Grand or Supreme Council' on which the members 'sit indissolubly'. It is not to be called a 'parliament', because that Norman or French word is 'a monument to our ancient servitude'. Quite why anyone should be thinking in those long terms in this excited period is not clear. It is characteristic of Milton's attitude, though, always to have one foot in the present and the other in history.

Milton's measured tone is in contrast with the giddy feel of some of the other intense debates that were currently taking place. Gathering over coffee, the newly fashionable drink, a group named the 'Rota' held meetings every night at the Turk's Head in Whitehall. John Aubrey attended, along with Cyriack Skinner and the young Pepys, and reports that 'the discourses in this kind were the most ingenious and smart that ever I heard or expect to hear, and bandied with great eagerness: the arguments in the Parliament house were but flat to it'.[1] The name Rota came from the theory of James Harrington, the most prominent member of this circle, that a system of a rotating senate would be the best way to ensure impartial government. Harrington and Milton (who did not attend these meetings, it seems) disagreed over this point and over the church, which Harrington thought should be official and established. Milton soon took issue with him in writing, and then quickly both were satirized in another tract, Royalist this time, perhaps by Samuel Butler.[2] These were exciting times to be thinking politics, but rather ominously, Aubrey comments on the meetings of the Rota that in their lack of foresight, these men thought 'there was no possibility of the king's return'.

Events now ran away with them all. Riots and military manoeuvres were accompanied by petitions denouncing the army or the Rump. Rumours of a Royalist uprising were rife, and some former supporters of Cromwell even called for the return of the monarchy.

Monck's troops moved relentlessly toward London. He was receiving a steady flow of petitions asking him to support this or that cause, and in February 1660 he gave the Rump an ultimatum: they were to issue writs for elections to fill up their depleted number, and then to disband. Joyful bonfires were lit in the streets, and after a few days the Rump did indeed vote to fill up the vacancies. When he arrived Monck was assigned choice apartments in the Palace of Whitehall, right by the river. Just a few months earlier, the palace had been put up for sale to find a way to pay the army's back-pay. Now that sale was abandoned. The army was Monck's, and so was the country.

In this overheated atmosphere Milton wrote a draft of *The Readie and Easie Way to Establish a Free Commonwealth*. It contains two specific proposals: that the Rump is to be augmented by elections – but only those who are of good intent can vote – and secondly that the newly expanded Parliament perpetuate itself (unlike the Rota's senate). Many similar tracts and pamphlets were appearing in these days, and Milton was in touch with the authors of some at least, such as Harrington and Vane. He also wrote a further tract, apparently addressed to Monck, urging him to impose a new procedure for establishing the grand council, and in view of the Royalist threat, by force if necessary. Milton was constantly responding to the debates around him.

Within a few days, in April 1660, a second and much enlarged edition of the *Readie and Easie Way* appeared, casting Milton as Jeremiah warning the Israelites against their coming slavery to Nebuchadnezzar in Babylon, and elaborating the argument for an aristocratic republic: he cites as precedents the Sanhedrin 'among the Jews', the Athenian council on the Areopagus, and the Roman Senate. He also points to the model of the Netherlands (*YP* VII 436-7). But he almost despairs of the degenerate English people and his terms are those a blind man – 'the noise and shouting of a rude multitude'. He fears they are seeking a new thraldom under a king. Even Monck would be better, he now admits. The tract bore on its title page the bold announcement of 'the author J. M.' He added both at the beginning and the end that these might be 'the last words of our expiring liberty'. In Gordon Campbell's words, the pamphlet is 'England's greatest monument to a lost political cause'.[3] Milton reiterated the idea about electing Monck rather than submitting to Charles Stuart a week later in *Brief Notes upon a Late Sermon*, his last publication while he still had access to print.

Milton was regularly the target of both witty and scurrilous attacks. One writer, perhaps again Samuel Butler, called him 'an old Heretick both in Religion and Manners, that by his will would shake off his Governors as he doth his Wives, four in a Fortnight', and anticipated that, because everything he stood for was so unusual, 'when he is condemned to travel to *Tyburn* in a Cart, he will petition for the favour to be the first man that ever was driven thither in a *Wheel-barrow*'.[4] The same author made fun of his insistence that Christ was a supporter of the republic: 'notwithstanding the Scripture everywhere calls his Government the Kingdom of heaven, it ought to be Corrected, and Rendered, the Common-wealth of this world'.[5] He was now so well known as prime spokesman for the remaining radicals that even anti-Royalist tracts that were not by Milton were now fathered on him. Roger L'Estrange answered an anonymous but published letter to Monck, *Plaine English,* which implies he should oppose the clamour for Charles's return, as if it had been at least partly Milton's.

On 1 May Parliament heard read the declaration issued by Charles at Breda in the Netherlands (based largely on what Monck had secretly proposed). It promised general amnesty for all but those designated by Parliament itself for punishment. They immediately voted for the proposal that England's government be 'King, Lords and Commons'. The return of Charles II was imminent and Milton was in great danger. He risked losing most of his money (which he did), and even his life. Seven of the regicides were selected for immediate execution, and others were being considered. His last tract, issued just a few days before, had denounced monarchy in the strongest terms: 'a king must be ador'd like a Demigod'; he will set out 'to pageant himself up and down in progress among the perpetual bowings and cringings of an abject people, on either side deifying and adoring him'. The king landed at Dover on 25 May. Celebrations throughout the month culminated in his entry to London on 29 May. Milton went into hiding. He moved from Petty France, where he had lived longer than any house except his childhood home in Bread Street, to a friendly house in Bartholomew Close near Smithfield. No one knows who the friend was, perhaps a member of the Diodati family, who had lived near Little St Bartholomew's during the 1640s. We do not know whether his three young daughters, now aged fifteen, twelve and nine, went with him, or whether, as is more likely, they went to stay with their grandmother, Anne Powell, who was now back in London and no doubt relishing the return of the monarch. A story was told later that Milton's friends staged a mock funeral to put the authorities off the scent. When he heard of the trick later, the king was said to have laughed heartily. There are many such colourful and unlikely stories told about the period. But Milton was really in hiding, and really in danger.

Within a few weeks of the Restoration John Dryden had switched sides. He had worked for Cromwell, and written a glowing tribute for his funeral: now he wrote happily for the return of His Sacred Majesty Charles the Second, for whose 'long absence Church and State did groan'. Milton was of course more prominent than his younger friend and former colleague, but in any case his constancy of character would not have permitted such abject action. His widow tells us that he considered Dryden, who sometimes visited, 'no poet, but a good rimist'. However that may be, he must have wondered whether he would survive the vengeance of the new king.

17

With Dangers Compast Round

During the next few weeks Milton was in grave danger. He had, after all, been the first to defend the regicide in *The Tenure of Kings and Magistrates* and Royalists had good reason to find other tracts treasonable, especially the ones he had written at the behest of the Commonwealth government, *Eikonoklastes* and the *Defensio*. Only a few days before he had tried to persuade the people in *The Readie and Easie Way* and in *Brief Notes* not to accept the return of the king. And now many polemical and satiric texts made out he was one of the worst offenders, one of them placing him in Hell, ready to write for the devil as he had for Cromwell.[1] He could not emerge from hiding until he and his friends knew Parliament's decision about who was to be executed.

The regicides (those who had signed the king's death warrant) and those closely associated with them were brutally put to death. Hanged but taken down while still alive, they had their 'privy members' cut off and their entrails taken out and burnt before their eyes. The sentence concludes (this one on Major-General Thomas Harrison, a radical Fifth Monarchist from Staffordshire who had long had an uneasy relation with Cromwell, but was probably known to Milton) with the instruction that 'your head to be cut off, your body to be divided into four quarters, and head and quarters to be disposed of at the pleasure of the king's majesty, and the Lord have mercy on your soul'. At his trial Harrison had made a great impression. Unrepentant, he stated: 'I followed not my own judgment, I did what I did as out of conscience to the Lord.' On his way to the scaffold, the crowd had cried, 'Where is your Good Old Cause now?' He replied: 'Here in my bosom, and I shall seal it with my blood.' Eight more of the regicides suffered the same fate as Harrison.

The options open to Milton were various. Fifteen of the forty-one surviving regicides and their friends had fled to the American colonies, Switzerland or the Netherlands. George Downing (1623–84), formerly Cromwell's director of military intelligence and now Charles's ambassador to the Netherlands, tracked down and arrested three of them: John Barkstead, John Okey (his former friend) and Miles Corbet, who were extradited and executed in April 1662. Even Pepys called Downing a 'perfidious rogue'. His name is famous for the source of his family fortune, speculative building in central London, including Downing Street itself. John Lisle, another regicide, was murdered by a fanatical Irish Royalist at Lausanne, Switzerland in 1664. William Cawey died in Vevey, along the lake from Lausanne, in 1667. The last survivor of the regicides was probably Edmund Ludlow, who died also at Vevey in 1692, and is buried there. Two clerks of the High Court, Andrew Broughton and John Phelps, also escaped to Switzerland (Broughton died there in 1688). There is a memorial to both in St Martin's church in Vevey, erected by American descendants of Phelps, which calls them 'an exile to the cause of human freedom'. Although he was not directly involved in the trial and execution, the puritan preacher Hugh Peter was prosecuted and executed because of his enthusiastic support for the regicides. Others brought to trial – though not associated directly with the regicide – were the leader of the Scottish Covenanters, the marquis of Argyll, executed in 1661, and Major-General John Lambert, brought to trial alongside Sir Henry Vane in June 1662 and accused of high treason. Although sentenced to death, Lambert appealed to the King's mercy and the sentence was commuted to life imprisonment. He was moved from the Tower of London to Castle Cornet on Guernsey, and finally to Drake's Island in Plymouth Sound, where his wife visited him regularly till she died in 1676. He died insane in February 1684 at the age of sixty-four, having spent the last twenty-four years of his life in prison. There are streets named after three of the regicides in New Haven – Edmund Whalley, William Goffe and John Dixwell. For the hiding of these dangerous men, so displeased was the king that in 1665 he suppressed New Haven as a separate colony and joined it to Connecticut. There is now a Regicides hiking trail in the nearby country. The identity of the executioner who actually beheaded the king was sought but never discovered.[2]

Milton, however, stayed put. He neither turned his coat, like Dryden, nor tried to flee. He was a well-known republican and the authorities must treat him as they would. On 8 June 1660 Parliament decided the names of twenty regicide associates to be rigorously punished, short of death. They included Milton's friend Henry Vane. Milton's name was mentioned, but not seconded. According to Edward Phillips, he owed his escape to friends and supporters in Parliament, especially Andrew Marvell, who was the member for Hull, and who had worked with Milton for the Commonwealth bureaucracy. Another source, more distant, says that Sir William Davenant also had some influence, since Milton had helped save his life in 1651 when he was awaiting execution in the Tower as a Royalist conspirator. Poets stick together in hard times.

Nonetheless, a resolution of 16 June urged Charles to order Milton arrested and his books burned. A royal proclamation of 13 August gave orders that both *Eikonoklastes* and the *Defensio*, along with a book by John Goodwin, should be publicly burned – apparently in lieu of the authors, who 'are both fled, or so obscure themselves, that no endeavours used for their apprehension can take effect, whereby they might be brought to Legal Trial, and deservedly receive condigne punishment for their Treasons and Offences'.[3] The word 'Treason' in that indictment is a sign of how close Milton came to a death sentence or a punishment so severe it might have killed him. On 27 August the books were indeed burned at the Old Bailey. Other copies were confiscated throughout the country.

The next day Parliament passed the 'Act of Free and general Pardon, Indemnity, and Oblivion'. It excluded by name 102 persons, but not Milton. The king signed it immediately. Milton could now suppose himself free from danger. He emerged from hiding, and took up residence near Red Lion Fields in Holborn. The past, though, was catching up with him. In September Salmasius' own posthumous response to Milton's *Defensio* finally appeared. It insults Milton as a dwarf, blind with rage in mind as in body, an insignificant teacher with a poor command of Latin: someone else must have written the *Defensio*. One can imagine Milton's outrage, but he could not make any public reply. His friends and associates were being arraigned: some escaped punishment (like), others fled (like Nedham), but all told twenty-nine of the regicides and associates were executed. Then, one day during all this commotion, Milton was arrested.

The sergeant-at-arms, James Norfolke, did not allow that the Act of Oblivion had cancelled the proclamation against Milton and his books. Several weeks imprisonment in the Tower, now followed, and it is not difficult to imagine how a blind man suddenly deprived of his friends' support and at the mercy of his gaolers would feel. There were no doubt petitions and appeals for his release at work behind the scenes, probably also from his impeccably Royalist brother Christopher, who was called to the bench on 25 November. On 15 December the Commons ordered that 'Mr. Milton… be forthwith released, paying his Fees.' There was a delay, perhaps because of these fees. Marvell supported Milton's protest that the fees (£150 for his upkeep during his time in custody) were exorbitant, while the solicitor-general who had prosecuted the regicides, Sir Heneage Finch, 'observed, That Milton was Latin Secretary to Cromwell, and deserved hanging'. Nonetheless, on 17 December 'the celebrated Mr John Milton', as the parliamentary record calls him, was released.

On 30 January 1661, the anniversary of Charles' execution, amid 'the universal outcry of the people' (as a newsbook put it), the corpses of Cromwell, his son-in-law Ireton and Milton's friend and former lawyer Bradshaw were dug up from the Henry VII chapel in Westminster Abbey and carried through the streets to Tyburn. There they were pulled out of their coffins and 'hang'd at the several angles of that Triple Tree'. They stayed there till sunset, when 'they were taken down, their heads cut off, and their 'loathsome Trunks thrown into a deep hole under the Gallows'. The hangman placed their heads on poles outside Westminster Hall, where they remained till 1684. Milton was lucky not to be among them.

There was indeed a flurry of satirical or polemical pamphlets linking him with the regicides. He was the 'Image-breaker', and along with Nedham, Bradshaw and others, his best 'divorce' would be to commit suicide. He was also imagined in the Greek classical underworld at Pluto's court. Some contemporaries were surprised at his escape. A leading bishop, Gilbert Burnet, who had little reason to love Milton but who clearly respected him in his fair-minded way, wrote in his memoirs that 'Milton had appeared so boldly, tho' with much wit and great purity and elegancy of style, against Salmasius and others, upon that Argument of putting the King to death, and had discovered such violence against the late King and all the Royal family, and against Monarchy, that it was thought a strange omission if he was forgot, and an odd strain of clemency.'[4]

Milton soon moved away from Holborn and back to his old neighbourhood near Aldersgate, to a house in Jewin Street. But he cannot have felt safe. One of the early biographers, Jonathan Richardson, though he was writing long after Milton's death, says he 'was in Perpetual Terror of being Assassinated' in these years.[5] Printed attacks on him multiplied. Apart from Salmasius, a new edition of the *Regii Sanguinis Clamor* appeared, this time with the clergyman Pierre de Moulin as its acknowledged author. Other texts that had earlier denounced him were reprinted. His old foe Alexander More himself came and preached two sermons before the king.

Once again, Milton's response was to write. This time he could not reply directly, and in any case his interests were now elsewhere. He tried to bring to a conclusion the theological tract he had been working on intermittently for many years, and that was eventually to become *De Doctrina Christiana*. He had also begun *Paradise Lost*. According to Phillips he had begun it in 1658, and this may be true. But he had little leisure for it in those final chaotic years of the republic, and the bulk of the writing of the poem must have been done during these years of withdrawal from the public sphere of action. From now on he did not cease, in spite of the difficulties,

> to wander where the Muses haunt
> Clear Spring, or shady grove, or sunny hill,
> Smit with the love of sacred Song. (III 27-29)

The new regime became more and more repressive. The Church of England was re-established and the bishops were restored to the House of Lords. In September 1661 the corpses of twenty Puritans, including friends of Milton such as the Stephen Marshall of 'Smectymnuus' and even the wife of John Bradshaw, were dug up and thrown into a common pit. Quakers were especially targeted, but all radical sects were persecuted. John Bunyan, who took the line that spiritual insight was superior to 'humane learning', was gaoled for preaching in Bedford and stayed in gaol for several years. Henry Vane was brought to trial, refused to submit to the court's authority, and defended the Good Old cause loudly and boldly. He was beheaded on Tower Hill. A biography appeared almost immediately, and included Milton's sonnet to Vane, though neither book nor sonnet could bear the authors' names.

When Charles married the Portuguese Infanta, Catherine of Braganza, in May 1662, that and the presence of the queen mother, Henrietta Maria, increased paranoid fears about Catholic influence. This marriage had a more important effect in the long term: part of the dowry was Bombay, Portuguese at the time, and thus began the Indian stretch of what became the British empire. It was Catherine who is said to have introduced the drinking of tea to Britain, which had come via her compatriots' far-eastern explorations. But this is not the place to pursue that legend. I doubt if Milton ever drank tea, originally a Royalist beverage.

Charles himself, rumour had it, was a secret Catholic. Parliament and the crown increased the repression of sects – no group of more than five persons could meet for a service of worship that did not conform to the Church of England liturgy. The Act of Uniformity obliged even Presbyterian incumbents, whom Milton had long seen as latter day Pharisees and as in part responsible for the Restoration, to resign their ministries on the day known as 'Black Bartholomew' (24 August 1662, the anniversary of the notorious St Bartholomew's day massacre of French Huguenots in 1572). And later non-conformists found themselves banished from towns to obscure villages.

Milton's household during these years included his three daughters (as we have seen, aged fifteen, twelve and nine in 1661), plus a servant and a mistress to teach the girls. If they had stayed with their grandmother during the troubles, they returned to their father now. Word has got about that he mistreated his daughters, and the notion is enshrined in the fictions of Robert Graves, Eve Figes and others. The main source is Edward Phillips, who in his chatty way tells us that, Anne the eldest excepted, they were 'Condemn'd to the performance of Reading, and exactly pronouncing all of the Languages of whatever Book he should at one time or another think fit to peruse'. He adds that, since they did not understand one word, this 'must needs be a Tryal of Patience, almost beyond endurance', and that 'the irksomeness of this imployment could not always be concealed, but broke out more and more into expressions of uneasiness; so that at length they were all (even the Eldest also) sent out to learn some Curious and Ingenious sorts of manufacture, that are proper for Women to learn, particularly Imbroideries in Gold or Silver'. Deborah's daughter, Elizabeth Foster, reported in later years that he did not have them taught to write because it was 'unnecessary for a woman', but this is evidently untrue of her own mother. John Aubrey reports that Milton taught Deborah Latin, and to read Greek (Aubrey also wrote 'Hebrew' but crossed it out). She may also have served as one of her father's scribes, or amanuenses, during his blindness. Aubrey says so – though she may herself be the source of his information. (No one has identified her handwriting among his papers.) Later she even opened a school, and told Jonathan Richardson, who interviewed her in 1734, that her father was 'Delightful Company, the Life of the Conversation, and that on Account of a Flow of Subject, and an Unaffected Chearfulness and Civility'.[6] So the evidence is contradictory.

It does seem odd that Milton would withhold an education from his daughters, who could have been so useful to him. Anne, the eldest, had a speech defect as well as a limp, and was excused from reading: she also signed her name with a mark. Mary could at least sign her name. Deborah, the youngest, told later interviewers that Milton believed and often repeated that 'one tongue was enough for a woman'. She could, nonetheless, recite some of Homer, Isaiah, Euripides and the opening of Ovid's *Metamorphoses*. These reports all suggest that the daughters resisted what learning Milton offered them, or resented they did not get more. Milton was a friend of educated women like Lady Ranelagh and Lady Margaret Ley, and an admirer of Queen Christina of Sweden. Perhaps this increased his irritation with his dull daughters, who could not learn to read Latin properly, or at least in a way he found acceptable.[7] They seem not to have appreciated his genius, nor perhaps the bodily services a blind man, aging and perhaps still with digestive troubles, required. His disgrace at the Restoration will have deprived them of domestic comfort and dowries (the collapse of the Excise Office took with it Milton's savings, the substantial sum of £2,000). The comments reported are typical of an unhappy family. There may have been many at the time.[8] While Milton's friends tell us of a temperate man who ate and drank little, but enjoyed what he ate, Deborah remembers that he always insisted on the best of everything. Milton's small healthy portions were put down to faddishness, as Samuel Johnson recognized. Nothing in the surviving documents suggests any affection between father and daughters. Deborah's daughter reported, when asked, that he 'kept his daughters at a great distance'.

How true all of this is we cannot know, but in 1662 the resentment of their status led Milton's daughters to steal from the household expenses and to start selling his books. The evidence for this comes from Milton's last maidservant, Elizabeth Fisher. At the probate hearing for Milton's will, she claimed that all his children 'did combine together and counsel his maidservant to cheat him the decedent in hir Marketings, and that his said children had made away some of his bookes and would have solde the rest of his bookes to the Dunghill women.' With the loss of Milton's savings, money must indeed have been a problem for the whole family. The story of secretly trying to sell the books to the Dunghill women has a ring of truth about it, however shocking, and suggests how coldly unpleasant Milton's home must have felt to live in.

Nonetheless, Thomas Newton, a later biographer, tells us that, of an evening, Milton liked to play the organ and sing until he went up to his study. Friends came to visit till eight, and then he would eat supper, 'usually olives or some light thing; and after supper he smoked his pipe, and drank a glass of water, and went to bed'. He also had some kind of swing operated by 'a Pulley'. If his daughters were as cold and uncooperative as they sound, then he would have depended on these visiting friends to read and write for him.

Edward Phillips continued to visit, even though he had become a Royalist, and he sometimes read to his uncle or wrote for him. But he moved away to become tutor to John Evelyn's son in Essex in 1663. A young Quaker, Thomas Ellwood, was introduced to Milton through Isaac Pennington, himself a Quaker, and in return for the Latin education he felt he lacked, he read and wrote for Milton every afternoon. But he was arrested as a Quaker in October 1662, and soon after his release in 1663 agreed to go as tutor and companion to the Pennington household in Buckinghamshire. Ellwood had met the radical Quaker James Nayler on his release from prison in 1659: he admired this eccentric heretic, a victim of ill treatment in prison and brigandage on the road home to Yorkshire. Nayler died a year later, but he handed on to Ellwood and other young Quakers a sense that, in the words of Proverbs 3:2, 'God giveth grace to the lowly.'

In July 1663 Andrew Marvell went as secretary for the ambassador to Muscovy. So there was no regularity or reliability about the visits of any of Milton's friends. Yet these were the years when *Paradise Lost* was being composed, a task which thus became especially difficult. Richardson says

Milton was 'perpetually Asking One Friend or Another who Visited him to Write a Quantity of Verses he had ready in his Mind'.[9]

Milton himself, or his narrator, describes the composition of *Paradise Lost* as taking place mostly at night: in Book IX 21-4, the Muse 'deignes / Her nightly visitations unimplor'd, and dictates to me slumbring, or inspires / Easie my unpremeditated Verse'. Cyriack Skinner confirms that Milton 'waking early (as is the use of temperate men) had commonly a good Stock of Verses ready against his Amanuensis came; which if it happened to be later than ordinary, he would complain, Saying, *hee wanted to be milked*' (my italics).[10] It is a striking and revealing phrase, not only because he likens himself to a cow, but because like that cow he must wait to be milked. To stand and wait, he had early stated, was also part of serving the Lord, and now again, he and his Muse had to sit, or lie abed, and wait.

One of his friends, Dr Nathan Paget, who had also become his personal physician, now proposed a third marriage – to his own cousin, a young red-headed woman called Elizabeth Minshull. She was 24 and Milton 54, though on the marriage certificate Milton reduces the difference, describing himself as 'about 50' and his bride as 'about 25 years'. He signed the application himself, with an oddly blotted signature. They were married on 24 February 1663. Apparently he did not think to tell his daughters, and when the servant girl told them, Mary said 'that that was no news to hear of his wedding but if she could hear of his death, that was something'. John Aubrey, the conciliator, who met the new Mrs Milton later, describes her as gentle and 'of peaceful & agreable humour'. Though there was soon a good deal of affection on both sides, and they were wed for twelve years, Milton's unpleasant daughters resented the marriage, fearing the will would replace them. It did. Elizabeth outlived her husband by more than half a century, dying only in 1727.

Once again, the family moved, this time to a house in Artillery Walk near Bunhill Fields. It was smaller than the Jewin Street house but had a large garden – something Milton had always enjoyed. He could also walk in the fields. In warm weather he would sit at the door and receive visits. In the winter months he worked on the great poem. His widow reported this, and said 'his vein never happily flow'd' except from the autumn equinox to the spring. In the summer, therefore, he was probably trying to complete *De Doctrina Christiana*. He refused a request to write for the new government, since that, his widow reported, 'would be very inconsistent with his former conduct, for he had never yet employed his pen against his conscience'.[11]

18

Plague, and *Paradise Lost*

In the summer of 1665, a new threat forced Milton and many others to leave London – the plague. One of the worst afflicted parishes in London was Milton's, St Giles Cripplegate. In total, one-fifth of the population of London died. Samuel Pepys was keeping track of the effects in his diary, and reported a mass exodus in June. Houses were boarded up with red crosses placed on the doors, cemeteries had no more room, entire households were shut up and died behind their locked doors. Milton would have heard the regular cry in the streets of his neighbourhood: 'Bring out your dead.' One of the huge burial pits for the dead was, Daniel Defoe reported in his *Journal of the Plague Year,* in Bunhill Fields. So Milton's young Quaker friend Thomas Ellwood arranged for a small cottage in the country at Chalfont St Giles, near where he himself now lived in Buckinghamshire.

The charming house, the only residence of Milton's which still survives (though somewhat altered, and now only just outside the M25), was owned by a daughter of George Fleetwood, one of the regicides, who had fled to America, and whose brother, lieutenant-general Charles, Milton had known a long time, and had praised in *Defensio Secunda.* Milton moved his household to Chalfont probably in June, before the worst of the plague broke out in London in August and September. If Milton took his four womenfolk with him, then the house was crowded. Milton probably slept downstairs, since upstairs was reached by a ladder into one of the bedrooms. That will have helped the domestic tensions, since Milton rose early, at 4 a.m. in summer, to read the Hebrew Bible. But who read it to him?

A few cases of the plague were reported even in Chalfont St Giles, so it is unlikely that Milton walked out very much at first, even as far as the lovely Norman church, still less to his Quaker friend Isaac Pennington's house in the neighbouring village of Chalfont St Peter. We do not know whether Milton ever attended a Quaker meeting – indeed we have no evidence that he belonged to any church or attended any after the Restoration. But there was a large Quaker community in the area, and many features of the Quaker meeting would have been to his liking: its informality and lack of authoritarian structure, the absence of a clergyman, the quiet waiting on the spirit to move the people, the freedom to speak one's mind. Thomas Ellwood, the Quaker friend who had arranged for the cottage, was released from prison in August and returned to his house, Bottrell's Close. He immediately went over to Milton's cottage to welcome his distinguished guest and mentor. There he tells us 'After some common Discourses had passed between us, he called for a Manuscript of his; which being brought he delivered to me, bidding me take it home with me, and read it at my Leisure, and when I had done so, return it to him, with my Judgment thereupon.' When he got it home he found it was 'that Excellent POEM which he entitled PARADISE LOST'.

Imagine being the first reader (apart from the scribe) of that extraordinary masterpiece! Imagine carrying it home, the only manuscript, to read and give Milton himself your opinion! Did the great Milton really ask shyly for the opinion of a young pupil in his early twenties? Apparently so. Ellwood says he acknowledged the favour done him but is frustratingly vague about his judgment: 'He asked me how I liked it, and what I thought of it; which I modestly, but freely told him.' He does mention, though, one comment: 'I pleasantly said to him, Thou hast said much here of *Paradise lost*, but what hast thou to say of *Paradise found*? He made me no Answer, but sate some time in a Muse; then brake off that discourse, and fell upon another Subject.' This brilliant little cameo is revealing. It suggests that the excellent Ellwood had not managed fully to understand the poem, or perhaps to finish it, since it does indeed announce, near its end and quite explicitly, the potential recovery of paradise, both for Adam ('a paradise within thee, happier farr' (XII 587), and for humankind as a whole through the sacrifice of the Son.

Ellwood would not be the last reader to miss important aspects of the poem on a first reading. What Ellwood thought of Milton's silent 'Muse' he tells us later: he, Ellwood, in his 'modest' way, had given Milton the idea for *Paradise Regained*. Or so Milton himself told him 'in a pleasant Tone' when he later showed him that poem. Of course Milton's 'Muse' may simply have been determining to make clearer the meaning or subtext of the poem, the bringing of good out of evil, which is the overall theme of *Paradise Lost*. What Ellwood read was probably not the final form of the manuscript, which Milton could have continued to work on in Chalfont and perhaps also back in London. He did not give it to the printer for another eighteen months.

What evidence we have tells us he had already been working on the poem intermittently for a long time. Edward Phillips even says he had seen the lines that are now in Book IV, the opening of Satan's address to the

Sun ('how I hate thy Beams'), several years before, and as the beginning of a tragedy, not an epic. Milton had indeed sketched out several plans for tragedies in the Trinity manuscript, including more than one on the Fall. John Aubrey heard from Phillips that he had begun the poem 'two yeares before the K. came in, and finished it 3 yeares after the K's Restauracion'. If so, it was substantially complete in 1663, the year of his third marriage. It is not obvious how Milton could have written (or composed – we must remember his blindness) during those five years of turmoil and anxiety and hard work.

There are several autobiographical moments in the poem. In one of them he imagines himself voyaging as narrator down into Hell and back again, via Chaos, to the earth. He is, he claims (or hopes) 'Taught by the heav'nly Muse to venture down/ The dark descent, and up to reascend' (III 19-20). The composition of the poem becomes a perilous task. He has fortunately escaped the Stygian pool, and now revisits the light of Heaven, but Thou

> Revisit'st not these eyes, that rowle in vain
> To find thy piercing ray, and find no dawn;
> So thick a drop serene hath quencht thir Orbs.
>   … Thus with the Year
> Seasons return, but not to me returns
> Day, or the sweet approach of Ev'n or Morn,
> Or sight of vernal bloom, or Summers Rose,
> Or flocks, or herds, or human face divine. (III 23-44)

He consoles himself with the thought that he may find fame like the blind ancients, Homer or Tiresias. He begs the celestial light to shine inward, so that 'I may see and tell / Of things invisible to mortal sight' (III 54-55), and goes on immediately to imagine God and the Son chatting in Heaven. These words could have been written at any time since the onset of his blindness in 1652.

In another autobiographical intervention, as the second half of the poem opens, he continues the linking of writing and danger, but this time:

> More safe I sing with mortal voice, unchang'd
> To hoarse or mute, though fallen on evil dayes
> On evil dayes though fall'n, and evil tongues;
> In darkness, and with dangers compast round,
> And solitude. (VII 25-28)

Those resonant words link the narrator, perhaps not altogether consciously, to the allegorical figure of Sin who described herself earlier as 'With terrors and with clamors compasst round/ Of mine own brood, that on my bowels feed' (II 862). This parallel suggests a deep-rooted anxiety, as does the prayer that he be spared the fate of Orpheus, drowned in a 'savage clamor' of Bacchanalian Maenads (VII 37). But the narrator's words also sound like Milton's situation immediately after the Restoration, and if so, he boldly asserts that, in spite of the danger, he is politically 'unchanged'. We might therefore infer that, if he composed the poem in something like the sequence in which it was published, he had written the first half before, and wrote the rest after, the Restoration.

Yet there is nothing to confirm this, and some of the passages in the first half may well have been added later. The long description of Belial in Book I 490-505 looks as if it was written during the Restoration as a covert denunciation of Charles and his court. It says of Belial that

> In Courts and Palaces he also Reigns
> And in luxurious Cities, where the noyse
> Of riot ascends above thir loftiest Towrs,
> And injury and outrage: And when Night
> Darkens the Streets, then wander forth the Sons
> Of Belial, flown with insolence and wine.

No one can miss the present tense. The passage continues with a reference to the Sodomites of Genesis 19 who tried to rape Lot's angel guests: he offered them his daughters instead, but no rape took place and Sodom was destroyed. As often in the Bible, there is a parallel to this story at Judges 19, to which Milton also refers, having noticed the similarity. Here a Levite gives 'certain Sons of Belial' his maid, or concubine, in an effort to protect his male visitor from a homosexual attack, the 'worse rape' mentioned: the woman, having been abused 'all the night', soon died.

Milton was fascinated by this biblical horror story. He had referred to it early, in the stage directions following *Comus* line 22, where the rout of Comus is described in the same terms. It may also have been in his mind, I suggested earlier, when he refers to 'evil absolutely' in *Areopagitica*, an abomination not to be tolerated.[1] Significantly, he changed the *Paradise Lost* passage between the first and second editions of the poem, since he got the reference wrong in the first: he wrote that it was plural 'Matrons' who were raped, not just one, and not a concubine, as she is in Judges. He also changed 'Yielded' to 'Expos'd', since the poor woman is set outside the door defenceless:

> Witness the Streets of Sodom, and that night
> In Gibeah, when the hospitable door [Dores]
> Expos'd [Yielded] a Matron[s] to avoid worse rape.

Mistakes are usually revealing, often of something that the writer's unconscious is obscurely moved by. Here the sexuality is blatant, both violent and homosexual. The passage reaches in two directions – inward, to Milton's psyche, and outward, to puritan distaste for Cavalier riot, those casually cursed 'sons of Belial, flown with insolence and wine'.

The first edition of the poem has only ten books, not twelve. Yet the two editions are hardly different except for the reorganization of the second half, by rough line count, into six books instead of four. Critics who have tried to understand the shift have speculated (as I shall in a later chapter) that the first version is closer to the tragedy Milton initially envisaged: a five-act tragedy becomes a ten-book epic, with the crisis, the moment of Aristotelian periphrasis, in the fourth act, or book 8. This is indeed, in the first edition, the book of the Fall, what we know as Book IX.

But there may be another, political reason for the ten books of the first edition, one that in recent years has come to dominate the discussion. Royalist epics tended to follow Virgil and fall into twelve books. An example is Abraham Cowley's unfinished *Davideis* – a poet Milton admired, according to his widow, along with Spenser and Shakespeare. The poem retells the story of David and establishes obvious parallels with Charles. And the Restoration was celebrated with many references to Virgil, whether to the new Golden Age anticipated in the Fourth Eclogue or to the *Aeneid*, the poem that announces the triumphant foundation of the Roman empire out of the ruins of Trojan civilization. John Denham had already set the tone and translated Book II in 1656 as *The Destruction of Troy*, making the sad death of Priam coincide with the death of Charles I. Now the Royalist perspective had changed, and Dryden's *Astraea Redux* makes the coronation of Charles II overlap with the more glorious aspects of Aeneas and Augustus.

Lucan, on the other hand, whose anti-Caesar epic called *Pharsalia*, or *The Civil Wars*, is written in ten books, was for Milton, it has been argued, a politically closer model.[2] Lucan's poem is hostile to the *Aeneid*, though it does not exactly repudiate its form. It is explicitly hostile to Caesar and Caesarism as tyranny, and favours the losing side in the civil war that ended the Roman republic. Lucan was writing under Nero, and was obliged while still a young man to commit suicide for trying to overthrow him. For this reason, Milton, like Lucan's friend Statius, seems to have identified him with Orpheus, whose violent end he explicitly feared as early as 'Lycidas'.[3] The *Pharsalia* had been translated by Thomas May in 1627 and was widely read by republicans as a story of what happens in the world of civil war and efforts to overthrow tyranny. But there are other possible models. Camoens's *Os Lusiadas*, for example, is also in ten books, a poem that celebrates Portuguese empire-building as the triumph of Christianity. Milton had been closely involved, through his official letters, with Cromwell's efforts to recall the authorities in Portugal to their European responsibilities over the attempted assassination of the English ambassador, and the great Portuguese epic of what was then modernity had a special resonance for him.

The plague had waned and Milton returned to London, to the house in Artillery Walk, in early March 1666. It is extraordinary that we do not know who wrote out or corrected the final version of *Paradise Lost*. Edward Phillips was available only occasionally, since he was now at Wilton House as tutor to Phillip Herbert. His younger brother John had become a satirist in the service of the new government, but may have visited Milton infrequently. Perhaps Marvell also helped. Meanwhile the new war with the Dutch raged and a four-day naval battle killed large numbers on both sides. Given his earlier correspondence, Milton will have been saddened by this war with a Protestant republic. Peter Heimbach, whom he had recommended in 1657 as secretary to the ambassador to the Hague, now wrote to him to say he was state councillor to the elector of Brandenburg, and also to say he was glad Milton was not dead, as rumour had told him. Milton's reply is the last surviving letter he wrote. He congratulates Heimbach on his success, pokes gentle fun at his bad Latin, and jokes that he is glad not to be dead just yet. He is happier with the earthly than the heavenly *patria*, and says that 'A man's *Patria* is wherever it is well with him.' He also remarks that, if the letter arrives in bad Latin or with errors, Heimbach is to blame it on the ignorant boy who wrote it down at Milton's dictation. He had to spell out every letter.

19

Fire and War

In early September 1666 London burned. The Great Fire broke out soon after midnight in Thomas Farriner's bakery on 2 September, a Sunday, in Pudding Lane, and burned for four days. At first it did not seem so bad. The mayor, Sir Thomas Bloodworth, peeved at being roused from sleep, had seen worse fires: 'A woman could piss it out', he claimed. But the winds and hot, dry weather soon carried the flames everywhere. Sparks jumped and quickly ignited the largely wooden, tightly packed buildings. John Evelyn wrote in his diary that the flames burned 'the churches, public halls, exchange, hospitals, monuments, and ornaments, leaping after a prodigious manner from house to house and street to street, at great distance one from the other, for the heat (with a long set of fair and warm weather) had even ignited the air, and prepared the materials to conceive the fire, which devoured after an incredible manner, houses, furniture and everything'. It did not, in the event, reach Milton's house, but it came within a quarter of a mile. He must have been, in his blindness, as fearful as most Londoners at what might happen, for the noise of the flames and the cries of the people were prodigious. Samuel Pepys's invaluable diary tells of blinding smoke and firedrop showers, of the unsuccessful efforts to stop the fire by blowing up buildings in its path, of the terror and chaos it caused, and of the bookshops burned and the leaves of books flying everywhere. It sounds like Hell. Was it the imminent Apocalypse? Had it been caused by Jesuits, the French, the dissolute behaviour of the court? Rumours were rife, but the duke of York as king's representative took charge and controlled the people's reactions and gradually reorganized the fire-fighting.

The fire was checked in the east by gunpowder explosions, which created large firebreaks and saved the Tower of London. But the fire kept spreading west. It leapt the river Fleet and for a while threatened to spread to Whitehall and the royal palaces. It burned St Mary-le-Bow, sending the Bow bells to the ground, where they melted in the heat. The medieval guild buildings,

Grocer's Hall, Merchant Taylor's Hall, Draper's Hall, the Guildhall itself, the Exchange, all burned. The old Gothic church of St Paul's was consumed, together with the books and other goods people had tried to store in the crypt. 'The stones of Paul's flew like granados [grenades],' wrote John Evelyn, 'the melting lead running down the streets in a stream and the very pavements glowing with fiery redness.'

At last, on Wednesday morning, the wind dropped and the fire lost intensity and broke up. It became possible to douse the flames, but people battled for another thirty-six hours before the last of the fires were finally extinguished on Thursday night. More than 13,000 houses, eighty-seven churches and the main buildings in the City had all been destroyed. Amazingly, only five deaths were documented, including the housemaid in Farriner's bakery and people who thought to shelter in St Paul's. But over 100,000 people were left homeless and destitute. Milton's old school and his birthplace, the Spread Eagle in Bread Street, were burned to the ground. The destruction was widely seen as God's judgment on the people or on their government.

Slowly, the rebuilding of the city began and life re-established some kind of pattern. Near the end of April 1667, Milton signed a contract for his new poem, *Paradise Lost*, with the printer and publisher Samuel Simmons in nearby Aldersgate, one of the few such shops to have survived the fire. This is in fact 'the first recorded formal contract assuring intellectual property rights and payment to an author: five pounds when copy was delivered, five pounds when 1300 copies were sold',[1] then further provisions for second or third editions. Payments at the time were most irregular, and some authors were paid with free copies of their book. Copyright was granted only through entry in the Stationers Register, and then only to the publisher.

Milton's contract with Simmons was thus a departure from normal practice, yet it was typical of Milton's personality, which those of a psychoanalytic bent call 'anal-retentive'. All through his life he tried to exert control over what appeared for him in public. Not only did he include long, and sometimes not clearly relevant autobiographical passages (often defensive) in his polemical prose, but he donated copies of his books, even his topical pamphlets, to the Bodleian Library; he preserved his juvenilia; and made sure he knew his printers. Samuel Simmons was the son of Matthew Simmons, who had earlier published two of Milton's tracts. Only Ben Jonson, among major seventeenth-century authors, had as much knowledge of how books were made, signed for, sold and presented. One of Milton's friends was George Thomason, the archivist who collected all the ephemeral political pamphlets published in the revolutionary period (and now in the British Library). So we should be grateful for this controlling, retentive aspect of Milton's psyche. It made him thrifty and frugal, perhaps rather difficult to live with and certainly awkward to differ from, but it gave him his meticulous, scholarly attitude to all his work, and his phenomenal memory. It also marked him as a member of the new capitalist middle class. His father, the scrivener, lawyer and money-lender, had taught him well. Because of the contract with Simmons, in this market-oriented system of book production, he had something close to what we think of as intellectual property rights.

Milton's long-standing enemy, Roger L'Estrange, who had already mocked Milton back in 1660 in the days just before the Restoration, was one of the licensers in 1667, but Milton's manuscript was handed for approval by the censors to a younger man, Thomas Tomkyns. He was a strict and ardent Royalist, chaplain to the archbishop of Canterbury no less, and no friend to toleration. At first, we are told by John Toland, he objected (from 'Ignorance or Malice') to a passage in Book I: he found there 'imaginary Treason'. This sounds as if it means that the treason was simply in the eye of the beholder, but in fact it probably means, as the phrase often did, the imagining of the king's death or overthrow, a serious charge. There are plenty of passages on which Tomkyns might have fixed his attention, such as the one quoted above about the sons of Belial in courts or palaces 'flown with insolence and wine'. But in fact what he objected to, it seems, were the lines comparing Satan to the Sun in eclipse, which

> disastrous Twilight sheds
> On half the nations, and with fear of change
> Perplexes Monarchs. (I 597-99)

Probably Tomkyns was moved to act by the anxieties occasioned by the recent eclipse of 22 June 1666. Eclipses were often taken to be of political, as well as cosmic, significance. When the king was born, the one who became Charles II, there was an eclipse (29 May 1630). Royalists later proclaimed the event as a good omen (as did Dryden in *Astraea Redux* 288-91) but Edward Phillips recalled that, conversely, it had been seen as a portent of the Commonwealth.[2] In 'Lycidas' the eclipse was a bad omen: the ship in which Milton imagines his friend as having made his last voyage was 'Built in th' eclipse and rigg'd with curses dark' (101). Eventually, we do not know why, Tomkyns relented and allowed registration with the Stationers.

In June the Dutch sent a large fleet up the Medway and burned the ships of the English navy that had laid up in Chatham dock to avoid expense. The attack was in revenge for the burning of their own fleet the previous year and the destruction of the port of Schelling. The *Royal Charles*, the very ship that had brought the king back from exile in France, was burned and towed away by the marauding Dutch. They then blockaded the Thames and impeded supplies to London (one of the causes of the war was the trade rivalry). The mood of the English people was still low from the Great Fire of the previous year, and a combination of depression and indignation now afflicted many. A treaty was quickly signed at Breda ending this Second Anglo-Dutch War and trading the tiny but valuable nutmeg island of Run in Indonesia in return for another island colony, still known to the Dutch as New Amsterdam, even though Peter Stuyvesant had earlier surrendered it to a surprise British attack. It was renamed New York in honour of the king's brother James, duke of York. James's father-in-law, Edward Hyde, earl of Clarendon, whose restrictive Code imposed a harsh order on dissident churches, had become distinctly unpopular. Even though he had opposed it as financially ruinous he became the scapegoat for the war. On the night that Chatham docks burned a crowd attacked his home. He was impeached by Parliament, in part for sending prisoners out of England to places like Jersey and holding them there without the benefit of trial. He was forced into exile and fled to France in November. There he lived out his life and finished working on his *History of the Rebellion and Civil Wars in England*.

In the wake of all this disastrous action, *Paradise Lost* was finally registered with the Stationers on 20 August 1667, and it appeared in print within a few weeks. The book is the classic 'slim volume of verse', an oddly diminutive quarto in view of its expansive contents. There is no preface to encourage people to buy it, nor commendatory verses, not even the name of the printer. The title page does contain a notice in large letters announcing the poem is 'Licensed, and Entred according to order', which is obviously designed to reassure potential buyers. It also announces the names of the booksellers where the book is for sale:

Peter Parker under Creed Church near Aldgate; And [in much smaller type] by Robert Boulter at the Turks Head in Bishopsgate-street; And Matthias Walker, under St. Dunstons Church in Fleet-street, 1667.

Since these places are all within or on the edge of the area devastated by the fire, we may infer that London's business life was returning to normal, even if much of the city, including the old focus of the book trade, St Paul's, was all in ruins.

The book began to sell, slowly at first, then more rapidly as it went through three more impressions. In a re-issue of 1668, Simmons redrafted the title page, without the 'Licensed and Entred' line but including his own name in full and that of the author. Evidently he was gaining in confidence: he had not been arrested, nor had Milton. He added a brief note explaining that he had obtained from Milton the 'Argument', a prose summary of each book all printed together at the front, along with an explanation of the use of blank or unrhymed verse. With typically strong language, Milton writes of

> Rime being no necessary Adjunct or true Ornament of Poem or good
> Verse, in longer Works especially, but the Invention of a barbarous Age,
> to set off wretched matter and lame Meeter; grac't indeed since by
> the use of some famous modern Poets, carried away by Custom, but
> much to their own vexation, hindrance, and constraint to express many
> things otherwise, and for the most part worse than else they would have
> exprest them.

Who are the 'famous modern poets' he has in mind? Perhaps Camoens, author of the Portuguese epic *Os Lusiades*, or his translator Richard Fanshawe, Abraham Cowley, John Denham, William Davenant, whose unfinished *Gondibert* was modelled on Tasso and who had defended rhyme as 'more pleasant to the reader in a work of length', and almost certainly his former colleague John Dryden: his *Of Dramatic Poesie* claims rhyme as the poetic norm and was also published in 1667. Dryden in fact had become the leading poet of the new court, where his heroic dramas were especially popular. So Milton's note on the verse continues: 'our best *English* tragedies' [Marlowe and Shakespeare?] have long since rejected rhyme as

> a thing of itself, to all judicious eares, trivial and of no true musical
> delight, which consists only in apt Numbers, fit quantity of syllables, and
> the sense variously drawn out from one Verse into another, not in the
> jingling sound of like endings.

The rest of the note confirms the buried polemic against the Royalist fashion:

> this neglect of Rime... is to be esteem'd as an example set, the first
> in English, of ancient liberty restored to Heroic poem from the
> troublesome and modern bondage of Riming.

Early readers approved, but with an important proviso. 'Milton is a poet too full of the Devill', said the minister John Beale in letters to John Evelyn in November 1667. Though he thought *Paradise Lost* 'excellent', he found 'great faults' in it, and preferred the earlier poetry, less obviously political: he wrote that Milton had 'put such long & horrible Blasphemyes in the Mouth of Satan, as no man that feares God can endure to Read it, or without a poysonous Impression'. For the Presbyterian John Hobart in letters of

January 1668, Milton's prose was 'criminal', but he thought the poem would prove morally beneficial in a wicked age. Indeed it is 'equall to any of the Ancient Poets'.[3]

Apparently unaffected by this new success, Milton's daughters finally left home. His brother Christopher testified at the proving of Milton's will in 1674 that they had lived away from their father four or five years, and that on his deathbed Milton had said they were 'undutifull and unkind to him'. The analogy with King Lear has occurred to more than one critic. Milton clearly felt 'how sharper than a serpent's tooth it is to have a thankless child'. Years later, his granddaughter Elizabeth Foster claimed that Milton's third wife, Elizabeth Minshull, had sent them out to apprenticeships without his knowledge, and that though 'he was no fond father', he had been made uneasy by his wife's 'ill Treport is unreliable. One wonders where the money came from for the apprenticeships if Milton did not know, but it is nonetheless likely the idea was his wife's.[4] His youngest daughter Deborah left to become the companion of a lady with an estate in Ireland. On 1 June 1674 she married one Abraham Clarke in Dublin. Milton probably never learned of the wedding. At the probate hearing, Milton's maid said she recalled Milton saying that he thought he had made good provision for his daughters all his life, but indeed the remains of his worldly goods and property were intended to go to his wife.

20

Adam and Eve – and Satan

Why is *Paradise Lost* such a 'great' poem? There is no simple answer. The beauty of the language, the richness of reference, the intensity of the emotions described and evoked, the uplift that anyone feels as he begins to figure out the remarkable meanings this poem makes, all are part of the story. Add in, to begin with, the tingle you feel as you start reading aloud, and remember that is the only way the blind Milton himself could ever 'read' it. The poem is full of cross-references, which means Milton had to hold it all in mind: as he was dictating the passage in which Adam, in his misery, compares himself to Satan, descends into an abyss of fears and imagines he finds no way out, 'from deep to deeper plunged' (X 845), Milton had to recall the language of Satan's 'Myself am Hell' speech (IV 75) and even the philosophical devils who find no end to their speculation, 'in wand'ring mazes lost' (II 561).

Milton retells the story of Adam and Eve from Genesis, but as a marriage, of which he had varied experience by now. It is a love story at the human level, and at the divine, because of Satan, a hate story. As in classical epic, the two levels interact. Angels visit Eden and tell the story of what happened earlier in Heaven, the mother of all wars, and what will happen later on Earth. They warn and educate Adam and Eve, and one of them even sits down to a light lunch ('no fear lest dinner coole', V 396). And Satan visits the garden and eventually insinuates himself into the serpent.

'Happiness writes white', said a wise Frenchman, meaning that if you try to write about happiness, nothing comes out onto the paper. Milton succeeds, briefly: he has his Eve say to Adam,

> With thee conversing I forget all time,
> All seasons and their change, all please alike. (IV 639–40)

Adam and reader believe her and share the joy. Adam and Eve partake in the loving conversation that Milton thought to be the true reason for marriage.

But their happiness is credible partly because it is under constant menace, and we know it will be brief.

The Genesis story had been recast in the years of late antiquity, especially by Augustine, as the story of original sin, and Milton follows that conception. The leading figures of the Protestant Reformation took the Augustinian idea of original sin very seriously. The Fall had devastated all human life. We all inherit sin from Adam. In abolishing monasticism, Martin Luther insisted that patriarchal marriage was the necessary result of the Fall. Once equal partner to the man, woman was obliged through Eve's sin to subject herself to her husband. For Jean Calvin also, 'Thou shalt desire nothing but what thy husband wishes.'[1] Calvin had a complex understanding of the text of Genesis, which he read in the light of the New Testament passages, largely Pauline, which mention it. Thus on the one hand 'Adam was not deceived but the woman' (I Timothy 2:14), so it was his wife's allure, not Satan's, that persuaded Adam. He was not even present when the serpent tempted Eve (a matter about which the text of Genesis 3:6 leaves some doubt, since 'she gave also unto her husband with her'). On the other hand Paul says in Romans 5:12 that 'sin came not by the woman but by Adam himself' (on Genesis 3:6). 'No excuse was left to him who had obeyed his wife rather than God' (on 3:17).

Paradise Lost makes explicit use of these ideas, but reworks them into an entirely new pattern. Adam is made to bear the larger part of the blame, since he falls 'not deceaved/ But fondly overcome with female charm' (IX 999). However, the dramatic focus of the story is Eve. She has the two most beautiful lyrics in the poem. In their innocent, unfallen, state she sings to Adam a delicate sonnet-like poem 'Sweet is the breath of Morn' which ends, after a long list of all the things that are indeed sweet in Paradise, with the loving and remarkable lines that tell Adam that none of this,

> Nor grateful Eevning mild, nor silent Night
> With this her solemn Bird, nor walk by Moon,
> Or glittering Starr-light without thee is sweet. (IV 641-56)

The longer we wait for that conclusion the greater its impact: 'without thee is sweet'. Mostly we are led to think that it is Adam who is more in love, but this little poem suggests they are equals in love. It is Eve, too, who proposes the brief separation to which Adam reluctantly agrees, she who is therefore the target of Satan's temptation in a marvellously seductive dialogue, and after the Fall, it is she who leads Adam back to his better nature with the moving appeal, 'Forsake me not thus, Adam' (X 914-36). Her proposal of joint suicide is what finally awakens Adam to the treasure that she is, and to his reasons to go on living. Eve also has the poem's last word (almost a love-sonnet from wife to husband of fourteen unrhymed lines, XII 610-23) – before the narrator leads us, and them, out of Eden.

Some readers have found a specifically Miltonic misogyny in the treatment of Eve, most obviously in the statement that introduces the human couple: they are both

> Not equal, as thir sex not equal seemd;
> For contemplation hee and valour formd,
> For softness shee, and sweet attractive Grace,
> Hee for God only, shee for God in him. (IV 295-9)

One word might give us pause here – 'seemd'. To whom? Well, the way the story is told makes us arrive at Paradise with Satan and see it first through his eyes. So 'seemd' could imply 'seemed to Satan'. And therefore distorted? However firmly the narrator himself makes these statements about sexual difference, can we be sure he is not contaminated by the Satanic perspective? Nevertheless the poem says that Eve is created not only different but 'not equal', which seems to mean inferior, or so most Christian theology implies: that will be the source of her dissatisfaction, what Satan will exploit. He gets her to believe, both in the dream he inspires in her, and in the temptation itself, that the difference between Adam and Eve, on which so much turns, is not just along a horizontal scale of difference, with Eve toward the graceful and softer end, Adam toward the valorous and contemplative. It is also a vertical scale, with Adam superior. Indeed the poem generally assumes that 'not equal' means they have different positions in a hierarchy. The explicit statement a few lines later reinforces this, that she was made for 'subjection', even if 'requir'd with gentle sway' (IV 308).

Others see such statements not as unconscious revelations of Milton's private misogyny but as the ways in which Milton honestly faced the implications of the story, and of Western misogyny in general. The harsh language of the Bible is actually modified: 1 Timothy 2:11 reads: 'Let the woman learn in silence with all subjection' – there is nothing about 'gentle sway'. Milton thus explained Eve's sin on the grounds of her feeling of inferiority: as she herself says while debating whether to give Adam the fruit to share with her, 'for inferior, who is free?' (IX 825). Most of the overtly misogynist statements are put into Adam's mouth after the Fall, as when he aligns Eve with the serpent, as indeed did much of the tradition: 'out of my sight, thou Serpent!' (X 867) or when he makes the pun on her name that is available only in English, 'O *Eve*, in evil hour thou didst give eare/ To that false Worm' (X 1067). Adam it is too, in his bitterness, who imagines (falsely) that God 'peopl'd highest Heaven/ With spirits masculine', and who therefore wishes God had not made woman, 'This noveltie on Earth, this fair defect/ Of nature' (X 889-92).

Milton, as I see it, balances the egalitarian and hierarchical traditions of reading Genesis. One is based on the Priestly author's 'male and female created he them', the other on the Yahwist's story of the rib. Milton did not know about the two authors of Genesis, but he sensed, along with many other readers of the Bible, a discrepancy. So on the one hand, he has Adam ask God for an equal companion rather than an animal ('Among unequals what societie?', VIII 383), and God so understands him (VIII 407). Adam thinks of Eve as 'the last and best/ Of all God's works' (IX 896-7).

On the other hand, he is explicitly reproved for having been so moved by passion that he listened to his wife, whom he should have ruled. There is an uneasy tension throughout the poem between two notions of gender relations: on the one hand is the tradition of male dominance, on the other the newer ideal of companionate marriage that Milton defended in the divorce tracts, and which led Adam to ask for a mate like himself, 'fit to participate/ All rational delight' (VIII 390-1). In *Tetrachordon*, for example, Milton acknowledges that there are two accounts in Genesis of the creation of man and woman, but thinks that Paul 'ends the controversie by explaining that the woman is not primarily and immediately the image of God, but in reference to the man' (*YP* II.589). He thus echoes the traditional view that a wife should normally be subjected to her husband, but he also takes a more progressive approach and allows for exceptions if she 'exceed her husband in prudence and dexterity…, [since] the wiser should govern the lesse wise, whether male or female'. It is a matter for the reader to decide which of the two appears/is the wiser, and in what respects, in *Paradise Lost*.

Milton imagines the first man and woman as sexually mature from the first, and making love. It is this which makes Satan so jealous as he spies on them.

> Sight hateful, sight tormenting! thus these two
> Imparadis't in one anothers arms
> The happier *Eden*, shall enjoy thir fill
> Of bliss on bliss, while I to Hell am thrust,
> Where neither joy nor love, but fierce desire
> Among our other torments not the least,
> Still unfulfill'd with pain of longing pines. (IV 505-11)

What he sees immediately is that Paradise is both a place and a state of mind or being, and what makes it so is love. Adam and Eve are 'imparadis't' in being with each other, physically. To this lonely voyeur, excluded from Paradise ('while I to Hell am thrust'– note the present tense), a man and a woman in each other's arms is 'the happier *Eden*'. Satan's own feelings, he knows, contrast miserably: he experiences only 'fierce desire/ Among our other torments not the least'. And why? Because 'still unfulfill'd'. Satan adds a phrase which may seem simply to repeat what he has said in other words (*variatio*): 'with pain of longing pines'. But if you listen to those words, you will hear a pun on 'pain' and 'pine', which in Milton's London dialect may have been pronounced almost the same. More important 'pain of longing' is another way of saying not just desire but 'nostalgia'– so important to Satan's experience here, and also to ours: we too are both present to, and excluded from, this *Paradise Lost*.

The point of view from which we first see our first parents, then, like all of Paradise itself, is Satan's. Of course we forget this point of view as the narrative develops, and are harshly reminded, for example, just as the narrative introduces Adam and Eve ('where the Fiend/ Saw undelighted all delight' IV 285). This raises the question of whether what we see is without distortion, and this question becomes especially important when Eve is described, she who wears her hair as a veil down to her waist 'Dissheveld, but in wanton ringlets wav'd' (306). Wanton? Can we possibly read that word and not relate it to 'fallen' sexuality? As if to underline the point, the narrator now intervenes, telling us that Adam and Eve are naked, but experience no shame, and thus reminding us of our own disturbed consciousness and the distance between what we are being told and what we have become:

> Nor those mysterious parts were then conceald,
> Then was not guiltie shame: dishonest shame
> Of nature's works, honour dishonourable,
> Sin-bred, how have ye troubl'd all mankind
> With shews instead, meer shews of seeming pure,
> And banisht from man's life his happiest life,
> Simplicitie and spotless innocence. (IV 312-18)

So not only is the Satanic point of view the way we see Adam and Eve first, but this perspective, in which Satan's is like ours, will not let us see clearly and simply – for shame.

This passage about nakedness is an example of how much Milton both adds to and comments upon the biblical story. Of course it is Eve's nakedness that is most interesting. Even the narrator seems to be rather smitten by Eve. At the end of her famous speech about her own birth and first awakening, about the love she first felt, like Narcissus, for her own image and which might therefore have 'pin'd with vain desire' but for the voice which led her to Adam (IV 467), the narrator describes how she

> with eyes
> Of conjugal attraction unreprov'd,
> And meek surrender, half imbracing leand
> On our first Father, half her swelling Breast
> Naked met his under the flowing Gold
> Of her loose tresses hid: hee in delight
> Both of her Beauty and submissive Charms
> Smil'd with superior Love, as *Jupiter*
> On *Juno* smiles, when he impregns the Clouds
> That shed May Flowers; and press'd her Matron lip
> With kisses pure. (IV 493-503)

The Jupiter-Juno simile interposes reading space between smile and kiss, drawing out the erotic moment: like the adjective 'Matron' rather than *maiden* for Eve's lip, the allusion leaves little doubt as to what happens next between the couple, even as Satan himself turns aside, with an exclamation about this 'Sight hateful, sight tormenting!' The narrator, like Adam here, and Satan, seems to be attracted to Eve, by that half of a swelling breast naked and touching Adam's but (to increase the erotic charge) *hid* beneath her loose tresses.

As the simile shows, the word 'superior' literally refers merely to physical position, like Jupiter's in relation to Juno. But beyond this unsettling Homeric comparison, in this Miltonic language, it is Adam who smiles with 'superior Love', and Eve whose 'submissive Charms' delight. Desire, even in this innocent paradise, is enmeshed in the polarities of dominance and submission.

As if the narrative knows we are unlikely to be equal to the struggle in these erotic passages, it almost turns on itself to insist that, whatever our reaction may have been to those words and this nakedness, '*Then* was not guilty shame'. The lines repeat the familiar doctrine from Genesis 3 that shame came into the world with the Fall ('sin-bred'), but also seem to imply that it is the very feeling of shame itself that prevents us from enjoying the innocence of nakedness. There was apparently one puritan sect at the time, the Adamites, which practised nudity in search of just such Edenic innocence. At any rate, words like 'wanton', which is used both for Eve and for Paradise, show how clearly the world of the garden is bodied forth in its inhabitants. Critics divide, understandably given the intimate sensitivity of the issues raised, on whether these passages allow the reader access to what

Milton 'considered a relaxed and natural form of sexual delight', or whether the intrinsic fallenness of rhetoric is an impenetrable barrier. These issues are perhaps at their most poignant and powerful through all this welter of powerful sexual emotions.

This pattern of presentation and response is repeated later, that evening in fact, when Adam takes Eve to bed – or at least to their bower – and we are reminded they had no need to undress: we are told that they 'Straight side by side were laid' (IV 741), neither turning away nor refusing the other – phrases which show the mutuality of this sexual encounter and rather undermine the suggestion we heard earlier about Eve's 'sweet reluctant amorous delay' (IV 311). It sounds as if Adam does have, in the helpmeet he asked God for, an equal. The language of Proverbs or the Song of Songs is close: this is even a kind of universal language of sexual attraction.

But instead of continuing the description the narrator goes negative on us, and directs us away to ourselves and our own impoverished and deprived sexuality:

> nor turned I weene
> *Adam* from his fair Spouse, nor *Eve* the Rites
> Mysterious of connubial Love refus'd:
> Whatever Hypocrites austerely talk
> Of purity and place and innocence,
> Defaming as impure what God declares
> Pure, and commands to som, leaves free to all.
> Our Maker bids increase, who bids abstain
> But our Destroyer, foe to God and Man? (IV 741-9)

So Satan, foe to God and man, becomes what the word *puritan* has come to mean, a sexual hypocrite.

At moments like these we recognize that the narrator, who pretends to be Milton, is a complex modern personality, and as he views the scenes he constructs for us, he often comments – on sexuality, on politics and on sexual politics. In the midst of the above passages, for example, he intrudes a political and characteristically distancing comment in an effort to restore his independence and his adversarial relation to Satan. In Satan's first speech of reaction to the loving couple, he memorably begins with the exclamation, 'Oh Hell! What doe mine eyes with grief behold' (IV 358), and he then claims to melt at their innocence. Nonetheless he feels compelled by his imperial mission to do what else, though damned, he would abhor. At the end of the speech, the narrator remarks: 'So spake the Fiend, and with necessitie,/ The Tyrants plea, excus'd his devilish deeds' (IV 393-94). Given the immediacy of the scene Satan has just been witnessing, the comment invites us to spot a further motivation concealed by the 'excuse'– not politics but sexual jealousy.

Another example of this complex narrator is the remarkable passage in Book V when the angel Raphael has come to visit. The narrator clearly knows all about predatory male gazes. Yet he also separates the 'then' from the 'now' of the narration – insistently:

> Mean while at Table Eve
> Ministerd naked, and thir flowing cups
> With pleasant liquors crown'd: O innocence
> Deserving Paradise! if ever, then,
> Then had the Sons of God excuse to have bin
> Enamour'd at that sight; but in those hearts
> Love unlibidinous reign'd, nor jealousie
> Was understood, the injur'd Lovers Hell. (V 443-50)

The narrator imagines a fallen personality like himself unable to resist Eve's charms, and quickly adds a 'but' as if to withdraw himself and the equally enchanted reader from this drooling. These Sons of God come in curiously to take over the guilt, and we can get back to innocence:'but in *those* hearts/ Love unlibidinous reign'd' (unlike the kind of love that *we* know when in our 'pleasant liquors').

The reference within this narratorial aside has a long reach. The story the narrator refers to here is in fact one of the original stories that accounted for the fall toward our current state, that the so-called Watcher angels (supposed to protect us) fell for the beautiful daughters of men. The parallel between this story, deriving from the fragment of it remaining at Genesis 6:1–4, preceding the flood narrative, and the Eve story, had often been noted, and Milton here shows himself fully aware of it. Largely because of Paul's citations of it, the Adam and Eve story had supplanted the Watcher story within the early church as the one that explains how the world got to be in its current lousy state. But the older Watcher story was never entirely forgotten; it survives in the church fathers, especially Origen, and in medieval literature (especially through the survival of parts of the *Book of Enoch*, where the story is told at some length). Thus into the relations of narrator/reader and Eve is folded an older and still resonant version of the primal sin. Yet, the narrator appears to forgive those original Sons of God, so caught up is he in the powerful charge of Eve's naked innocence.

What is more the passage requires us to ask who it is that makes the comment about jealousy as the injured lover's Hell? Satan's jealousy has already been amply demonstrated, and there is a curious parallel established by the reference to hypocrisy in Book III, 683–4 between Satan, narrator, and at least some readers, those who are loath to admit to an unfallen sexuality in Eden. So here, even though Satan is himself absent from the encounter with Raphael, at least from the outer narrative, here in this scene is the most powerful and destructive of the emotions he experiences, and which the narrator – for this is his comment – knows only too well. Is this Milton himself? Like Satan, the narrator understands how complicated is his own reaction to these people in this place, and also like Satan longs for a time of loving innocence. Satan in fact has just told us he could love these beautiful people,

> so lively shines
> In them Divine resemblance, and such grace
> The hand that formd them on thir shape hath pourd. (IV 363-5)

Does that mean Satan is also admitting a love for God?

The whole poem, not only the relation of Adam and Eve, is imbued with a pervasive erotic appeal. There are many examples. Satan meets the results of his own licentious feelings in a moment of black comedy at the gates of Hell: he does not recognize his own lover or offspring (Sin and Death). The presiding Spirit of the poem is apparently androgynous or bisexual, as the initial appeal to the Muse implies: dove-like the Spirit sat 'brooding on the vast Abyss' yet it also made the abyss pregnant (I 31-2). The successive acts of creation by the Son are erotically charged. Creation of poem and universe are brought into parallel. The poem also invokes something quite different from its own warm and loving sexuality, which is to be found

> not in the bought smile
> Of harlots, loveless, joyless, unendear'd,
> Casual fruition, nor in court amours
> Mixed dance, or wanton mask, or midnight ball,
> Or the serenade, which the starv'd lover sings
> To his proud fair, best quitted with disdain. (IV 765-70)

The narrative then returns to Adam and Eve, who 'lulled by nightingales embracing slept'. On their naked bodies rose petals gently fall.

Another peculiarity of the Miltonic version of Paradise is that Adam and Eve are generally subject to error, not simply the one big mistake that will prove fatal. They can be surprised, and they can learn and grow. Eve especially begins learning almost immediately: in her first view of the world, a wonderful scene that is entirely Milton's invention, she sees her own image in the lake and finds it so lovely she needs to be led away from there to Adam, whom at first she finds not so appealing (IV 460-91). She can also learn (does she?) from the Satanic dream (V 30-93) which Adam interprets for her – but which seems to increase her dissatisfaction. Adam also has much to learn: he can ask questions about astronomy and be answered, but also needs to be set right by the visiting angel Raphael about the proper moral hierarchy – a crucial passage for the theme of forbidden knowledge. Whether the Ptolemaic or the Copernican systems are correct, or even more radical theories, those are matters for scientific inquiry, not for divine revelation. What matters to Adam, says the angel, is to take care of what before him lies, 'this Paradise/ And thy faire Eve' (VIII 171-2). Eden is a lush and lovely garden, but Adam and Eve must work to maintain it. Humankind cares for the natural world from the beginning, not merely as a labour imposed after the Fall. By a marvellously original idea, Milton makes this need to work part of the pleasure of the garden, but also the reason Eve proposes, on the fateful morning, that they separate so as to work more efficiently. Otherwise, she says, they keep pausing to enjoy each other's company, and get almost nothing done.

The scene in which they discuss this separation (IX 205-386) is one of the great moments of the poem. The dialogue is dramatic, perhaps imagined originally for a tragedy, but it is also psychologically subtle. Adam tries to dissuade her from going off alone, and hurts her feelings. 'As one who loves and some unkindness meets' she replies how surprised she is he could doubt her firmness. Eve uses arguments similar to the ones Milton had used in *Areopagitica*, that she ought to be free to test her virtue even though they have been warned about the Satanic enemy. Adam keeps up his side of the argument for a while, but finally, afraid to lose her love, he convinces himself she is right: a trial will make them stronger once resisted. 'Go, for thy stay, not free, absents thee more.' She is indeed free. Adam can no more insist that she stay than a censor can prevent reading or God intervene to prevent the Fall. And away she goes. The serpent can then find her alone at her task, and the temptation proceed. Again the dialogue is subtle and intelligent. Satan (in the serpent) makes himself as sexy a serpent as he can, but mostly appeals to Eve's logical sense: God can't have meant to deny you the fruit I have eaten and that has given me the ability to talk. Imagine what it would do for you! You could become the admired goddess you deserve to be. Once she has eaten, he knows he can leave the rest to her, and depart. Eve will easily persuade Adam to follow her.

Satan is the most memorable character of the poem, often taken to be the real hero (see my book *The Satanic Epic*). 'Better to reign in Hell than serve in Heaven' (I 263) is one of the best known lines in English poetry.

He evokes sympathy not only because of what he says himself, but of what the narrator, perhaps not quite intentionally, says about him. He is capable of love and jealousy, and despair. Even though he leaps into Paradise like those detested hirelings into the church (IV 184-7), recalling quite deliberately the wolves of 'Lycidas', and the angel Gabriel reminds him, in an angry speech, what he had been like in Heaven, a toady to God who 'Once fawn'd, and cring'd, and servilely ador'd/ Heaven's awful monarch' (IV 959-60), that is not the Satan we remember. It is he who early on embodies the whole epic tradition (and so calls it into question), who rebels against what he regards as tyranny and fights a heroic war, who drives the poem into motion by his reaction to finding himself in God's Hell, who devises the plot to colonize Eden, who undertakes a bold and dramatic voyage through Chaos, who invents the plan to corrupt Adam and Eve by noticing how they love each other and now innocent they are, who returns to Hell like a conquering epic hero and finds that he and all his angel colleagues can do nothing, briefly, but hiss. It is especially his speeches to his fellow devils, and later to himself, in the first quarter of the poem that help us understand why Eve is so impressed when he comes to tempt her. His rhetorical skill makes him an unequal match for the first lovely but innocent woman. All her points of vulnerability he manages to discover and exploit. Milton has him invent a cunning story about how he has already eaten the fruit, and so has learned, unusual for a snake, to speak. He convinces her eventually that the prohibition is unfair: it is an injurious withholding of knowledge. The poem bends a little to try to counter this claim, but this is what we remember, and continue to think. It was not only Romantic readers who constructed a sympathetic Satan. He was put there by Milton.

21

Milton's Womb: Chaos, Hell and the Ribs of Gold

On a second reading of the poem, people begin to notice the wealth of cross-references, which becomes one of the most insistent features of the language. As you read you run out of fingers to mark the passages you are invited to compare. This book is a biography rather than a work of literary criticism, so we cannot explore Milton's language in more than a preliminary way. It is remarkable for many reasons: for the way it deploys the sounds of English, for its deeply informed allusiveness, for its syntactical inventiveness. To demonstrate all that, we can begin from one passage, one line even, and follow its links round the poem and the history of the language.

One of the most original ideas in the poem is Chaos. Typically, it is a blend of Milton's classical learning with his heterodox theology. It is a region of inchoate matter, constantly warring elements, out of which the Son creates the universe. It is memorably described as 'the Womb of nature and perhaps her grave' (II 911). The phrase translates a line in Lucretius's Epicurean poem, *De Rerum Natura* (V 259), a provocative allusion itself in a Christian poem. It implies a lurking and potentially hostile force, monstrous and untamed, not simply an abstract concept. The ability to control Chaos is a primary sign of God's power and a key political idea: Hobbes had invoked 'the first Chaos of Violence and Civill Warre' in his *Leviathan* of 1651, precisely to deplore the consequences of rebellion against the monarch. But Milton's Chaos is also an independent being, personified as a cosmic character whom Satan meets on his journey. In this respect he reactivates the mythical root latent in the biblical *tehom*, the abyss of Genesis and the book of Revelation. It is also the Chaos of Hesiod and Vergil, who invokes, even prays to, Chaos and Phlegethon as Aeneas enters the underworld (VI 265). And there is a trace of the feminine in that phrase just quoted: Chaos is 'the womb of nature'. The phrase is worth following up.

Before we look at the meaning of the phrase itself, we need to consider the context. The phrase occurs at the moment in the poem when Satan begins his journey. He pauses on the brink of the abyss. Here Chaos is the hostile space he must cross in order to get from the gates of Hell to earth. His journey is Milton's variant of the required odyssey in an epic, and very exciting and dangerous it is. Commentators since the eighteenth century have noticed a particular feature of Milton's style that is most readily accessible in this passage. 'The Poet Himself seems to be Doing what he Describes, for the Period begins at 910. Then he goes not on Directly, but Lingers; giving an Idea of *Chaos* before he Enters into it.'[1] The unpredictability of rhythm and syntax takes us into Satan's energies and struggles. Here is the passage.

> Into this wilde Abyss,
> The Womb of nature and perhaps her Grave,
> Of neither Sea, nor Shore, nor Air, nor Fire,
> But all these in thir pregnant causes mixt
> Confus'dly, and which thus must ever fight,
> Unless th'Almighty Maker them ordain
> His dark materials to create more Worlds,
> Into this wild Abyss the warie fiend
> Stood on the brink of Hell and look'd a while,
> Pondering his Voyage. (II 910-19)

We share the experience of 'the wary fiend' in his anxious hesitation on the very brink of Hell. The syntax stalls for line after line while the nature of Chaos is explored in subordinate clauses heaped together 'Confus'dly' (II 914), until at last the opening phrase returns, 'into this wild Abyss', as in a musical composition, and the narrative resumes. Even then there is a mild surprise, since Satan still does not complete the movement implied by 'into'; rather he 'Stood' (as Bentley irascibly pointed out in 1732[2]). The next verb completes the syntax properly (he looked into the abyss) but still doesn't give us the jump we've been waiting for.

That jump doesn't actually come until line 929, where the long wait is stressed by the phrase that opens the sentence:

> At last his Sail-broad Vannes
> He spreads for flight, and in the surging smoak
> Uplifted spurns the ground. (II 927-9)

Even then we may blink momentarily before we see that 'spurns the ground' means 'jumps'. This whole passage exhibits that close relationship between form and meaning which readers have often felt to be one of the desirable, if not definitive, characteristics of poetic language. 'Milton can be said to be making the form *significant*.'[3] The particular significance it takes on here is that it brings the Satanic hesitation directly into the narrative, and makes it textual. The reader cannot but experience it as Satan does. We too teeter on the edge of Chaos.

Just as pygmy devils, or Galileo's telescope, deliberately introduced early into the narrative, disturb our sense of perspective or proportion, so the noise of Chaos that Satan now hears performs the same function for the ear. Blasting noise immediately assaults Satan's ear like the seige of a city in time of war – repeating the recent trauma of civil war for the first readers of the poem.

> Nor was his eare less peal'd
> With noises loud and ruinous (to compare
> Great things with small) than when Bellona storms,
> With all her battering Engines bent to rase
> Som Capital City; or less than if this frame
> Of Heav'n were falling, and these Elements
> In mutinie had from her Axle torn
> The stedfast Earth. (II 920-27)

It is with a sense of relief (and gratitude) that one reaches that fine phrase 'the stedfast Earth'. Such resting places stud the narrative of the Chaos-journey, but one must, like Satan, earn them. The noise of Chaos here is first compared to the war Milton's readers knew at firsthand (the Bellona reference) before it is magnified to become the disruption of the earth's 'Axle', the *axis mundi* of countless myths.

Since going blind, in the way that our other senses compensate when we lose one, Milton's susceptibility to loud noise had been enhanced: it is the converse of his delicate and highly wrought atunement to the harmonies of music and poetry. The materials of Chaos are not only 'dark' but 'loud'. We are reminded, as we noted before, of the 'barbarous dissonance' (VII 32) or 'savage clamour' (VII 36) of the Restoration court, like the lawless fury that impelled the Maenads to destroy Orpheus.[4]

Milton has often been praised as the great poet of sound in our language. His resistance to rhyme allowed him to create flexible blank verse lines organized into paragraphs where 'true musical delight', as he calls it in his own note on 'The Verse', is derived from 'apt Numbers, fit quantity of Syllables, and the sense variously drawn out from one Verse into another'. That is, the basic iambic rhythm of five strong, five weak syllables to a line is frequently varied to the point where there may be only three, or as many as eight, strong stresses. Sound and syntax are related. The enjambement and flexible Latinate syntax allow many effects like the one in the lines just quoted in which the word 'Uplifted' (II 929) can come at the beginning of the line as Satan finally soars away into Chaos.

The effects are many. Eve can meet Adam's advances 'with sweet reluctant amorous delay', where the extra adjectives vary the rhythm and delay 'delay'. She can sing delicate and beautifully affecting love lyrics, like the one mentioned before that begins 'Sweet is the breath of Morn' (IV 449-91). Later, her touching lament 'Forsake me not thus Adam' (X 914-36) at one of the great turning points of the poem begins to move Adam back towards herself, and towards reconciliation and rediscovered love. Or in the terrible terrain of Hell, monosyllables choke the verse: 'Rocks, Caves, Lakes, Fens, Bogs, Dens, and shades of death' (II 621: a line with eight stresses). Satan's voyage through Chaos is similarly difficult:

> Ore bogs or steep, through strait, rough, dense, or rare,
> With head, hands, wings, or feet pursues his way,
> And swims or sinks, or wades, or creeps, or flyes. (II 948-50)

In a famous essay, T. S. Eliot turned this praise of sound upside down and accused Milton of being unable to visualize anything. He was blind, after all. The vulgarity of this charge is breathtaking, and has often been answered. Perhaps the best reply would be that of Sergei Eisenstein, the pioneering Russian filmmaker, who showed from a passage in the War in Heaven how Milton's imagination worked in cinematic terms. In retrospect it is obvious that Eliot was reading Milton as he had become since the eighteenth century - the poet of the sublime - and the sublime, it had been thought at least since Burke's 1757 treatise on the sublime and the beautiful, was produced by obscurity. Hell and Chaos are especially full of passages which fit that definition, like the 'surging smoak' into which Satan flies up. Praised by Burke, denounced by Eliot, the language of moments such as these when Satan spreads his wings and 'Uplifted spurns the ground', has been captured and reproduced by countless painters and illustrators. That would be odd if Eliot were right, and Milton had, in his words, 'never really seen anything'.

So Satan flies off and into the frightening 'Womb of nature'. This is not the first time we have heard about a womb. Like most great writers, Milton can exploit, even without consciously realizing it, the state of the language in his time. In Milton's poetry words can retain their older meanings, often Latinate, while they also suggest their more modern sense. Milton's language reflects a period of rapidly changing usages (especially enhanced by the Civil War and everything that went with it), so that we often find words in which an older and a more modern meaning are both available. In the opening part of the poem, the devils set out to build a new palace for themselves, to be called Pandemonium (the word means 'all the demons' and is Milton's invention). They go looking for materials and the text continues with the following passage:

> There stood a Hill not far whose grisly top
> Belch'd fire and rowling smoak; the rest entire
> Shon with a glossie scurff, undoubted sign
> That in his womb was hid metallic Ore,
> The work of Sulphur. Thither wing'd with speed
> A numerous Brigad hasten'd. As when Bands
> Of pioners with Spade and pickax arm'd
> Forerun the Royal Camp, to trench a Field
> Or cast a Rampart. (I 670–78)

This language shows evident familiarity with basic military techniques, since these 'pioners' are advance sappers who go ahead to dig trenches or built ramparts: Milton could have seen this kind of action during the civil warfare he had lived through before he went blind, although he could equally well have read about it in Caesar's *Gallic Wars,* like many another schoolboy. But what are we to make of that very odd phrase indeed –'his womb'?

First we should note that, by now (1667) in the development of the English language the pronoun *his* had largely been replaced by *its* for the neuter gender. Shakespeare regularly uses *his,* but *its* was a recent innovation; *his* did not reflect the human/nonhuman distinction found elsewhere in the pronoun system (as in *what/who*). An expert on the history of the language says '*its* obviously fitted the system ideally, as can be deduced from its rapid spread in the first half of the seventeenth century'.[5] So is Milton just lagging behind the times? Perhaps he is, since there are only two uses of *its* in *Paradise Lost,* and not many elsewhere. So 'his womb' is really just the way Milton would say 'its womb'.

Nonetheless, we might well ask what a hill is doing with a *womb*. It could be just the looser use of 'womb' as stomach, current till the nineteenth century, and yet surely in this loaded context the phrase must bear more weight. Once you begin to think along those lines, you may want to connect it with 'the Womb of nature', but also with that other very striking metaphor which soon follows, in which these mining angels

> Rifl'd the bowels of thir mother Earth
> For treasures better hid. Soon had his crew
> Op'nd into the Hill a spacious wound
> And dig'd out ribs of Gold. Let none admire
> That riches grow in Hell; that soyle may best
> Deserve the precious bane. (I 687-92)

The hill is now seen as part of 'mother Earth'. The physiology may be a little odd, since the miners find treasures in the earth's bowels. Perhaps this is an instance of the common psychoanalytic equation of money and faeces that goes under the wonderful generic title of 'Filthy Lucre'.[6] 'Bowels', though, is commonly extended to mean all of one's internal organs, and was frequently and famously so used by D. H. Lawrence, especially in more intense passages. But above all, this female earth, be it noted, has ribs.

Now of course one wants to explain that the ribs are 'just a metaphor' for the veins of gold in the rocks. But if we start making connections again, we'll soon realize that the image is carefully chosen, and not only because it extends the anatomical language of the whole passage. An eighteenth-century critic, not Richardson this time but Pearce, commented that this phrase 'alludes to the formation of Eve' recounted later by Adam: he tells how God 'op'nd my left side, and took/ From thence a Rib, ... wide was the wound' (VIII 463). A very great critic, William Empson, picked up this splendid perception ('I call this a profound piece of criticism'),[7] and makes the connection between Eve as universal mother and the concept 'mother Earth'. One editor, Fowler, in spite of the wonderfully erudite battle with Empson he carries on in his footnotes, one of the minor pleasures of reading heavily annotated editions of Milton, agrees with the Pearce-Empson connection. He omits, however, the further connection between Eve's birth and that of Sin, born from 'the left side op'ning wide' (II 755) of Satan's head. Thus the passage brings together the poem's three main female figures – Eve, mother Earth, Sin – who are all implicated in the image of this strange birth. Strange indeed, and yet none of the commentators takes the next logical step and points out that, though the parallel with Eve's birth is indeed close in the language of these scenes, she is 'born', in the story Milton elaborates from Genesis, not from a woman but from Adam. His is the womb, or the wide wound, from which she is taken. The sexes are reversed.

Many cultures in fact have what anthropologists call 'male birth myths' like this, but Milton won't let us ignore (unless we are not attending) the half-submerged ideas. Here, as in Genesis, though sanitized and adapted to the idea of an all-powerful male God, a divine 'mid-husband' reaches in with his bare hands and brings out the material of life. What Milton does, if we take seriously the implication of 'his womb', is to align these various passages where we have been keeping our fingers with the ambivalent sexuality that pervades the poem, beginning with the very recreation in the opening lines of the cosmogonic myth itself. There the spirit of God, as we saw in the last chapter, sits dove-like brooding on the vast abyss (the first appearance of what later becomes Chaos) and makes it pregnant, giving both male and female functions to this cosmic bird-god (I 21-2) – but making the abyss, if we think about it, a cosmic egg and definitely female. So here in Hell it is mother earth who has productive ribs of gold within her, whereas in the parallel passage for the birth of Eve, the productive innards are Adam's. There is no need to read 'his womb' in this way, but it makes the text a lot more interesting if we do.

The point will be even clearer by contrast. The poem does contain a few quite proper wombs. Sin has her womb with its growing burden (II 767, 778, 798), even though what is growing there is Death, the result of her impregnation by her father Satan. The whole scene is painful and perverse, self-love replacing mutual love, but the genders are not bent. A healthier variant occurs in the first words the angel Raphael addresses to Eve: 'Hail Mother of Mankind, whose fruitful Womb/ Shall fill the World' (V 288-89). And a few lines before, mother earth has an unexceptional womb in the midst of a remarkable passage of poetry. As the angel makes his approach to the garden, he passes through

> A Wilderness of sweets; for Nature here
> Wantond as in her prime, and plaid at will
> Her Virgin Fancies, pouring forth more sweet,
> Wilde above Rule or Art; enormous bliss. (V 294-97)

The language gets even more erotic as Adam sees him coming at noon,

> while now the mounted Sun
> Shot down direct his fervid Raies to warme
> Earths inmost womb, more warmth than Adam needs.

That 'inmost womb' is comfortably surrounded by two instances of 'warm': Milton loves to play with sound, and here it is quite gratuitous, since there was no reason to add how much warmth Adam did not need. The implied sex here is quite 'normal', with a sun that shoots its rays into the receiving womb of earth, though we may perhaps wonder why, in the midst of all this fertility, Nature is oddly described as having 'Virgin Fancies'. In any case, the erotic implications of 'wantond' enhance the conventional gender equations.

There is no blurring of the kind we found in the Hellish passage, and that may be a reason for the contrast.

Gender confusion is not infrequent in Milton. Sometimes it can be explained on purely linguistic grounds, as with 'his womb'. Thus in the phrase we quoted before from *Areopagitica* England is 'a noble and puissant Nation rousing herself like a strong man after sleep and shaking her invincible locks' (*YP* II 558). In this case the Latin word behind 'Nation' is feminine, so when she rouses herself, we hear only Milton's (and his century's) familiarity with Latin. But the second time, the pronoun 'her' follows immediately that 'strong man', and 'his' would have been more appropriate.

At this point we may want to refer back to the quotation above (I 687-92) as we go a bit further afield. Just as 'his womb' might be understood as the vestige of older usages no longer current in modern English, but a more modern meaning is equally valid, so, in the narrator's immediate warning about the riches of Hell, the word 'admire' clearly retains its Latin sense (*admirari*) of 'wonder' (even if the word was often used in this sense in Early Modern English). This sense is what requires the conjunction *that* immediately afterwards: 'Let none admire/ That riches grow in Hell' (I 690-91). On the other hand, and just as clearly, the word is developing the modern sense in which one stands in admiration before something remarkable. It is this sense, even more than the older one, which leads to the warning not to do it: 'Let none admire'. The phrase comes at the end of the line, and by a characteristic use of double syntax, we first read it in its modern sense before, with the word 'That' at the beginning of the next line, we correct and supply the older meaning. First we hear a warning, appropriate enough here in Hell, not to admire the gold or the mining or the opening of the spacious wound, before we adjust to the meaning 'wonder'. And the warning extends to the oxymoron 'precious bane' in the next line.

The angel who led this 'Brigad' to their mining activities was Mammon (appropriately enough, since his name is a generic term for worldly riches). About him we have just heard the following extraordinary information, extraordinary at least if we imagine that the poem always distinguishes carefully between Heaven and Hell. Mammon is called

> the least erected Spirit that fell
> From heav'n, for ev'n in heav'n his looks and thoughts
> Were always downward bent, admiring more
> The riches of Heav'ns pavement, trod'n Gold,
> Then aught divine or holy else enjoy'd
> In vision beatific; by him first
> Men also, and by his suggestion taught,

> Ransack'd the center, and with impious hands
> Rifl'd the bowels of thir mother Earth. (I 697-87)

Not only was Mammon ripe for the Fall, then, but he seems already to have been 'fallen' even in heaven! Jesus was right, no doubt, about the fallen world of the Roman empire, when he averred that 'Ye cannot serve both God and Mammon' (Matthew 6:24; Luke 16:13), but Milton's bold decision to invent for his (equally invented) Mammon a prelapsarian existence leads to a real difficulty. Mammon sees little difference between Heaven and Hell, as he tells us in his speech during the Parliament in Book II.

> As [God] our darkness, cannot we his Light
> Imitate when we please? This Desart soile
> Wants not her hidden lustre, Gemms and Gold;
> Nor want we skill or art, from whence to raise
> Magnificence; and what can Heav'n show more? (II 262-70)

The answer to Mammon's splendidly perverse question should probably be 'Nothing', but then Heaven is not so exclusively concerned with *show* as is Mammon. Mammon is another of those several figures in Milton who look and cannot see.

Mammon is faulted, as Stanley Fish noted in a brilliant piece of criticism,

> not for admiring Heaven's riches but for admiring them in and for themselves and not as signs of the power ('divine or holy else') that made them. In his eyes they are riches that just happened to be in Heaven rather than *Heaven's* riches. It is their 'lustre' (II 271) not their source that impresses him, and that is why he is so pleased to find that same lustre in the 'gems and gold' of Hell's soil. 'What can Heav'n show more?' (II 273), he asks, making it as plain as could be that 'show' names the limit of his perception even as it names his desire.[8]

At the same time, I suggest, Mammon has lost the older sense of the word *admire* – wonder. That is a sign of his problem: he simply admires riches. The contrary sense occurs when we hear how Adam and Eve react to the story of how it all began, how Satan rebelled. They listen to the angel Raphael's story of the War between God's troops and the rebel angels and are filled

> With admiration and deep Muse to heare
> Of things so high and strange, things to thir thought

So unimaginable as hate in Heav'n,
And Warr so near the seat of God in bliss
With such confusion. (VII 52-56)

The story is beyond them. For them, hate in Heaven is *unimaginable*. This points to the role of Milton's Satan and to the problem he poses his audience. Evil arises in bliss.'Admiration' here means 'wonder', but specifically without any understanding.

The narrator of Book I, describing Mammon for the first time, while he was still in Heaven, is thinking of the book of Revelation, where the City of God has streets of pure gold (21:21), but the result of Milton's reframing of the idea is that we see that none of us know very well how to distinguish the riches of Heaven's pavement, trodden gold, from the gems and gold of the Hell hill's womb. We need the warning not to admire. The famously hellish oxymoron, then, in which these words issue, is entirely appropriate: 'that soyle may best/ Deserve the precious bane' (I 691-2). Like 'darkness visible',[41] and partly for the same reason (imitation of heaven), 'precious bane' describes the attractive ambivalence of Hell.

Ovid's *Metamorphoses* I 125-42 is the *locus classicus* for the idea that digging for golden wealth hid underground among 'Stygian shades' initiates the corrupt iron age of modernity. This was one of Ovid's many clever adaptations of Virgil's underworld realm of Hades, though the idea is widespread, and reiterated often in the Middle Ages and the Renaissance. But Milton's language bears closer attention, for it is not a tired reiteration of a commonplace. Milton's phrase makes a new metaphor. Riches *grow* in Hell.[9] Hell thus imitates the natural world, though for many in the period this function of usury was still regarded as a perversion appropriate only for Jews. This is one of the contentious issues between Shylock and Antonio in *The Merchant of Venice*. Milton, however, was the son of a money-lender. He lived on the proceeds, and had met his first wife while collecting a debt. He feels called upon to defend usury in the *De Doctrina* (*YP* VI 776). Thus not only does the word 'admire' point backward and forward at once, but the image of riches growing in Hell both looks back to the Ovidian original and also suggests something about Milton's own life.

Hell is not just a place. It *is* a place whither

all the damn'd
Are brought: and feel by turns the bitter change
Of fierce extreams. (II 597-9)

– language that sounds as if it refers to people as well as fallen angels. But

Milton's Hell, like his paradise, is also a state of mind, and one that infects not only the devils who live there. Milton's narrator is eager to separate himself from it, and one of his means is this reiterated system of warnings that he sets up about such matters as the riches of Hell and the womb of Chaos – and sex in the garden.

22

Emptying the Desk

The last years of Milton's life were intensely and marvellously productive. Three of his greatest poems were published. He was not an old man, so there was no real parallel with the final years of a Sophocles or an Ibsen in their creative eighties. But he was blind, he was suffering from increasing pain caused by gout (which was not understood at the time), and he could not walk at ease in the public street. He used to sit at the door of his house in Bunhill Fields when the weather was warm, and there receive the visits of people of high social position, including foreigners.

He also needed money. He started selling some of the collection of books he had amassed on his travels and in more recent years. He even briefly lived with an antique bookseller called Millington in Little Britain. Another solution to his relative poverty was to empty his drawers of unpublished work. So 1669, perhaps June, saw the publication of the Latin grammar he had worked on when he was teaching (or perhaps begun even earlier at Cambridge, as a way to overcome the boredom). The standard work in use was Lily's grammar, and Milton revised it to eliminate texts that seem to support royal or church structures and substituted a lot of Cicero, short and longer texts that address the struggle for justice or civil rights.

He worked up his *History of Britain*, adding a kind of moral at the end: 'And as the long suffering of God permits bad men to enjoy prosperous daies with the good, so his severity oft times exempts not good men from thir share in evil times with the bad.' So in our present times we should 'fear from like Vices without amendment the Revolution of like Calamities'. The thought reproduces famous lines from the last book of *Paradise Lost*

> so shall the World goe on,
> To good malignant, to bad men benigne,
> Under her own waight groaning till the day

Appeer of respiration to the just,
And vengeance to the wicked. (XII 537-41)

The *History* was eventually published in November 1670 but it had first to cope with problems from the censor. This time Milton's old foe Roger l'Estrange presumably took a direct hand, and suppressed certain pages that were 'too sharp against the Clergy'. Probably this concerned, as John Toland explained, passages which 'expos'd the Superstition, Pride, and Cunning of the Popish Monks in the *Saxon* Times, but apply'd by the sagacious Licensers to *Charles* the Second's Bishops'.[1] The 'Digression' denouncing the Long Parliament and the Presbyterian Westminster Assembly was also not published, and saw the light only in 1681 after Milton's death (mangled apparently for political purposes, perhaps by L'Estrange). It was eventually re-edited from the manuscript now at Harvard and published in the Columbia Milton.

The *History* as published has an engraved portrait by William Faithorne of Milton at age sixty-two. His wife did not like it, but his daughter Deborah, years later, was said to have cried 'in a Transport, – 'tis My Father, 'tis my dear Father! I see him! 'tis Him!' She also claimed that visitors, including Joseph Addison, commented on her likeness to her father's portrait.

When a few months later Milton produced for the press a version of his old treatise on logic, *Artis Logicae Plenior Institutio* (announced for sale in May 1672), it included, in some editions, a portrait by William Dolle, based on the Faithorne engraving. It also included a brief life of Peter Ramus, the logician whose work inspired the treatise. He was – and Milton seems to have identified with him quite strongly – a bold and unorthodox thinker, a Protestant who was forced into hiding by his Roman Catholic opponents, and eventually martyred in his Paris office at the St Bartholemew's Day massacre in 1572. The treatise itself is derived mostly from a Latin commentary on Ramus by George Downham, and the life condensed from one by Johann Freige.

Milton was notorious as the author of the divorce tracts, and this now became of immediate political importance. Charles II had fathered more than one bastard by other women but had no children by his barren queen, and he was now seeking to 'put her away'. A bill was introduced in Parliament as a trial balloon to allow another man, Lord Roos, to remarry after divorcing his wife for infidelity. A certain member of the House of Lords approached Milton for his expert advice. The bill eventually passed and was signed by Charles on 11 April 1670, but the king then did nothing to further his own case. Milton would almost certainly have supported the bill, since it would have allowed Charles to produce a legitimate heir and so prevent his overtly Catholic brother James from succeeding him.

It is likely that the peer who came to solicit Milton's counsel was the earl of Anglesey, Arthur Annesley, who had become a frequent visitor. He was, we are told by Anthony à Wood, 'a man of superior tastes and abilities' who enjoyed talking books and religion. He was, according to Edward Phillips, one among many such members of the nobility or 'persons of eminent quality'[2] who came to visit. Sir Robert Howard also came frequently, and once asked Milton what made him side with the republican cause. Milton answered that, among other reasons, it was the most frugal government, 'that for the trappings of a monarchy' a whole ordinary commonwealth could be set up. 'He pronounced the letter R very hard'. *Trrrappings.*

On 2 July 1670 another new book of Milton's was licensed for publication and then registered with the Stationers in September. It contained two remarkable poems, *Paradise Regained* and *Samson Agonistes.* Ellwood had already seen a draft of *Paradise Regained* in 1666, and it is likely that *Samson* as we have it was also composed in the years after *Paradise Lost.* It is true that Edward Phillips says it 'cannot certainly be concluded' when the poem was written, and it is indeed possible that Milton had begun *Samson* much earlier and now reworked it in the same way as the other books he was publishing at this time.[3] We have seen how Milton had used Samson as a metaphor even back in 1641 in the *Reason of Church-Government*, for Charles I seduced by 'the strumpet flatteries of Prelats' and thereafter, once his hair ('the bright and weighty tresses of his laws'), is cut off, is made to 'grinde in the prison house of their sinister ends' (*YP* I 859). The metaphor is repeated in the poem, though not for its sexual implications, when Samson must 'grind in brazen fetter under task.../ Eyeless in Gaza at the mill with slaves' (*SA* 35-41). The tempted and fallen Samson had been a part of Milton's imaginary life for a long time. Now things were different. Milton was, like Samson, blind.

It is hard to resist seeing the blind hero of *Samson Agonistes* as a version of Milton himself after the Restoration, and the language sometimes echoes that used of other republican victims of the monarchy such as Algernon Sydney or Henry Vane. Samson is at the mercy of his enemies the Philistines and required to participate in what he regards as their idolatrous rituals, much as the puritans were now forced to attend Anglican services and as ministers had publicly to declare their acceptance of the Book of Common Prayer. In this light the poem, cast as a Greek tragedy, is a kind of revenge fantasy, with the English monarchy and aristocracy, all the Royalists in fact, herded together into the theatre and then crushed under the weight of the falling masonry. The temple of Judges Milton does indeed call a theatre, perhaps to signal to his readers how different was the poem they were reading from the sexy, clever and heartless plays currently being performed in Restoration theatres. Imagine if you were watching a satirical comedy by William Wycherly, with its indecent talk of oranges and back entrances, when Samson came to do his business. Fortunately for the reader who is not in sympathy with such violent religious terrorism, there is a good deal more going on in the depths of the poem. Just as in *Paradise Lost*, there is a kind of countermovement that calls into question all this destructive energy. His original in Judges 13–16, the biblical Samson, reworked in the New Testament letter to the Hebrews as a hero of faith, acts with God's approval. Milton's Samson is different. He tunes into various impulses that he imagines to be God-driven, and finally convinces himself, but not necessarily the reader. As Gordon Campbell puts it, he is 'a Restoration nonconformist struggling to discern a pattern of divine intervention in his life'.[4]

To what extent does Milton construct Samson as a version of himself? In his first *Defensio*, chiding Salmasius for quoting Aeschylus's *Supplices* without regard to context, he had written:

> We should consider not so much what the poet says as who in the poem says it. Various figures appear, some good, some bad, some wise, some foolish, each speaking not the poet's opinions but what is appropriate for each person (*YP* IV.1 459).

In the *Apology* he had written 'The author is ever distinguisht from the person he introduces' (*YP* I 880). But he also says in the *Pro Se Defensio* that 'it is the custom of poets to place their own opinions in the mouths of their great characters' (*YP* IV.2 446). In this case some kind of overlap is obvious. Milton's fascination with Samson and his hair goes back at least to *Areopagitica* in which England, with that curious confusion of genders mentioned in the previous chapter, is 'a noble and puissant Nation rousing herself like a strong man after sleep and shaking her invincible locks' (*YP* II 558). Now the defeated republicans, Milton included, are subject to renewed self-scrutiny in the same figure, a faded hero, and blind.

As a young man Milton was, like Samson, set aside by his father to be a man of God. He had not gone into the church, but poetry he thought of as a divine vocation, and he imagined himself to be inspired by the Holy Spirit. He had fallen in love with a Royalist girl (not quite a Philistine, but close) in the months before the outbreak of war. And married again. And again. Broken in health and 'blind, dishearten'd, sham'd, dishonour'd, quell'd' (*SA* 563), he was assaulted, led bound, derided by his foes, imprisoned. Milton's auburn hair, of which he had been quietly proud, becomes

> redundant locks
> Robustious to no purpose clustring down,

> Vain monument of strength; till length of years
> And sedentary numbness craze my limbs
> To a contemptible old age obscure. (568-72)

Milton had known his father live on into his eighties, and 'without the least trouble imaginable' (as Phillips tells us). The idea of old age as 'contemptible' reflects a gratuitous moment of self-pity – and does not apply to the poem's Manoa.

Unlike Samson, at least on the face of it, Milton doggedly refused to doubt God's Providence. Yet the Old Testament God, Samson's, is often absent, or deserts his servants. Had Milton's life been a waste? Are these his own doubts allowed to find form in the guise of Samson's complaints? Which way would the story turn?

The Samson of Judges is quite a different figure from Milton's. He is a folkloric, superhuman savage, almost a berserker from an Icelandic saga. He is not a poet of the feelings. Milton's rewriting turns him into just that, an eloquent thinker, capable of self-analysis, emotionally appealing in his need to castigate himself for his folly. Blindness is mentioned only briefly in Judges. In Milton's poem blindness is a torment, fully articulated in Samson's moving opening soliloquy, with its far-reaching experiments in metre and line-length.

> O dark, dark, dark, amid the blaze of noon,
> Irrecoverably dark, total Eclipse
> Without all hope of day!
> O first created Beam, and thou great Word,
> Let there be light, and light was over all;
> Why am I thus bereav'd thy prime decree?
> The Sun to me is dark
> And silent as the Moon,
> When she deserts the night
> Hid in her vacant interlunar cave.
> Since light so necessary is to life,
> And almost life itself, if it be true
> That light is in the Soul,
> She all in every part; why was the sight
> To such a tender ball as th' eye confin'd? (80-94)

Samson's father, Manoa, is perhaps a voice of good sense, reminding his son, with a touch of Milton's own self-deprecating humour, of the mistakes he has made:

> I cannot praise thy Marriage choices, Son,
> Rather approv'd them not; but thou didst plead
> Divine impulsion. (420-22)

Manoa asserts all the conventional values (he must be a little like Milton's own father) and thus allows the poem, and Samson, to depart from them clearly and with good reason.

At the centre of the poem is the encounter between Samson and Dalila. Biographers, hungry for insight into Milton's marriages, want to read Milton's intimate feelings for women into Samson's self-reproach: like Adam, though with very different effects, Samson sees himself as a slave of passion.

> This base degree to which I now am fall'n,
> These rags, this grinding, is not yet so base
> As was my former servitude, ignoble,
> Unmanly, ignominious, infamous,
> True slavery

and he imagines a spiritual

> blindness worse than this,
> That saw not how degenerately I serv'd. (414-19)

But the situation is dramatized in ways distant from any situations Milton had known. It is not clear quite why Dalila comes to Samson, though ostensibly it is for a reconciliation, and a newly sensual life. She offers to have him released from prison and to nurse him at home, offering renewed sensual pleasures.

> Life yet hath many solaces, enjoyed
> Where other senses want not their delights. (915-16)

The meeting provides a way into the centre of Samson's psyche, into what has been keeping him sane, or driving him close to madness, all these years. He is portrayed as a man who likes women, and who suffers for that – but who somehow, bizarrely, remains chaste. Milton changes the biblical account by making the woman of Timna and then Dalila into Samson's wives, not whores or concubines. He eliminates entirely the episode in the Bible about Samson and a harlot in Gaza (Judges 16:1-3). He thus develops the emotional centre of the play, in the same way he did in *Paradise Lost*, into a kind of bourgeois domestic drama, and he also allows that new centre to be as potentially destructive as had been his own first marriage. He exploits the sexual intensity of marriage and the feeling of intimate betrayal. Samson describes his decision to marry beyond his tribe, especially important for a Judge and a Nazarite, someone consecrated to the service of his (nationalistic) god, as obeying an 'intimate impulse' (223) – a phrase in which both words have sexual implications. Above all he invents a revealing moment, near the end of the interview and when Dalila has tried everything else, in which she offers to touch him, and Samson's reaction is immediate and hostile:

> *Dalila*: Let me approach at least and touch thy hand.
> *Samson*: Not for thy life, lest fierce remembrance wake
> My sudden rage to tear thee joint by joint.
> At distance I forgive thee, go with that. (951-54)

The moment recalls Dalila's first coming onto the scene: the chorus announce her arrival, and Samson says 'My wife, my Traitress, let her not come near me' (725). In each case the possibility of being touched (in both senses) stings him into remembering the good times with his woman, and into the knowledge he would wreak a terrible revenge for the betrayal if he could, or if he lost control of his emotions. All this is Milton's invention: he makes it seem that the snare of 'fair fallacious looks, venereal trains' has made a public fool of him – 'turned me out ridiculous' like a shorn sheep (539). He shouts 'Out, out, *Hyaena*', and he (Samson, not Milton) likens her wonted arts to 'every woman false like thee' (749). At the end of the interview, the chorus call her 'a manifest serpent by her sting' (997), both phrases recalling Adam's denunciation of Eve.

Dalila is not a portrait of Mary Powell, but the link with the language of the divorce tracts has led some readers to think that the poem, or these parts of it, may have been written a long time before it was published. Milton there speaks of marriage as 'a drooping and disconsolate household captivitie, without refuge or redemption' (*YP* II 235). Remembering this, Samson manages to refuse the offer of renewal. His words recall *Comus*, oddly enough.

> Thy fair enchanted cup, and warbling charms
> No more on me have power, their force is null'd,
> So much of adder's wisdom I have learn'd
> To fence my ear against thy sorceries. (*Comus* 934-37)

Milton had also used the cup metaphor in *Apology*. But in *Samson* the cup has been drunk before, Samson has fallen, and he must now resist: the resistance helps to revive his strength.

The next encounter, with Harapha, has also been identified with Milton's duel with Salmasius. Indeed Milton himself says he met Salmasius 'in single combat… and bore off the spoils of honor' (*YP* IV.1 555-56). Harapha, a bizarre Philistinian giant whom Milton invented, is both the traditional cowardly *miles gloriosus*, and an embodiment of what the biblical Samson of Judges had himself been, a figure of legend or saga from a different, distant world, a bit like the Hercules of Greek myth. He is also an embodiment of Royalists denouncing Puritans before and after the Restoration for rebellion, while Samson represents armed resistance. The parallel makes a certain sense, with Milton as a kind of pamphleteering prize-fighter. Except – and it is a major exception – Samson allows that his current 'evils I deserve and more,/ Acknowledge them from God inflicted on me' (1168-69). Milton never acceded to the charges his blindness was inflicted by God. Nonetheless, Samson's inner confidence revives. Invited to the feast, he refuses: 'Can they think me so broken, so debas'd… that my mind ever/ Will condescend to such absurd commands?' (1335-37) The moment recalls Milton's refusal to write for the court of Charles II. He would never, his wife said, choose to write against his conscience.[5]

The conclusion of the poem begins to develop as soon as Samson feels those mysterious 'rouzing motions' (1382) and, unlike Milton, suddenly changes his mind: he will after all go along with the messenger to the Dagon festival, and senses that something extraordinary is about to happen. For all that some readers want to see in those words the direct intervention of God, we should be clear that God is not mentioned at this point. And these rousing motions recall the ones that earlier led Samson into the clutches of his wives, whether that 'intimate impulse' (223) that made him marry the woman of Timna, or the 'divine impulsion' mentioned by Samson's father Manoa with disapproval (422). Too kind to say so directly, Manoa clearly doesn't think much of his son's pleading of 'divine impulsion' since it led directly to Samson's captivity and the Philistine triumph. The irony (in a Greek tragedy) is that this is what allows Samson into the enemy camp and puts him in a position to wreak the destruction with which the play concludes.

The concluding scene is the crisis where interpretation must focus. From one point of view Samson's end is suicide. As John Donne had said, those who, like St Augustine, wish to protect both 'Samson's honour and his own conscience' have to explain how it is that Judges has him die with these words on his lips: 'Let me lose my life with the Philistines'.[6] Yet Milton appears cunningly to challenge this view. He omits the words from Judges that Donne quotes, and uses the terms of Greek tragedy to protect Samson: the Messenger says he 'inevitably/ Pulled down the same destruction on himself' and the chorus of loyal Israelites comment:

> Among thy slain self-kill'd
> Not willingly, but tangl'd in the fold
> Of dire necessity. (1664-66)

In the 'Argument' prefixed to the beginning of the poem, Milton specifies that his messenger relates what Samson did to the Philistines, and *by accident* to himself.

Even if Samson does not commit the sin of suicide, and even if Milton's portrait of Samson is broadly sympathetic, even if it is psychologically profound as it probes the possibilities for a maimed and beaten man to discover a way towards regeneration, it is still plausible that Milton was troubled by Samson's deed, as troubled as he so clearly was by civil war and self-serving politicians by the time he wrote *Paradise Lost*. Milton had written earlier that 'no man can know at all times [the spirit] to be in himself'[7] and there is no obvious reason why the situation should be different for Samson. The messenger who recounts the destructive event calls it a 'horrid spectacle' (1542). Even Manoa, Samson's father, says

> O lastly overstrong against thyself!
> A dreadful way thou took'st to thy revenge. (1590-91)

Milton and his fit audience knew, after all, that Samson's act did not in fact lead to the liberation of his people. Philistine rule simply continued.

One revealing sign of how he felt about all those slaughtered Philistines is that Milton changes the account of the destruction in Judges. There both Lords and people are killed, but in Milton's account, the building collapses on 'Lords, Ladies, Captains, Councellors, or Priests' (1653), but 'The vulgar only scap'd who stood without' (1659). The qualification shows that Milton was relaxed about the destruction of the ruling class, but he saves the innocent 'vulgar'. He may have been no sentimental democrat, as we have seen, and the chorus sings of the 'ingrateful multitude', but still, we would not want them all wiped out. Whether to protect his own or his readers' sensibilities, Milton so arranges it.

Milton wrote two poems on what we would nowadays call terrorism. One is the Gunpowder Plot poem, the other is *Samson*. The issue of Samson as terrorist has been much in the news of late, for obvious reasons. He has in common with the others, both the Catholic conspirators around Guy Fawkes and our Islamist contemporaries of 11 September 2001 or 7 July 2005 that he acts from religious motives, that his act would or does kill a number of innocents, and that he is himself killed. Walter Benjamin, the great German critic, said that 'There is no work of civilization that is not also a monument to barbarism'. He was thinking of the trophies brought home in Roman triumphs, or perhaps the Louvre, or the British Museum. But the phrase applies well to *Samson Agonistes*. It is a great poem, a work of civilization, perhaps because it is also a moment of barbarism. Whatever Milton himself thought (we cannot know), we can ourselves see how desperate Samson becomes, sympathize with his predicament, and yet still find his act repellent. It is, after all, not a tract but a tragedy.

Nonetheless, it seems that 'the demons of self-hatred and uncertainty have been purged'. The poem ends with two perfect classical tropes. One is the marvellous image of the 'evening dragon' to which the semichorus compares Samson (1692), attacking 'tame villatic fowl', but which is then rapidly transmuted into that of the mythical Phoenix, 'that self-begotten bird', which is consumed in the fire only to be reborn, 'then vigorous most when most unactive deem'd' (1704-45). This is a recurring idea in Milton, most famously at the end of Sonnet xix: 'They also serve who only stand and wait'.

The other classical trope is one of the elements of the poem that make it perhaps as near perfect a Greek tragedy as ever written. For the poem ends with a serious gesture towards reconciliation. After all this destructive turmoil, especially that reported by the Messenger as the temple crumbles and so many die, Manoa first comments that 'Nothing is here for tears' (1721), and then the last lines of the poem recall us to ourselves, or to our ideal selves. A sonnet by the chorus brings the poem to an end with the memorable

> His [God's] servants he with new acquist
> Of true experience from this great event
> With peace and consolation hath dismissed,
> And calm of mind, all passion spent.

Samson's excess of passion has left the audience with 'just measure', if we recur to the language of Milton's own Prologue, reiterating the Aristotelian theory of catharsis:

> Tragedy... [was] said by Aristotle to be of a power by raising pity and
> fear, or terror, to purge the mind of those and such like passions, that
> is to temper and reduce them to just measure with a kind of delight,
> stirred up by reading or seeing those passions well imitated.

Stirred up by passion – and then spent. The metaphors are both sexual and medical for the effects of tragedy on the reader, but the most important idea is that seeing passion 'well imitated' produces delight. The paradox is inherent in Aristotle's theory, and in Milton's poem.

23

Paradise Regained

Though Satan is one of the two main characters in *Paradise Regained*, the other opem published with *Samson Agonistes*, the poem is very different from *Paradise Lost*, and is not in any respects a sequel. The other main character is the Jesus of the synoptic gospels in the New Testament. Milton had not written a poem with Christ as its central theme for forty years. But now he had gained a new confidence. At the beginning he, or his narrator, prays for inspiration not to some Heavenly Muse but directly to the Holy Spirit, the same spirit that guides Jesus into the desert. That is not the only overlap of Milton with Christ. His Jesus, who is never actually called Christ in the poem, embodies everything Milton believed to be good, and once again Milton is tucked away within the main character.

> When I was a child, no childish play
> To me was pleasing, all my mind was set
> Serious to learn and know, and thence to do
> What might be public good. (I 201-4)

In the *imitatio Christi* tradition that is so important within Christianity, and that this poem takes up and extends, one tries to be like Christ. But Milton inverts the relation: he describes Christ's life as *mutatis mutandis* an idealized version of his own. Perhaps Milton made a mistake or two, to be sure, but he never, in his own view, committed what might be called, strictly speaking, a sin.

The subject of the poem is not the crucifixion, where most orthodox Christians would have focused their version of what matters in the New Testament. Milton no doubt took for granted that this was the important moment, as the end of *Paradise Lost* shows. But it did not interest him aesthetically, and perhaps he shared some of the puritan suspicion of the iconic representation of the crucifixion. No, the focus of *Paradise Regained* is on the desert scenes, which occur in all three synoptic gospels, but not in John, and in Mark only in very brief form. Matthew and Luke tell the 'full' story, but they differ. Milton chose to follow Luke's version, at least for the order of the three temptations. Matthew makes the kingdoms' temptation come last, but Luke's climax, more dramatically, takes place on the pinnacle of the temple.

So the main subject, as of many of Milton's poems, is temptation, through a long extended verbal battle with Satan. But temptation to what? The best quick answer perhaps would be: to ill-considered action. This man, so Satan thinks, will want to liberate his country from the heathen empire, just as Milton had helped to throw over the yoke of monarchy and episcopacy. But he rejects the temptation to the Good Old Cause in favour of submission, or rather in learning rule over the self. Now is not the time for uprisings (like the Fifth Monarchists, savagely repressed in 1661). All in God's good time. He sees the massed troops

> In coats of mail and military pride;
> In mail their horses clad, yet fleet and strong,
> Prancing their riders bore, the flower and choice
> Of many provinces. (III 312-15)

Milton might have been impressed by such shows in the early years of Cromwell's rise to power, but not Jesus now.

What is really extraordinary about this poem is that Milton puts the focus where none of the gospels do, on Christ's inner being, and on his humanity. He is a little like a young knight of romance who meets his first test in the wilderness before being recognized as a true champion. But here, going into the desert is equivalent to going into the self (III 190-95). Mary's son 'with holiest Meditations fed,/Into himself descended' (II 109-11). The threats are external, perhaps, but his manner of resisting them is entirely inner, indeed depends upon his sense of himself. Jesus discovers this inner self in the course of the poem, because of Satan's temptations. Satan presents clever parodies of his possible nature/mission, thus inadvertently teaching him the true one. The tentative tone of his first meditation, 'O what a multitude of thoughts at once/ Within me swarm' (I 197-293), shows he has only two sources of knowledge, what his mother Mary has told him, and the prophecies in scripture (what was to become the Old Testament). He also expects guidance from the Spirit. In a sense Satan is a trickster-teacher, from whom the hero learns who he is, even if neither participant understands the process fully. Jesus himself becomes a special version of Everyman. Certainly it is his humanity, not his divinity, which is emphasized. God calls him a 'perfect Man, by merit call'd my Son' (I 166) – whatever that means. His divine nature becomes an issue only in the final scene, and there the event is enigmatic.

The drama, then, in so far as *Paradise Regained* has any drama, is mostly internal, and such action as the poem represents is psychological. The reader is driven to expect action of a more conventional kind and is constantly disappointed, frustrated, perplexed – like Satan, who asks 'thinkst thou to regain/ Thy right by sitting still or thus retiring?' (III 163-64). It all leads finally to Satan's wonderfully exasperated cry, 'What dost thou in this world?' (IV 372)[1] Satan is a faded character now, a Worldly Wiseman like a character in Bunyan rather than an epic hero or ruined archangel. Jesus himself has also been seen as an unsatisfactory hero, uncertain of who he is or what he is to do. And the temptations are not tempting, especially given Christ's nature.

These criticisms can be answered, although they retain some force. The point is that the poem is a kind of philosophical tussle, a bit like a traditional Jewish disputation. The key question is about the nature of Christ: it is posed within the poem, both in the 'holy meditations', and more especially by Satan – and answered only indirectly. Both Son and Satan are ignorant of his identity as 'first-begotten Son' until informed ambiguously by the descent of a dove at the opening of the poem. Satan then asks what it means to be a 'Son of God'. He well says that 'All men are sons of God' (IV 520). We need to remember Milton's Arianism, which means the Son is a separate, created being, not simply a manifestation of the Godhead; he is radically inferior to the Father, and so mutable (as the Incarnation shows); he remains good by his own free will. He has no memory of his earlier status (as the Son in *Paradise Lost*). He has to discover himself.

The second temptation is the longest and most revealing. It begins with the banquet or feast scene (II 320), obviously following from the first stones-to-bread temptation but going much further. Belial characteristically suggests that he might tempt Jesus with sex: 'Set women in his eye'. Satan rejects the idea, but nonetheless the banquet is served by lovely nymphs and even 'Tall stripling youths rich clad, of fairer hew/ Than Ganymed or Hylas' (II 352-3). In his youthful Latin poem, Elegy VII, about his encounter with Cupid, Milton imagined the god as looking like the same pair of comely young men from Greek amd Roman myth (21–24), though he is made to fall for a young Venus-like girl in the poem. Unlike the young Milton (who had already repudiated the *Elegy* even as he published it in 1645), Jesus is unmoved. Nonetheless, as the temptation continues, it is splendidly ambivalent and recalls *Paradise Lost*: Satan assumes the Son must want an earthly throne, or at least the power to deliver Israel from heathen servitude, just as he had tempted Eve with the kind of power that suited her need – a desire for equality with Adam.

In this part of the poem Milton does not make it easy to like his hero. He seems aloof, cold, inflexible. At one point he reiterates what had long been Milton's opinion about the popular uprising he had lived through, views he had expressed before in *Eikonoklastes*, where he called the people 'a credulous and hapless herd, begott'n to servility' (*YP* III 601). Jesus says:

> For what is glory but the blaze of fame,
> The peoples praise, if always praise unmixt?
> And what the people but a herd confus'd,
> A miscellaneous rabble, who extol
> Things vulgar, & well weigh'd, scarce worth the praise,
> They praise and they admire they know not what;
> And know not whom, but as one leads the other;
> And what delight to be by such extoll'd,
> To live upon thir tongues and be thir talk,
> Of whom to be disprais'd were no small praise? (III 47-56)

Granted that the context makes these words a reply to Satan, the words are chilling not because of their undemocratic spirit but because of the unflinching sense of superiority. There was something heroic when Abdiel took the position of the 'one just man' defying Satan and all his armies in *Paradise Lost*. Here there is merely wounded arrogance.

Many readers feel that Satan is but a pale copy of the wonderfully eloquent character in *Paradise Lost*. But in this part of the poem, stung by Jesus's tone, he bursts back into the fully complex figure of the earlier poem. When the Son resists his offer of temporal power by making light of 'glory', Satan makes a splendid short speech about how glory is after all what God the Father seeks, and indeed is the main reason he made the world:

> Think not so slight of glory; therein least
> Resembling thy great Father: he seeks glory,
> And for his glory all things made, all things
> Orders and governs, nor content in Heaven
> By all his Angels glorifi'd, he requires
> Glory from men, from all men good or bad,
> Wise or unwise, no differences, no exemption;
> Above all Sacrifice, or hallow'd gift
> Glory he requires, and glory he receives... (III 111-17)

Try reading the speech aloud and giving increasingly sarcastic emphasis to the word 'glory' each time. Not only is the Son impermeable, however, but he even replies 'fervently' to this appeal, reminding Satan inadvertently that he had himself lost all for his own desire of glory.

Nonetheless he presses on, and in the same heroic and despairing mode of the earlier poem. Warned of his own future destruction, he says to himself ('inly rackt'):

> Let that come when it comes; all hope is lost
> Of my reception into grace; what worse?
> For where no hope is left, is left no fear;
> If there be worse, the expectation more
> Of worse torments me then the feeling can.
> I would be at the worst; worst is my Port,
> My harbour and my ultimate repose,
> The end I would attain, my final good.
> My error was my error, and my crime
> My crime; whatever for itself condemn'd,
> And will alike be punish'd; whether thou
> Raign or raign not; though to that gentle brow
> Willingly I could fly... (III 204-16)

The desperate echo of Edgar in *King Lear* ('Who is't can say I am at the worst?' IV I.27), and of *Macbeth* (as he decides to return to the weird sisters: 'for now I am bent to know,/ By the worst means, the worst' III IV.136-37) is one of many signs in the great poems that Milton can deploy Shakespearean allusions as he pleases. He had absorbed Shakespeare early and can use him late. But above all Milton here is echoing himself, one of the greatest of the speeches he had given the Satan of *Paradise Lost*. On Mt Niphates, as he arrives for the first time on Earth, Satan reflects on his condition with searing honesty and realizes he cannot repent: 'Myself am Hell', he sees, and

> The lower still I fall, onely Supream
> In miserie; such joy Ambition findes.
> But say I could repent and could obtaine
> By Act of Grace my former state; how soon
> Would hight recall high thoughts, how soon unsay
> What feign'd submission swore: ease would recant
> Vows made in pain, as violent and void.
> For never can true reconcilement grow
> Where wounds of deadly hate have peirc'd so deep. (PL IV 91-99)

The speech concludes with the famous cry:

> So farewel Hope, and with Hope farewel Fear,
> Farewel Remorse: all Good to me is lost;
> Evil be thou my Good.

This new Satan remembers it, and sees just as clearly his new situation, closer to the end as it is. Even so, he is tempted, and it is a remarkable moment, to beg forgiveness, seeing that 'gentle brow'. But soon he accepts it is too late, as before. He must drive himself onwards, not from hope, nor even from despair, but now from a desire finally to understand his adversary. Knowing he cannot succeed, he goes through the motions of the tempter, and it is that divided sense of his need and his hopelessness that makes the character still tragically appealing. Satan goes on to offer Jesus the rule of the Roman empire, and finally the wisdom of Athens (*PR* IV 213-365).

The climax of this central 'kingdoms' temptation is a puzzle for readers sympathetic to Milton, since the Son here appears to reject, eloquently, what Milton had loved and reworked all his life long: the learning that is the main gift of the Greco-Roman world to the modern, via the Renaissance. For the Son, the most difficult temptation to resist, because it is closest to his own temperament, is to be the Roman Stoic's

> virtuous man,
> Wise, perfect in himself, and all possessing
> Equal to God.

This ideal had appealed to the young Milton, and so the Son is especially harsh on the Stoics: 'their tedious talk is but vain boast,/ Or subtle shifts conviction to evade.' But the most powerful temptation of all is the beauty of Greek and Latin literature. The Son rejects all these in favour of the biblical psalms:

> Remove their swelling Epithetes thick laid
> As varnish on a Harlot's cheek, the rest,
> Thin sown with aught of profit or delight,
> Will far be found unworthy to compare
> With Sion's songs, to all true tastes excelling,
> Where God is prais'd aright, and Godlike men. (IV 343-48)

He seems to think, as had many in the early church, and as many still thought in the Renaissance, that the arts of Greece were imitated from Hebrew.

Milton had indeed turned more and more to the rigours and dignified simplicities of the Old Testament. By now this world was certainly what he valued highest aesthetically. During the century, a Hebraizing movement had grown within Protestantism. In an extreme case, the followers of John Traske were imprisoned in 1618 for 'Judaizing'. On their release, they went to Amsterdam and joined the synagogue. Milton did not go this far, but he did read the Hebrew Bible, we are told, every morning. He may even have been involved, as we saw earlier, in negotiations with Rabbi Menasseh ben Israel for the official readmission of the Jews to London (unofficially they had been present for many years). Pepys went to the newly established synagogue more than once to hear the ancient chants. Perhaps Milton too went out from the privacy of his study to hear the living language he had learned only in books. And in the poem, he imagined himself back into the consciousness of a young man who had grown up with it in his ears.

> Or if I would delight my private hours
> With Music or with Poem, where so soon
> As in our native Language can I find
> That solace? All our Law and Story strew'd
> With Hymns, our Psalms with artful terms inscrib'd,
> Our Hebrew Songs and Harps in Babylon,
> That pleas'd so well our Victors ear, declare
> That rather Greece from us these Arts deriv'd;
> Ill imitated, while they loudest sing
> The vices of thir Deities, and thir own
> In Fable, Hymn, or Song, so personating
> Thir Gods ridiculous, and themselves past shame. (IV 331-42)

He alludes in particular to Psalm 137: 'By the rivers of Babylon, there we sat down, yea, we wept, when we remembered Sion.' Such beauties pleased the victor's ear, and so 'declare/ That Greece from us these Arts derive'.

It is not certain Milton fully believed such ideas as historical fact: he does have his Jesus say so, though only with that rather tentative verb 'declare'. There are two voices in that passage. One is the quiet acceptance of the beauty of Hebrew. The other is an anxious, angry repudiation of much of what Milton had spent his life enjoying, admiring – and imitating. It is a kind of sad purge.

The final rejection of classical learning sounds as if it comes not from a young man's growing consciousness but from an older man who could now transcend even that greatest of temptations. We who love books can all hear his wise words and wince.

> However many books
> Wise men have said are wearisom; who reads
> Incessantly, and to his reading brings not
> A spirit and judgment equal or superior
> (And what he brings, what needs he elsewhere seek)
> Uncertain and unsettl'd still remains,
> Deep verst in books and shallow in himself,
> Crude or intoxicate, collecting toys,
> And trifles for choice matters, worth a spunge;
> As Children gathering pebles on the shore (IV 321-30).

'Worth a sponge', that is, fit to be erased from the child's schoolroom slate. All those years of learning and teaching have come to this. In so far as he is thinking generally, or about himself, Milton is here somewhat ungrateful to the languages and education that had given him his pre-eminence in the world of European culture, not to mention his job under Cromwell. But we have seen the beginnings of this attitude before, when he is arguing, in *The Ready and Easy Way*, against paying ministers of the church and assessing how much they need to buy books. So if, as some more sympathetic readers have proposed, he is thinking of the needs of a country priest, the contemptuous dismissal of books as 'pebles on the shore' may appear less shocking.[2] Perhaps.

The final confrontation of Jesus and Satan on the pinnacle of the temple, the third temptation, uses two complicated epic similes, one about the struggle of Antaeus with Hercules, the other about the Theban monster, the Sphinx. The two allusions restore to the poem, strangely enough, the classical learning just banished by the Son — but now for a special purpose. Satan whisks Jesus up to the top of the pinnacle ('thy Father's house') and expects him either to fall, or to reveal his divine nature by magical intervention. Instead he stands, and it is Satan who falls, like Antaeus and the Sphinx. Greek myth may still help us understand the enemy. Angels then carry Jesus off to a banquet that makes up for the one he had rejected from Satan. At the end of the poem, there is, as in all Milton's great endings, a quiet simplicity. Not to his Father's house, where Satan frantically had tried to place him, but now our Saviour meek, 'unobserv'd/ Home to his mother's house private returned'.

Perhaps because of their quiet unobtrusiveness, these words are as memorable as any of Milton's endings. They evoke a house without a father, only a quietly adoring mother. Is that suggestive of what Milton's own fantasy life might have been like? We hear so little about Milton's own mother. And not nearly enough about his wives. Never mind. It is as poetry that the words have their appeal. The enjambement gives the words 'unobserved' and 'Home' especial prominence. And the subtle placing of the adjective 'private' as if it were an adverb brings to life a whole imaginary Milton, such as he might have projected for himself if he had not lived in such interesting times.

24

Final Accomplishment

We do not know how Milton's contemporaries read these last poems. But he could not stay away from controversy for long. Suspicion of Charles's Catholic sympathies was rife in the land. 'No Popery' was the cry from pulpits and chapbook. When Charles issued an apparently wise Declaration of Indulgence in March 1672, calling for freedom of worship for all dissenters from the Anglican Church, 'few people were so blind', as Bishop Gilbert Burnet observed, 'as not to see what was aimed at'. The Antichrist was at work again. The English Church would be annexed to the Church of Rome. Within a year, Charles had been obliged to sign into law the Test Act requiring all office-holders to take the oath of Allegiance, receive the Anglican sacrament and renounce the pernicious doctrine of transubstantiation. No, the bread did not really become the body of Christ, nor the wine his blood.

Milton was drawn into the controversy because of two people he knew well. One was Samuel Parker, who had earlier been a pupil but had since published two tracts from a strongly Anglican slant denouncing dissenters and claiming the absolute authority of the magistrates in religious matters. He now wrote a new tract attacking the Declaration of Indulgence. To these Andrew Marvell replied in the satirical *The Rehearsal Transposed,* which includes a witty characterization of Parker under the name Bayes, and supports liberty of conscience and the king's policy of indulgence. Dissenters are forced to take up their schismatic position by the persecution of the bishops. Going back to the earlier reign, Marvell blames the hard line of Laud and his advisers for the revolution against Charles I. Don't let it happen again. He follows this with the ringing phrase that the Good Old Cause 'was too good to have been fought for'.

Parker and his supporters, a *Posse Archidiaconatus* as Marvell mockingly called them, replied, charging that he 'had all this out of the Answerer of *Salmasius*', that is, that he is borrowing everything from Milton, whether the *Defensio* or *Areopagitica* or other treatises: all lead to 'the Rebellion and

Murther of the King'. Another reply, probably by Samuel Butler,[1] brings
Paradise Lost into the fray. Referring to the invocations to the Heavenly Muse,
especially the appeal 'Hail Holy Light' in Book III, he claims the poem relies
on inspiration, just like the 'enthusiasm' of these radical dissenters. Milton is
'a *Schismatick* in Poetry… *nonconformable* in point of rhyme'. The tract goes
on showing great familiarity with Milton's work: 'This doctrine of *killing
Kings*… is nothing but *Iconoclastes* drawn in little, and *Defensio Populi Anglicani*
in Miniature'. Butler's admiration shows clearly through the hostility: he was,
after all, the author of a mock-epic burlesque of 1664, *Hudibras*, written in
octosyllabic couplets. It ridiculed its buffoon of a Presbyterian hero, a kind
of Don Quixote manqué, and his squire Ralpho, an Independent. Butler
may have felt, perhaps rightly, that Milton's epic was an indirect reply to this
scurrilous attack on dissenting religion and its corrupt, unchivalrous and
'fanatick' representatives.

Marvell soon published a reply to Parker, extending his defense of
toleration, attacking the high church clergy as the main causes of the trouble,
and ending with a defense of Milton coupled with a denial of his role in
the quarrel. He claims, perhaps a little disingenuously, not to have seen
Milton for two years, and says he takes it ill that Parker should think him not
'competent to write such a simple book as that without assistance'. If Milton
had this read to him he would have been in two minds. On the one hand the
praise of Milton is warm and just, but on the other, Marvell attacks Parker
for laying his simple book to the charge of another 'without ever taking
care to inform your self better'. This was exactly the charge that Alexander
More and Pierre Du Moulin had made about Milton's *Defensio Secunda* and
its attack on *Clamor*. And Pierre Du Moulin had now acknowledged his
work again recently, and republished his satiric poem from *Clamor*: 'To the
beastly blackguard John Milton, Parricide and Advocate of Parricides'. He
also reminds his readers that More had supplied two witnesses who might
have revealed the true author. Du Moulin is ironically thankful Milton did
not follow suit, since in those days it would have brought him certain ruin.
What saved Du Moulin's life was Milton's pride. Milton 'could never be
brought to confess himself so grossly deceived' and 'preferred to have me safe
than himself ridiculous'. This is perhaps not far from the truth.

In the midst of all this rhetorical back and forth, another attack appeared,
Richard Leigh's *The Transposer Rehearsed* of 1673. He makes allegations about
the sexuality of Cromwell's two Latin clerks, Milton and Marvell. Marvell is
a gelding, Milton a stallion. Both are turned pure Italian, which in context
is an allegation about sexual promiscuity and perversion. The accusation is
one of sodomy, at least.[2] Probably few people actually believed this kind of
tabloid scandal-mongering, but it may have affected the reputation of both

men and neutralized their impact on the contemporary political landscape.

Milton himself now spoke up. *Of True Religion, Haeresie, Schism, Toleration, and What best means may be us'd against the growth of Popery* is Milton's last polemical tract and wears its content in its title. Though Milton nowhere refers directly to the current conflict, he makes plain that he takes a different line from Marvell, who had welcomed the Declaration of Indulgence and ignored the Catholic issue. He derides the very term Roman Catholic as a contradiction, as if the pope should say 'universal particular' or 'a Catholic Schismatic' (*YP* VIII 422). Popery, he claims is 'the only or the greatest Heresie'. It is committed to religious coercion because it relies not on scripture but on secular authority. It is mere idolatry. Protestantism, on the other hand, invites toleration through its commitment to *sola scriptura*, which encourages a dialogue among believers. The point of this polemic is that Milton wants to foster the Protestant nation for which he has worked all of his political life, but that nation is now defined more broadly along the latitudinarian lines of what was now known as 'comprehension': the Church of England should now 'comprehend' all sects except those egregious Catholics, the only true heretics.[3] Protestant sects are not made up of heretics, however various their views: these are all 'things indifferent' in Anglican terms, and have no implications for salvation. This doctrine allows the 'comprehension' of several of his own heterodoxies, including Anabaptism, Arianism and Arminianism.

There is an odd hesitation in the tract, and here we can see Milton's implicit awareness of the enormous consequences of the conflict. Private idolatry is not to be tolerated. Those who refuse the Test Act and thus confess their Catholicism should nonetheless not be punished with fines or corporal punishment. That would not accord with 'the Clemency of the Gospel'. Had he been writing in the 1640s, as A. N. Wilson puts it, 'he would have been less interested in the clemency of the Gospel'.[4] The solution now in 1673 is active argument, free inquiry, not coercion.

That fine solution did not work with the most important English Catholic of all. Parliament's Test Act was finally passed on 29 March, before Milton's treatise was published in May (it was licensed on 6 May). Within weeks the duke of York, heir to the throne, had resigned his commission as Lord High Admiral of the fleet rather than take the Anglican rite. In September he married Princess Mary of Modena, an Italian Catholic. The stage was set for the Exclusion crisis that would soon dominate English politics.

In the midst of all this, Milton prepared a new edition of his shorter poems, including those published together in 1645. This became necessarily a further political act even though it was still part of his efforts to earn money by seeing older material into print, some of it for the first time. He could not publish his republican sonnets to Cromwell, Vane or Fairfax, nor the one to Cyriack Skinner on his blindness. But he did publish several other sonnets, including 'On the Late Massacre in Piedmont' and the one to his late wife, 'Methought I saw my late espoused Saint'; the two psalm sequences (some of which call down God's vengeance on those who threaten the Lord's 'dear Saints'); and the Latin verse epistle which had accompanied the 1645 volume to the librarian at the Bodleian. He also dug out some very early poems such as 'On the Death of a Fair Infant Dying of a Cough' and 'At A Vacation Exercise'. The English part of the book ends with the translation of Psalm 88, of which the final lines also function, as Lewalski points out, as a poignant *envoi* for the volume as a whole:

> Lover and friend thou hast remov'd
> And sever'd from me far.
> They fly me now whom I have lov'd,
> And as in darkness are.

The volume concludes, somewhat strangely, with *Of Education*.

In the same surge of collecting and publishing earlier material Milton made copies of the letters of state he had written as Latin Secretary and offered them, together with some personal letters, to a bookseller. The resulting volume (*Epistolae Familiares*) has a preface by the bookseller, Brabazon Aylmer, explaining that he could not obtain permission to publish the official letters, only the private ones, but managed to obtain through a friend of Milton's (we do not know who) the seven orations Milton had written at Christ's College, Cambridge – and expects these droppings from the great poet's table now to be 'salable'. He did not include, though, that curious testament to the breadth of Milton's interests, the *Brief History of Muscovy*, which Milton also gave him, and which was not published till after his death. Some of the state letters were also published after his death, but in Amsterdam and Brussels, with a preface that distances the book from the hated politics of Cromwell: it claims that the main interest of the letters is their excellent Latin style. An inaccurate translation was corrected by Edward Phillips in 1694.

Milton did now publish one other curious item, the *Declaration, or Letters Patent*. This was actually a translation of a Latin text announcing the election of John Sobieski as King of Poland. Recently, Nicholas von Maltzahn has related this otherwise incomprehensible publication directly to the exclusion crisis: the way to stop the Catholic duke of York eventually becoming James II would be to imitate the Polish practice and elect the next king.[5] In this, his final work, religious violence has been exiled to the borders of Milton's wildly idealized

Poland with its reputation for religious tolerance, to be directed against the infidel Turks. But the inherent paradoxes of Milton's attitudes continue: he is extolling the virtues of one Catholic king to exclude the succession of another.

Fortunately for us all, in the same month as this odd pamphlet, June 1674, Milton also published the second edition of *Paradise Lost*. There, as Satan looks around him for the first time in Hell, he discovers the sublime cosmography that was so admired in the eighteenth century and so vilified by T. S. Eliot. There Satan sees a different Pole, and the contrast between the insignificance Milton's contemporary politics now has and the continuing power of the poetry is a measure of how far Milton's imagination could stretch: the narrator tells us Satan is

> In utter darkness...
> As far remov'd from God and light of Heav'n
> As from the center thrice to the utmost Pole.'.

A few lines later Satan, in one of his splendid speeches, is soon stressing God's 'utmost power' and his own

> unconquerable Will,
> And study of revenge, immortal hate,
> And courage never to submit or yield:
> ...To bow and sue for grace
> With suppliant knee, and deifie his power,
> Who from the terrour of this Arm so late
> Doubted his Empire, that were low indeed,
> That were an ignominy and shame beneath
> This downfall. (I 106-16)

It is hard to stop quoting Milton, especially his Satan, but beyond the obvious contrast between poem and *Declaration* there is an inherent connection: the distances are greater but the politics of Satan's struggle against what he regards as tyranny would not have been possible if Milton had not lived through its earthly variant.

For this new edition (*Ed II*), Milton decided to reappropriate the twelve book format of Virgil's epic. He divided the two longest books of the earlier ten-book format in half and merely added a few lines of transition. Yet the effect is quite different. The ten-book structure probably still suggested too much of Milton's original intention, recorded in the Trinity manuscript, to write a five-act tragedy (two books to an act, with the crisis in the fourth act), whereas the twelve-book structure subsumed the tragedy within the larger encyclopedic and redemptive possibilities of Virgilian epic. *Ed II* makes clear what was only implicit in the first edition (*Ed I*), that conversion, regeneration, the bringing of good from evil, are structural as well as doctrinal principles of *Paradise Lost*. The reorganization of the second edition is Milton's final illustration of this principle – as is the final shackling of Satan. Thus it is no longer, for example, the heroic and defeated Abdiel who spans the structural centre of the poem by book count (in Book V as lone resister, in Book VI as soldier in the War) but the larger action of the Son, first as warrior in Book VI and then as creator in Book VII.

If we summarize the plot of the poem as *Ed I* presents it, we can see the implications of the change. What we read as Book IX of *Paradise Lost* was originally Book 8, and thus the Fall of Man had its obvious and rightful place as the tragic *peripeteia*. Each of the first three acts moves toward anticipation of this crisis: in Book II Satan conceives the plan to subvert humankind and begins his journey to the new world; in Book IV he makes a preliminary attempt and the book ends with a face-off between Gabriel and Satan, the scales dangling enigmatically in God's sky; the third act, Books V and VI, contains the Rebellion and War, dramatic image of divine discord, and although it ends with Satan's defeat, we know this to be the immediate occasion for the revenge he is planning. By the end of the fourth act he has succeeded and can retire from the scene. Act Five, all of what is now the last three books, presented the consequences of his success: as that passage near the end of the poem puts it,

> so shall the World goe on,
> To good malignant, to bad men benigne,
> Under her own waight groaning. (XII 537-39)

Satan and his plot thus dominated the first edition. It is he who impels everything forward, right from the opening scenes in which he conceives a plan to colonize the newly created earth in revenge for the defeat he has suffered in heaven. The plot of *Paradise Lost* thus defined was what Milton was constructing from the time when he first conceived the idea of a tragedy, at some point in the late 1630s, according to the jottings in the Trinity manuscript, until *Ed I* was published in 1667. This is the version of the poem's *mythos* which makes it begin in Hell, so that Heaven appears as a parody of what the reader has already seen; which makes the War in Heaven precede the Creation, so that the Creation appears to be God's reaction to the depopulation of Heaven; and which makes Satan's success in the garden the cause of the Redemption. In sum, this is a plot that makes good and evil *balanced* opponents, and which shows God's goodness as required by Satan's badness.

The second edition changes this revenge tragedy more clearly into a classical epic. Yet since the shift of the second edition involved little more than renumbering and dividing the books of the poem, it is clear that the second plot emphasised by this new division was already present in the first edition. Milton's tinkering with the poem's external structure served merely to draw out in an explicit way what was already written into *Ed I*, the secret and mostly silent plot with which God and Milton had informed their creations, but which the power and dominance accorded, by their permissive wills, to Satan, had threatened to obscure. Good *emerges from* evil in the divine, benign scheme of things and in Milton's imitation and justification of that scheme.

It is true that none of the plans for a tragedy preserved in the Trinity manuscript bears much resemblance to the structure of the ten-book first edition. Nonetheless we recall that Edward Phillips tells us he saw the first ten lines of Satan's Niphates speech as the opening of a drama 'several Years before the Poem was begun', perhaps during the 1640s or early 1650s,[6] and this does suggest the idea of an Elizabethan revenge tragedy like *The Jew of Malta* and *Richard III*, which both open with soliloquies for the villain. And Milton still kept the essential idea of a plot which opens with powerful scenes for Satan, even when the epic scope allowed him to expand Satan's role, via the narrator, and set the scene in Hell. Thus the tragic figure of the lost archangel as well as the tragic five-act form persisted when Milton changed his mind and chose the epic genre.

The major changes in his perception and organization of the poem all occur in the second half and make more nearly accurate what the narrator says at the beginning of Book VII: 'Half yet remains unsung.' Three new pairs of books replace the two pairs that made up Acts Four and Five of *Ed I*. The first of these three pairs is the new Books VII and VIII, one long book in *Ed I*. The new arrangement reveals a previously buried or subordinate aspect of the poem, one which now begins to assert itself – the increasing focus on Adam and his progressive understanding. In *Ed II* one book is now devoted entirely to the magnificence of the creation, and then a further book to Adam's anxious questions about it, the astronomical speculations, and to his allied reflections upon his feelings for Eve (it was she who first posed the questions about the stars which Raphael answers). No longer only a preparation for the Fall, the dialogue with Raphael turns the otherwise mysterious and transcendent process of creation into something which has direct and decisive relevance, though problematic, to Adam's – and mankind's – situation. Indeed Adam has himself something to offer to this dialogue, his own account of the creation of

Eve. From this point of view, the dialogue that is Book VIII leads into Adam's assumption of the narrative duties and skills of Raphael, at least on a smaller scale, and so illustrates Raphael's hint that things on earth and in heaven may be 'Each to other like' (V 576).

The next new pair of books has a similar structure; the old climax of the Fall becomes now the first movement of a process which is compensated by the gradual repentance of Eve and Adam in Book X of *Ed II*. In that process Adam begins to realize the significance of the sentence passed on mankind by Christ, with its initially mysterious references to Eve's heel and the serpent's head. The repentance scene may now be seen more clearly to include within it the contrast with the unrepentant Satan's triumphant return to Hell. That return is no longer what it chiefly had been in *Ed I,* the beginning of Satan's power over earth, his successful colonization.

The final pair, also made out of one book in the original, may now be seen to turn about a similar pivot as the previous pair, and indeed as the whole poem now does: the break between Books XI and XII, newly established for *Ed II*, comes between the Flood and the Rainbow, or, as one of the new lines puts it, 'Betwixt the world destroy'd and world restor'd' (XII 3). Here too, Adam gradually moves toward a deeper understanding of his role in the larger scheme, and of the meaning of that scheme. So each of the new books created out of the second part of a long book in *Ed I* is devoted to Adam's education by an angel.

The twelve-book format, then, confirms and draws out what was present already in the poem. Yet there may be a further reason for the change – continued rivalry with Dryden. According to John Aubrey, Dryden 'went to him to have leave to putt his Paradise-lost into a Drama in Rhyme: Mr Milton received him civilly, & told him he would give him leave to tagge his Verses'. ('Tag' refers to the fashion of wearing ribbons with metal tags at the end to keep the stockings up.) A slightly more complete version of the story, clearly based on Aubrey, purports to give the actual words of Milton's reply:

> Well, Mr *Dryden*, says *Milton*, it seems you have a mind to *Tagg* my *Points*, and you have my Leave to *Tagg* '*em*, but some of 'em are so Awkward and Old Fashion'd that I think you had as good leave 'em as you found 'em.[7]

It is extraordinary that after the vehement defense of blank verse, directed in part at Dryden, Milton should accede so readily to a rhymed version. The story displays a kind of wry and tolerant humour, making the whole question one of fashion. But Dryden's visit may have provided the final impetus to republish the poem in a new Virgilian dress.

Dryden intended his play as an opera for the duke of York's bride, but since the match proved unpopular it was never produced. It was published in 1677 as *The State of Innocence*. Dryden acknowledges in the Preface that the original is 'undoubtedly one of the greatest, most noble, and most sublime *POEMS,* which either the Age or Nation has produc'd'. I suspect that Milton's accepting of Dryden's proposal had a lot to do with money, as a modern writer would find it hard to resist the Hollywood desire to turn his story into a film, even if he expects a travesty of his work. Whether Milton received any money directly is unknown, but he may have hoped that the opera would increase his sales. Indeed, Dryden's version went through nine editions before his death in 1700. It outsold Milton's original, at least until a beautiful and expensive folio edition of *Paradise Lost* was published for Jacob Tonson in 1688. It included illustrations for each of the twelve books, and even a short and typically inflated tribute – by Dryden.

One may gauge the distance between Milton and Dryden by a brief quotation. Milton's narrator, we saw, made explicit that no shame was attached to nakedness or sex in his Paradise. Dryden made the opposite decision, giving the discussion, and near-admission, of shame to Adam and Eve. They describe their erotic life in terms that approach the playful dialogues of Restoration comedy. When turned into direct speech, Eve's 'sweet reluctant amorous delay' (IV 311) becomes:

> Somewhat forbids me, which I cannot name,
> For ignorant of guilt, I fear not shame:
> But some restraining thought, I know not why,
> Tells me, you long should beg, I long deny.[8]

Milton's earlier plans for a drama on this subject were abandoned, but they would have certainly turned out nothing like this. Like Milton's Satan in the earliest version seen by Phillips, Dryden's opera opens with the singing Lucifer.

> These regions and this realm my wars have got;
> This mournful empire is the loser's lot:
> In liquid burnings or in dry to dwell,
> Is all the sad variety of hell. (I I.3-6)

The clunking rhythm is a gross violation of Milton's subtlety, though 'the sad variety of hell' is a memorable phrase. Dryden could be a much finer poet, but here one can see why Milton had, in his earlier belligerent mood, denounced rhyme.

The second edition of *Paradise Lost* in 1674 came with much more of a flourish than the first. It cost more, 3s, it had a frontispiece portrait (an engraving by William Dolle, based on the Faithorne portrait), and it was prefaced by two poems in its honour. One is in Latin by Samuel Barrow, the court physician but a friend of Milton's. He likes especially the War in Heaven, and dutifully recognizes Milton's superiority to Homer and Virgil. The other poem is by Andrew Marvell. It acknowledges the ancient tradition of praising rival or friendly poets. It begins by the rhetorical device of *concessio*, that is, confessing an anxiety that Milton would fall foul of the traps that awaited the writer of a Christian epic,

> That he would ruin (for I saw him strong)
> The sacred Truths to Fable and old Song.

The reference to Samson becomes explicit in the next lines:

> So Sampson groap'd the Temples Posts in spight
> The World o'rewhelming to revenge his sight.[9]

It shows that spite and revenge were available interpretations of his story at the time, interpretations which Milton managed both to include and to transcend in his own version, and in his life. Milton's blindness could have made him a Samson, but instead he is a Tiresias, the great prophet (43). Marvell also takes a swipe at Dryden, as 'some less skilful hand' who would try to 'ill imitate' Milton's poem and so seek fame. The phrase 'ill imitate' picks up the Son's condemnation of Greek imitations of Hebrew (as 'Fable, Hymn or Song') in *Paradise Regained* (IV 339). He ends by generously admitting his own love for rhyme, or what Milton had called 'tagging':

> I too transported by the Mode offend,
> And where I meant to Praise thee must Commend.
> Thy Verse created like thy Theme sublime,
> In Number, Weight, and Measure, needs not Rhime.

Praise of a fellow poet suits Marvell's talents perfectly, deeply read as he and Milton were in the Roman poets, or their Italian followers, who often celebrate each other and their friendships. The poem is one of his finest.

There was one other task that Milton set himself at this time: he took up and reworked the *De Doctrina Christiana* with a view to having it published. It opens with a kind of trumpet call to his readers, an epistle like those of Paul. 'John Milton, Englishman, To All the Churches of Christ and to All in any part of the world who profess the Christian Faith, Peace, Knowledge of the Truth, and Eternal Salvation in God the Father and in our Lord Jesus Christ.' But the heterodox contents may have dissuaded London printers, and it did not see the light until the nineteenth century. On Milton's death, it came into the possession of Daniel Skinner, a young man who had apparently been working as his amanuensis, and who had recopied the first 194 pages. He sent it along, with the state papers Aylmer had not been allowed to print to a Dutch publisher, Elsevier. On advice from a theologically alert friend and also under pressure from the English Secretary of State, Sir Joseph Williamson, about the 'treasonous' state letters, Elsevier returned most of the package to Skinner's father, who turned it all over to Williamson. Both bundles remained in the State Paper Office till 1823 when they were discovered by accident still in their original wrapping. *De Doctrina* was finally published two years later.

In July of 1674 Milton was having a bad fit of the gout. His wife cooked him a meal he enjoyed, and he commented: 'God have mercy Betty, I see thou wilt p'forme according to thy promise in providing mee such Dyshes as I think fitt whilst I live, and when I dye thou knowest that I have left thee all.' He was anticipating his death. His brother Christopher (perhaps already a Papist, rumour had it, as well as a successful lawyer) visited about 20 July, and found him in poor health. He said: 'Brother, the porcion due to me from mr. Powell, my former wives father, I leave to the unkind children I had by her but I have received noe part of it and my will and meaning is they shall have noe other benefit of my estate then the said porcion and what I have beside don for them, they having been very undutiful to me, and all the residue of my estate I leave to the disposal of Elizabeth my loving wife.' Milton expected his lawyer brother to return next time with the will to sign, after his summer in the country. The Powells had still not paid Milton the £1,000 dowry promised on his marriage to Mary, but they had indeed recovered their property, so leaving the 'porcion' to his daughters was not necessarily the empty or vindictive gesture it may seem. Both brothers will have expected that the will would force the Powells to pay up for their own kin. But Milton died on 9 or 10 November, before any will could be drawn up. A month longer and he would have been sixty-six.

Cyriack Skinner, Milton's long-time pupil and friend, author of the biography that was long called 'anonymous', describes Milton's death as if he were an eyewitness. It is reminiscent of the death of Socrates or of the 'virtuous men [who] pass mildly away' at the beginning of Donne's 'Valediction Forbidding Mourning'. 'Hee dy'd in a fit of the Gout, but with so little pain or Emotion, that the time of his expiring was not perceav'd by those in the room.'[10] He was buried in St Giles Cripplegate, where thirty years before he had interred his father. The little church, rebuilt, bombed and repaired, is still there, in the Barbican, surrounded by the commercial ugliness of modern London.

The daughters contested what Christopher and Elizabeth said about Milton's intentions, and the records of their testimony, and the replies, are vital evidence for the biographer. Much of it has been used in the previous pages, such as the testimony of the maid, Elizabeth Fisher, about the meal Betty cooked for him and which he connected with her expectations about the will, or the efforts of Milton's daughters to sell off his books to 'the Dunghill women'. The daughters were suspicious of their stepmother and uncle, who they thought were in cahoots. They prepared a set of questions for them at the hearing. They wanted to ascertain, for example, whether there was a conspiracy to have Milton's wife receive £1,000 and divide the rest among Christopher's children. In the event, Christopher seems to have admitted as much. They also wanted the witnesses to recall Milton's exact words at the time, and his state of mind and health, which accounts for the dramatic statements in the documents housed in the London Public Record Office. Was he calm or in a passion against 'some or one of his children by his former wife'? They also needed to prove their own good characters by the statements, and whether Anne's case in particular, 'lame and almost helpless', did not deserve some recognition.

Christopher's replies insisted that the daughters had not been present for several years, and that, as we have seen before, their absence was not because of their apprenticeships but because they were 'careless' of his blindness. We cannot tell how the court judged all this, though it is all, like most contested wills, fairly distasteful. In what looks like a classic compromise decision, and may have been an out-of-court settlement, it appears that Milton's wife should get two-thirds of the estate, about £600, with the other third going to the daughters, £100 each. Each of them soon signed releases to that effect, Mary and Anne (with her mark) on 22 February 1675, Deborah on 27 March, with her husband Abraham Clarke. Christopher also gave a bond to Milton's now successful brother-in-law, Richard Powell, probably to cover the payments to Milton's daughters, Powell's nieces. In her own will of 1678, Milton's difficult mother-in-law gave legacies to her granddaughters, Mary and Deborah. Poor Anne Milton had already died in childbirth.

It is not perhaps so surprising that Milton was buried near his father. What is a little odd is that he was buried in a church like this at all. For years he had not attended any church, and had indeed been a virulent opponent of the established Church of England. Probably the family had more to do with it than Milton's own wishes, even if he ever made them clear. His brother Christopher, whether he had in fact become a Catholic or not, would certainly have countenanced a burial in an established church, even one that had occasionally flirted with Dissent (a curate and a few Dissenting preachers had officiated), near their father.[11] Edward Phillips may have intervened even more decisively. He tells us proudly that his uncle received a 'very decent interment according to his Quality', and was 'attended from his House to the Church by several Gentlemen then in Town, his principal well-wishers and admirers'. This kind of ceremony might have jarred with a younger Milton, but perhaps in his age he might have acquiesced. Certainly it was what the nephew, eager to assert his own status within the new world of power, would have wanted – a distinguished uncle buried alongside his grandfather in a pleasant and official little church.

John Milton did not stay there. In the late 1780s Samuel Whitbread, the wealthy brewer, determined that a monument should be erected to him on the spot where he was buried, and had a bust sculpted to his orders. But where exactly was it to be placed? The structure of the church had been altered since the burial, and the marker lost. On Wednesday 4 August 1790, while the church was being renovated, some of the church members searched for and discovered the coffin. The next day, before it could be properly reburied, a few of the same churchmen, drunk on the great Whitbread product and having a high old time, cut open the coffin and discovered the bones. Hair, teeth, fingers, ribs and leg bones were offered to public view, with the sexton's approval, 'at first for 6d and afterwards for 3d. and 2d. each person', and were even sold as relics (supreme irony for the militant anti-Catholic) to souvenir hunters. One advertisement, reported in *The English Chronicle and Universal Evening Post*, offered to show to anyone who came to the place announced, 'within, *a hundred and four* real *teeth* of the famous Milton, vich the feller will make oath dat he took out of dat great poet's *mout* himself at Cripplegate'. Another, equally jokey, announced that an epidemic was now raging in the parish of St Giles Cripplegate, 'by the impudent opening of a coffin'.

Alongside the wit, there was general indignation in the press. William Cowper wrote a poem, of which the penultimate stanza reads:

> Ill fare the hands that heaved the stones
> Where Milton's ashes lay,
> That trembled not to grasp his bones
> And steal his dust away.

Details of the event tended to be rather various, as the reference to both ashes and bones shows. Some claimed that it was not really Milton's coffin which had been unearthed. George Steevens, the noted Shakespeare commentator, satisfied himself that 'it is all a flam, for that is the body of a Miss Smith'.[12] So even in death Milton became once again the 'Lady of Christ's'. Nonetheless, a quest began to collect the remains of the corpse, reminiscent of Isis as Milton describes her in *Areopagitica*, going about the country to collect the scattered and mangled fragments of Osiris, or Truth. We trust that most of the body was found and reassembled. A full-size metal statue, based on the bust, now adorns the church. A stone beneath the altar rail marks the spot where Milton was buried. Maybe he now is again. But the important remains of Milton, as Milton said himself about Shakespeare, are not in the ground but in his books.

Epilogue

The story of Milton's life has been told in many ways. Samuel Johnson, the great eighteenth-century critic and poet and compiler of a remarkable dictionary, admired Milton's poetry but disliked his politics and the man himself: he called him 'a surly republican'. He also opened a mare's nest by alleging Milton had 'a Turkish contempt for females'. Johnson, I hope to have shown, was wrong on both counts. Milton was indeed a republican, though not surly. As for his feelings about women, well, they seem to have been as complicated and various as most men's. The late Christopher Hill, on the other hand, the great Marxist historian at Oxford University who admired Milton's politics, re-examined all of his poetry, especially *Paradise Lost*, for signs that he was obliged to conceal his radical political views to protect them from the censors: he imagines Milton as a sympathetic man of the people spending his time in London pubs. Like Johnson, but in the opposite direction, Hill's own populist politics rather carried him away. Both were wrong (though Milton did sometimes visit a tavern), but the ways in which they were wrong are often more interesting than the dull biographer who tries to be right. Milton's life was, after all, an instance of that apocryphal Chinese curse: 'may you live in interesting times'.

Any reading of Milton's life story depends on the many surviving documents, increasing in number all the time through discoveries in various record offices. Some 2,000 references in 600 documents housed in fifty or more archives[1] make up an easily accessible collection of life records, and there are many references in seventeenth-century books, hostile, adulatory, puzzled, neutral. Many of the documents are records of his father's business or legal activities, but they sometimes tell us about Milton himself. A few he even signed, so they tell us where he was when. He was signing documents in London when he ought to have been at Cambridge, and this probably gives us the date of his rustication as spring 1627, not the 1626 which was previously thought and is still argued.[2] The letters of state Milton wrote in Latin while working for the Cromwell government are often revealing, but they raise the question, which comes back all the time, of where Milton himself stood, of whether Milton endorsed what he wrote. Sometimes there is no doubt about this, such as when he writes to protest the massacre of the sect known as the Waldensians in the valleys of Piedmont in 1655: Milton wrote that famous sonnet ('Avenge, O Lord, thy slaughter'd Saints') at the same time. Other sources suggest that Milton may have been more and more disillusioned with Cromwell, but for obvious reasons we cannot read that shift in the official correspondence.

A huge five-volume collection called *The Life Records of John Milton* was published by J. Milton French between 1949 and 1958. It includes lots of legal documents that French himself had discovered (in the preface to the first volume he says it will be in four volumes: much happened before he had finished). In 1968 William Riley Parker added many more such records in his two-volume *Milton: A Biography*. By the time Gordon Campbell updated this work in 1996, the number of records had increased, he says, by a third. All of this material means that we know, or at least have ways of knowing, far more about Milton than any great writer of or before his time. Milton is unique in the kind of material he has left to us, and we can rediscover it, combining the public world of politics and – though we always risk controversy – the more private world of poetry.

Lyric poetry we think of as private, but some of Milton's, like the Waldensians sonnet, is deliberately public. Epic we often think of as more public, yet there Milton is sometimes more revealing than any epic poet, even Dante, had ever been, not only in the passages where he seems explicitly to write about himself, but also in the comments of his narrator – 'oh when meet now/ Such pairs, in Love and mutual Honour joyn'd?' (VIII 37-38) – surely that tells us something about his emotional world? Or consider the apparently gratuitous comments about choosing a good wife that Adam suddenly inserts into a speech as he bewails his fate after eating the apple: he looks forward to a future when a man shall never find

> fit Mate, but such
> As some misfortune brings him, or mistake,
> Or whom he wishes most shall seldom gain
> Through her perverseness, but shall see her gaind
> By a farr worse, or if she love, withheld
> By Parents, or his happiest choice too late
> Shall meet, already linkt and Wedlock-bound
> To a fell Adversarie, his hate or shame. (X 899-906)

This sounds personal. We can fit parts of it to what we know about Milton's first marriage, but the rest is biographically obscure: we would love to know, and do not, who was so perverse as to refuse Milton, or who was withheld by her parents. Even more intriguing, was Milton already married when he met his happiest choice, so that his wife is his 'fell Adversarie'? Is this perhaps a covert reference to the mysterious Miss Davis, who Milton seems to have met just before Mary Powell came back to him? There are many passages in Milton's writings, both prose and poetry, in which he talks about himself. But in those passages Milton is usually creating some kind of public image: here, in the Adam passage, it looks as if he has given himself away, and in both senses.

The passages with clear autobiographical relevance from Milton's writings, both prose and poetry, were collected by John Diekhoff in a 300-page book, *Milton on Himself*, in 1939. Apart from the large number of things Milton said about himself, we construct our biographical picture partly from the so-called 'early lives', collected by Helen Darbishire in 1932. They include a preface to a 1694 edition of Milton's *Letters of State* by Edward Phillips, Milton's nephew, pupil and amanuensis (after Milton went blind) – he is chatty and a bit careless; an unpublished biography usually called 'anonymous' but in fact written by another pupil and amanuensis, Cyriack Skinner (as we know from two recently discovered letters in the City Record office in Hull!) – which makes use of Milton's own statements in the Latin treatises, but describes his physical appearance, his habits of composition, and his death; some invaluable notes taken in the 1680s by the antiquarian John Aubrey during interviews with people who had known Milton; a further biography by Anthony à Wood of 1691 which uses Skinner and Aubrey and reinterprets them in the light of his own unreflecting monarchism (Milton, Wood claims, justifies the murder of the best of kings at 'a monstrous and unparallel'd height of profligate impudence'); a brief account of 1698 by John Toland (the only one to tell us about that potential censorship of *Paradise Lost*); another by Milton's early editors, Jonathan Richardson, father and son, 1734; and finally two efforts at scholarly biography by Thomas Birch (1738, revised 1753) and Thomas Newton (1749), the last men who could publish information they had gathered from Milton's widow, his daughter Deborah Clarke and his granddaughter Elizabeth Foster, herself born years after his death.

Many other documents have come to light since then, sometimes in fortuitous ways, sometimes as the result of scholarly searches, such as those that Scots professor David Masson and his allies undertook as he was publishing his seven-volume biography in the nineteenth century (1859–94). Two were quite spectacular discoveries. In 1874 a certain Alfred Horwood, an antiquarian, was going through Sir Frederick Graham's collection of manuscripts at Netherby Hall, Cumberland, for the Royal Commission on Historical Manuscripts, and was surprised to find Milton's Commonplace Book, in which he kept a meticulous record of his reading. What was it doing there? Apparently Milton's last amanuensis, Daniel Skinner, a rather shady character, who inherited a few Milton manuscripts, had given it to Sir Richard Graham, Lord Preston, as a way to curry favour with him and perhaps get a job with him in Paris, and it simply stayed gathering dust in the family collection. The book was published two years later in facsimile and printed versions, and has been re-edited several times since.[3]

It is an enormously useful record. Milton began keeping the book in the 1630s, though there are few entries before September 1637, and he kept it going even after he went blind and had entries written in by others. Thus he included 19 quotations from Macchiavelli after 1650, that is, after he started losing his sight – an obvious sign of his increased interest in practical politics now that he was working for Cromwell almost every day. But there are also many entries on marriage and divorce, some of them from well before the period of his own marriage difficulties. These include references to the church fathers, to the permission granted for priests to marry by the Council of Vienne in France more than 900 years after Christ, and to Elizabeth's refusal of marriage to the duke of Anjou. He also notes, as om *De Doctrina*, that many writers approve of polygamy. Some entries show little more than the enormous breadth of Milton's reading, but many others, especially the longer ones (where he has returned many times to the same page and squeezed in extra entries) show his special interests. Apart from the entries on marriage or divorce, there is a very long one, and then a second, entitled 'King'. It shows his growing sympathy for republicanism. Another long one is headed 'Tyrant' and includes several references to English history, including both Anglo-Saxon times and what Shakespeare's source Holinshed discussed, such as the reign of Richard II. A later entry, not precisely dateable, argues in both Latin and Italian whether it is permissible to withdraw one's allegiance from a tyrant.

For one period, October 1651 to March 1652, there are almost daily accounts of Milton's activities because in 1877 Professor Alfred Stern of Berne came across and published the *Tagebuch* or diary of Hermann Mylius, a German diplomat who was in England to renew a treaty. Milton was his opposite number in the English bureaucracy. The diary also contained copies of invaluable letters in both directions. Stern published most of this material in his German biography *Milton und Seine Zeit* of 1877, and the whole treasure trove was thoroughly investigated and fully published, with informative notes and acknowledgments to the original German scholars, and thanks also to those who managed to read the almost indecipherable documents, in the great edition we know as the 'Columbia Milton' in 1936. Mylius, we learn, met Milton for the last time on 5 March 1652 and records that he was now wholly blind.

The Public Record Office for Hammersmith and Fulham yielded documents in 1996 which showed the Miltons lived there as early as April 1631, when Milton's father was assessed for poor relief. In the same archive, documents show that Bishop Laud, soon to be the cause of great trouble for the puritan wing of the church, founded the Chapel of St Paul in Hammersmith in June 1631. By May of 1633 John Milton senior had become a churchwarden of this chapel. Whether the poet worshipped there also in those years we do not know, but the information about his father rather scotches the idea, previously current, that our Milton might have been raised in a strictly puritan household.

Such, then, are some of the documents from which Milton's life can be partially reconstructed, and most are now integrated into recent biographies. We thus know more about Milton than about any other literary genius before the most recent period of our history. He is the most knowable and accessible of the world's great writers. He is not always likeable: even in the great poetry he is occasionally so vulnerable that we would turn away in embarrassment if we were not so enchanted. And in the polemical prose, as we have seen, he is sometimes very difficult to take. But if we are honest, we will usually recognize, behind his aggressive egotism, his broadly human sympathy; and he has wonderful fun with the English language as he denounces his enemies. The pleasure is infectious.

2008 is the quadricentenary of John Milton's birth (9 December 1608). For the first three of those 400 years his reputation stood high. It was a matter of satisfaction that English literature had produced two such different poets as Shakespeare and Milton. For Coleridge, 'Shakespeare became all things well into which he infused himself, while all forms, all things became Milton.' The contrast he makes is between a dramatist and what the Romantics thought a sublime poet should be. On the one hand is what Keats, in those brilliant letters of his, called Shakespeare's 'negative capability': on the other what he (rather unkindly) called the 'egotistical sublime' – though he was talking about Wordsworth, Milton's disciple in that as in so many respects. Matthew Arnold expressed the common opinion about Milton, yet with no sense that he was belittling Shakespeare, when he said: 'In the sure and flawless perfection of his rhythm and diction he is as admirable as Virgil or Dante… That Milton, of all our English race, is by his diction and rhythm the one artist of the highest rank in the great style whom we have; this I take as requiring no discussion, this I take as certain.' A few years later A. E. Housman said much the same thing.

That Victorian certainty evaporated with T. S. Eliot's attack on *Paradise Lost* just after the First World War, one of the founding statements of

Modernism – an effort to displace Milton in favour of John Donne, and to liberate poetry from what Eliot thought was Milton's oppressive influence. The key issues in the attack, developed and renewed with great vigour in a 1936 essay, were the sounds and images of poetry, and the focus was Milton's Satan and Hell. What Eliot had in mind was what Milton had become in the century after his death – sublime. There is a famous and contentious passage in Book I, for example, in which Satan is described through a sequence of similes that ends with a sun in eclipse, an eclipse which 'with fear of change/ Perplexes monarchs' (I 598-99). At the time of publication, the implications of these lines almost led to the suppression of the whole poem through the intervention of Charles II's censor, as we have seen. But before 100 years had passed, Edmund Burke, in his influential 1757 treatise *A Philosophical Enquiry into the Origin of the Ideas of the Sublime and the Beautiful*, almost ignores the politics in favour of the effect on the reader of the same passage.

> Here is a very noble picture; and in what does this poetical picture consist? in images of a tower, an archangel, the sun rising through mists, or in an eclipse, the ruin of monarchs, and the revolutions of kingdoms. The mind is hurried out of itself, by a croud of great and confused images; which affect because they are crouded and confused. For separate them, and you lose much of the greatness, and join them, and you infallibly lose the clearness. The images raised by poetry are always of this obscure kind.

In the same tradition, Wordsworth said that when he read these lines 'he felt a certain faintness come over his mind from the sense of beauty and grandeur', while William Hazlitt, reporting Wordsworth's comment, saw 'no extravagance in it but the utmost truth of feeling'.

Burke's reviewers, however, did not always agree with this point about poetry. An anonymous critic in *The Literary Magazine* wrote: 'Obscurity, our author observes, increases the sublime, which is certainly very just; but from thence erroneously infers, that clearness of imagery is unnecessary to affect the passions; but surely nothing can move but what gives ideas to the mind.' Similarly, the *Monthly Review* observed, 'Distinctness of imagery has ever been held productive of the sublime.' Mary Wollstonecraft could complain in 1787 that she was 'sick of hearing of the sublimity of Milton'. This did not stop her daughter, Mary Shelley, from recreating exactly that Miltonic sublime in the Alpine encounters between Frankenstein and his monstrous creature.

When T. S. Eliot launched his attack, it was this dubious sublime that he had in mind. Once again the comparison with Shakespeare is the key – but it is now an invidious one.

> The most important fact about Milton, for my purpose, is his *blindness*...
> At no period is the visual imagination conspicuous in Milton's poetry...
> From *Macbeth*:
>
> > Light thickens, and the crow
> > Makes wing to the rooky wood
>
> not only offers something to the eye, but, so to speak, to the common
> sense. I mean that they convey the feeling of being in a particular place
> at a particular time... In comparison, Milton's... language is, if one may
> use the term without disparagement, *artificial* and *conventional*... Milton
> may be said never to have seen anything. For Milton, therefore, the
> concentration on sound was wholly a benefit. Indeed, I find in reading
> *Paradise Lost*, that I am happiest where there is least to visualise.[4]

'Without disparagement'! Humph! F. R. Leavis took that last point a step
further, struggling to avoid the by-now debased word 'sublime':

> We say that the 'emphasis is on the sound' because we are less exactingly
> conscious in respect of meaning than when we read certain other
> poets...: it is not only our sense of sight that is blurred. The state
> induced has analogies with intoxication. Our response brings nothing
> to any arresting focus, but gives us a feeling of exalted significance, of
> energetic effortlessness, and of a buoyant ease of command.[5]

It is exactly that sense of trying to define greatness, of knowing somehow
where it lies, that captivated Leavis's Cambridge students in the twentieth
century and that has irritated many since. But note that the same ingredients
are used as when Milton was being praised. Wordsworth in his sonnet 'London
1802' says that his voice sounds like the sea; Arnold praises the rhythm of his
'great style'. But now the point is to belittle him. Talk of Milton's 'organ
music' implies that neither Milton nor his readers attend very closely to what
the verse actually shows. As an example, Eliot quotes from the first book of
Paradise Lost, a little earlier than the eclipse passage, when Satan awakes to
find himself in Hell and sees 'no light, but rather darkness visible' (I 63) – and
what Eliot dislikes is that he cannot imagine this hell: 'it is difficult to imagine
a burning lake in a scene where there was only darkness visible'.

Replies to these attacks have been various. They have called attention to the
variety of styles for God and Satan, to the subtlety rather than ponderousness

of the language (or if it is ponderous it is ironically so, as for Satan during the War in Heaven), to the appropriate use of Latin and Greek structures for poetic purposes, like the extended chiasmus around 'Will and Fate,/ Fixt Fate, free Will' (II 555-57). They have pointed out that this is an epic poem, and what C. S. Lewis called the 'ritual style' is appropriate: it is remote and artificial, but that is a good thing. Human beings like art. Douglas Bush defended the odd 'vegetable Gold' of Paradise and other such phrases as both general and arresting. And then Christopher Ricks challenged Eliot and especially Leavis on their own grounds. The style is indeed 'Grand', he allowed, but it is also sensitive and subtle. Ricks went back to the eighteenth-century critics and editors who had invented the Miltonic sublime and found that they had all discovered many other felicities as well, like the 'suspended Hell' of the angels' song in Book II, or the brilliant way the language makes Satan seem to teeter on the brink of Chaos before he flies forth. Other critics have even found a sophisticated visual imagination. The defenses were largely successful. Milton survived Eliot.

As it happens, three fine books entitled *Darkness Visible* have appeared in the years since Eliot wrote, all of them quietly answering him. One was a novel about war-torn England by William Golding, another was William Styron's moving account of surviving clinical depression, the third was an elegant comparison of Homer and Virgil by Ralph Johnson. All felt the force of the paradox in Milton's words, and wanted to make use of it.

And yet, what is surely a good thing, we can no longer recover the Victorians' certainty about Milton. Most interesting writing about him since Eliot has felt itself to be on the edge of dangerous ground. One common move in recent years has been to acknowledge what was mostly suppressed in all that aesthetic commentary from Burke to Leavis – Milton's politics. Part of the purpose of inventing the sublime Milton, it was realized, had been to save his poetry by suppressing his radical politics.

Not everyone colluded in the suppression. The implications of the eclipse passage had been no secret to Keats, who gloried in its anti-monarchist leanings. In his copy of *Paradise Lost*, which he was reading again and annotating around 1818, he wrote:

> How noble and collected an indignation against Kings – 'and for fear of change perplexes monarchs, &'. His very wishing should have had power to pull that feeble animal Charles from his bloody throne. 'The evil days' had come to him – he hit the new System of things a mighty mental blow.

Burke and the others who developed the commentary on the sublime had no such political and treasonous imaginings. Milton did.

A few years earlier, in a similar spirit to that of Keats, Jacques-Pierre Brissot, one of the Girondin leaders and a key figure in the French Revolution, honoured Milton on 14 July 1790 with the name of 'founding father of the French republic'. English republicans readily found their way into the discourse of the French Revolution. John Milton, Marchamont Nedham and James Harrington were translated or adapted by French revolutionaries to fit their own purposes. Mirabeau, the first President of the French National Assembly, translated *Areopagitica*, Milton's tract on the liberty of the press, and wrote a pamphlet called *Théorie de la royauté, d'après la doctrine de Milton*. In the context of debates over what to do with Louis XVI, this was soon re-edited by the Jacobins in 1792 and republished with a full translation of Milton's *Defensio*, the Latin treatise defending the right of the English people to behead their king. The title page adds that it is a work likely to clarify the situation in which France now finds itself.

The most famous words ever written about Milton are probably William Blake's aphorism in *The Marriage of Heaven and Hell* of 1793, that 'he was a true poet and of the Devils party without knowing it'. On the face of it, Blake was referring to Milton's Satan in *Paradise Lost*, since the devil, or the daemonic, was equated by Romantics like Blake with untrammelled Imagination, and Milton had as much of that laudable quality as Shakespeare. But Blake also had to be careful of the political repression which had imposed a heavy censorship in the years immediately after the French Revolution; he may have known that seventeenth-century republicans were sometimes known as the 'Devil's party'. For Blake at least, and for many since, Milton's politics and his poetry were not to be easily separated. Together, he hoped, they would help to build the new Jerusalem in what he called, in the poem that serves as an epigraph to his long poem entitled *Milton*, 'England's green and pleasant land'.

Milton's political influence continued. Whereas English republicanism may be said to have died on the scaffold with Algernon Sidney in 1683, Americans continued to call Milton to their aid. Benjamin Franklin evoked the Chaos of *Paradise Lost* in his diatribe against Britain's taxation of the colonies, Thomas Jefferson used Milton's arguments to attack the established church in Virginia, and John Adams denounced British rulers as embodiments of Milton's Satan – they were equally arrogant, and their policies futile.[6]

More recently, in fact just a few years ago, the French divorce laws were changed, and during the debate in the Senate, Milton's treatises on divorce, especially his arguments about the purpose of marriage, were introduced explicitly and persuasively into the discussion by one of the senators, Olivier Abel. For Milton, and, in those recent discussions, for the French, divorce was not merely a private matter, but a major political and public issue. Like the rights Milton defended in other contexts, his radical defence of divorce had to do with an early and unusually articulate commitment to the idea of a free individual. That, and the inestimable power of his poetry, are reasons for his continuing impact on all of us.

References

Introduction: Blind Love

1 John Milton, *The Doctrine and Discipline of Divorce*, in *Complete Prose Works of John Milton*, gen. ed. Don M. Wolfe, New Haven: Yale University Press, 1953–80, II, p. 258 (hereafter *YP*.)

2 *Samson Agonistes*, 35 in *The Riverside Milton,* ed. Roy Flannagan, Boston and New York: Houghton Mifflin, 1998.

3 *The Reason of Church Government, YP* I, p. 859.

4 *Areopagitica, YP* II, p. 493.

1 St Paul's

1 Helen Darbishire, ed., *The Early Lives of Milton,* New York: Barnes and Noble, 1965, pp. 4–5. (hereafter *EL*)

2 Cambridge

1 Arminianism, rooted in the theology of the Dutch Reformer Jacobus Arminius (1560-1609), emphasises that whilst salvation is by grace alone, a person is able to choose to receive and respond to it by faith.

2 Gordon Campbell, 'The Life Records', *A Companion to Milton*, ed. Thomas N. Corns, Oxford: Blackwell, 2001, pp. 486–7.

3 William Riley Parker, *Milton: A Biography*, Oxford: Clarendon Press, 1968, p. 30. If the poem does coincide with the time of his rustication, and Campbell is right about its date, then Milton was eighteen.

4 John K. Hale, *Milton's Cambridge Latin*, Tempe: Arizona Center for Medieval and Renaissance Studies, 2005, p. 195.

5 Biographers differ on this important issue. See the review of Barbara Lewalski, *Life of John Milton*, Oxford: Blackwell, 2000, 2003, by Thomas N. Corns in *Milton Quarterly* 41 (2007), pp. 25–7.

3 Early Signs of Genius

1 Gordon Campbell, 'Shakespeare and the Youth of Milton', in *Milton Quarterly* 33 (1999), pp. 95–105.

References (Pages 7-53)

4 Studious Retirement

1 William Kerrigan, *The Sacred Compex: On the Psychogenesis of* Paradise Lost, Cambridge, Mass: Harvard UP, 1983, p. 115.

2 The various theories are ably discussed by Barbara Lewalski, *Life* pp. 73–4, though she favours 1637. My own date coincides with that of John Carey, *Milton: Complete Shorter Poems*, Harlow: Longman, 1997, p. 154, and for the same reason – the present tense used or implied in lines 71–6, in which *abductum* must mean that father and son are together in this seclusion.

3 Barbara Breasted, 'Another Bewitching of Lady Alice Egerton, the Lady of *Comus*', *Notes and Queries* 17 (1970), pp. 411–12.

4 Leah S. Marcus, 'A "Local" Reading of *Comus*', in *Milton and the Idea of Woman*, ed. Julia M. Walker, Chicago: University of Illinois Press, 1988, pp. 66–85.

5 John Creaser, in 'Milton's *Comus*: The Irrelevance of the Castlehaven Scandal', *Notes and Queries* 31 (1984), pp. 307–17, argued against Barbara Breasted, 'Comus and the Castlehaven Scandal', *Milton Studies* 3 (1971) pp. 201–24, but his view is in fact close to mine, that Milton had to work hard to make sure that the audience did not think of the scandal.

5 Coping with Death: 'Lycidas'

1 James Holly Hanford, 'The Pastoral Elegy and Milton's *Lycidas*', *Publications of the Modern Language Association* 25 (1910), pp. 403–47, reprinted in C. A. Patrides, ed., *Milton's Lycidas: the Tradition and the Poem*, New York: Holt, Rhinehart & Winston, 1967, second edn Columbia: University of Missouri Press, 1983, pp. 27–55.

2 Samuel Johnson, *The Lives of the Most Eminent English Poets* (London, 1783), I, pp. 218–20, reprinted in Patrides, *Milton's Lycidas*, pp. 56–7.

3 The May, July and September eclogues all express indignation against corruption in the church. The Church of Rome is denounced in a passage in the fifth eclogue which Milton echoes:

Tho, under colour of shepheards, somewhile
There crept in wolves, full of fraud and guile,
That often devoured their own sheepe,
And often the shepheards that did hem keep.

4 Ruskin's explanation of this enigmatic phrase is worth repeating: This is a strange expression; a broken metaphor, one might think, careless and unscholarly. Not so: its very audacity and pithiness are intended to make us look close at the phrase and remember it. Those two monosyllables express the precisely accurate contraries of right character, in the two great offices of the Church – those of bishop and

235

pastor. A 'Bishop' means a 'person who sees.' A 'Pastor' means a 'person who feeds.' The most unbishoply character a man can have is therefore to be Blind. The most unpastoral is, instead of feeding, to want to be fed, – to be a Mouth. Take the two reverses together, and you have 'blind mouths.' We may advisably follow out this idea a little. Nearly all the evils in the Church have arisen from bishops desiring power more than light.

5 Virgil *Eclogue* III 27

6 Actually Milton changed that striking phrase in line 129 'nothing said' to 'little said', a more cautious phrase, for the poem's publication in the collective volume in 1638, and then reverted to 'nothing' in 1645 once the power of the established church had waned.

7 Merritt Y. Hughes, ed., *John Milton: Complete Poems and Major Prose*, New York: Odyssey Press, 1957, p.118.

8 I take issue with this view, but admit its force, throughout my *The Satanic Epic*, Princeton: Princeton UP, 2003.

9 John Leonard, "'Trembling ears": the Historical Moment of *Lycidas*', in *Journal of Medieval and Renaissance Studies* 21 (1991), pp. 59–81.

6 Foreign Parts

1 *Of Education*, in YP II, p. 414. 'Kicshoes' are trivialities derived from French *quelque chose*.

2 Gordon Campbell, *A Milton Chronology*, Basingstoke: Macmillan, 1997, p. 61 is my source for this as it is of much other information.

3 Roland Mushat Frye, *Milton's Imagery and the Visual Arts: Iconographic Tradition in the Epic Poems*, Princeton: Princeton UP, 1978.

4 James Grantham Turner, 'Milton Among the Libertines', in Christophe Tournu and Neil Forsyth, *Milton, Rights and Liberties*, Berne: Peter Lang, 2007, pp. 451-2, makes a case for the erotic flavour of the Diodati poems.

7 No Bishop, No King

1 This along with many other such texts is available on line from the Hanover Historical Texts project at http://history.hanover.edu.

2 See the two books by Joad Raymond for a thorough analysis of this exciting and dangerous world, *The Invention of the Newspaper*: English Newsbooks 1641–1649, Oxford: Clarendon Press, 1996, and *Pamphlets and Pamphleteering in Early Modern Britain*, Cambridge: Cambridge UP, 2003.

3 Christopher Hill, *The World Turned Upside Down*, Harmondsworth: Penguin, 1975, p. 35 cites a version from 1642.

4 Thomas Corns, *Regaining Paradise Lost*, Harlow: Longman, 1994, p. 128.

5 Mark Kishlansky, *Monarchy Transformed: Britain 1603-1714*, London:

Penguin, 1997, p. 135-6.

6 Hill, *The World Turned Upside Down*, pp. 27–8, 184–5, 395.

7 A. N. Wilson, *The Life of John Milton*, Oxford: Oxford University Press, 1984, p. 103. Thorough discussion of this Miltonic double self is in Steven Fallon, *Milton's Peculiar Grace: Self-Representation and Authority*, Ithaca: Cornell UP, 2007, p. 94.

8 Christopher Hill, in his fine book *Milton and the English Revolution*, New York: Viking, 1978, p. 59, 97-8, eager to paint Milton as a man of the people, goes too far in this respect. See the review by Quentin Skinner, 'Milton, Satan and Subversion', *New York Review of Books* 25.4 (March 23, 1978). Sonnet 20 (XVII) imitates and alludes to Horace's poems advocating friendship and good living, but sparingly – at least it does if the natural interpretation of 'spare' is not perverted, as it has sometimes been. See the notes in Carey, and especially Leonard.

9 See Stephen Fallon, *Milton's Peculiar Grace*, pp. ix–x.

8 Mary Powell

1 *Apology*, in *YP* I, p. 929. See the previous chapter.

2 Peter Thonemann, 'Wall of Ice', *London Review of Books*, Vol. 30:3, 7 February 2008, pp. 23–4, shows that the original of Eliot's Casaubon in *Middlemarch* was probably Mark Pattison, rector of Lincoln College, Oxford, author of a book about the Renaissance scholar, Isaac Casaubon, as well as a biographical study of Milton, London: Macmillan, 1879.

3 John Leonard, 'Thus They Relate Erring: Milton's Inaccurate Allusions', *Milton Studies* 38 (2000), p. 104, argues the allusion is to Lucian, who has Isocrates die suddenly on hearing the bad news.

4 Lucy Hutchinson, *The Memoirs of the Life of Colonel Hutchinson*, London: J.M. Dent, 1965, p. 75. A fine account is to be found at The Battlefield Trust website: http://www.battlefieldstrust.com.

9 Civil War

1 This is the third provision. The text is accessible online in several places; try http://www.constitution.org/eng/conpur058.htm

2 Since the two editions are quite different, I quote the first from *DDD 1* in J. Max Patrick, ed. *The Prose of John Milton*, New York: Doubleday Anchor, 1967, in this case p. 147. The second edition (*DDD 2*) is quoted from *YP* II.

3 Gordon Campbell, *John Milton*, Oxford: Oxford UP, 2007, p. 37. This 'Very Interesting People' (VIP) series reprints entries in the *Dictionary of National Biography*, of which Campbell's appeared in 2004.

4 Herbert Palmer, *The Glasse of God's Providence*, London, 1644, as cited

in Barbara Lewalski, The *Life of Milton*, Oxford: Blackwell, 2003, p.179, whose lucid account I have used extensively in this section.

5 Ephraim Pagitt, *Heresiography*: or, *A description of the Heretickes and Sectaries of these latter times*, London, 1645. The text is quoted in the marvellous compilation of J. Milton French, *The Life Records of John Milton*, New Brunswick, NJ: Rutgers UP, 1949–58, vol 2, p. 127. A recent book has brought together several discussions of these controversies, Sharon Achinstein and Elizabeth Sauer, eds. *Milton and Toleration*, Oxford: Oxford UP, 2007. For Pagitt, Williams and Milton, see the essay by Thomas Corns, 'John Milton, Roger Williams, and the Limits of Toleration', pp. 72–85.

6 Corns, 'Toleration', p. 73.

11 Rudest Violence

1 William Walwyn, *Gold tried in the fire, or the burnt petitions revived*, 4 June 1647. Reprinted in Andrew Sharp, ed. *The English Levellers*, Cambridge, Cambridge UP, 1998, and available on-line at http://www.constitution.org/lev/eng_lev_06.htm.

2 'Declaration of the New Model Army', in Sharp, *The English Levellers*, p. x.

3 Colonel Thomas Rainsborough, *Debates at the General Council of the Army, Putney*. 29 October 1647 at http://www.constitution.org/lev/eng_lev_08.htm. The Putney debates have become a *cause célèbre* in the history of English political ideas since their publication in A.S.P. Woodhouse *Puritanism and Liberty*, London: J.M. Dent (1938, repr. 1974). See now Philip Baker, ed. *The Putney Debates*, London: Verso, 2008.

4 Dating of these works is disputed. Barbara Lewalski, *The Life of Milton*, Oxford: Blackwell, 2003, p. 220, and p. 611, n. 109, argues for this dating of the 'Digression', along with the rest of this part of the *History*. Against her are two articles published as a 'debate' in *Historical Journal* 36 (1993), pp. 929–56: Austin Woolrich puts it much later, in 1660, while Nicholas von Maltzahn places it in February–March 1649, as also Gordon Campbell, *A Milton Chronology*, London: Macmillan, 1997, p. 97. A recent overview is by Andrew Hadfield in Thomas Corns, *A Companion to Milton*, Oxford: Blackwell, 2001, pp. 179–86.

12 Image Breaking

1 Pauline Gregg, *Free-Born John*, London: Greenwood Press, 1960, p. 313.

2 Text available at several places online, including at http://www.bilderberg.org/land/leveller.htm and see also http://www.spartacus.

schoolnet.co.uk/STUlilburne.htm.

3 Helen Darbishire, ed., *The Early Lives of Milton*, New York: Barnes and Noble, 1965, p. 28.

13 Blindness

1 *The Writings of William Walwyn,* ed. Jack R. McMichael abd Barbara Taft, Athens, Ga: University of Georgia Press, 1989, p. 242,

2 J. M. French, ed., *Life Records of John Milton*, New Brunswick, NJ: Rutgers UP, 1949–58, III, p. 206 – a report by the Hanseatic League representative.

3 Differing accounts of the meeting and Cromwell's remarks are printed in Wilbur Cortez Abbott, ed., *The Writings and Speeches of Oliver Cromwell*, Oxford: Clarendon Press, 1939, II, pp. 639–45. The most colourful version is that of the *Memoirs* of Edmund Ludlow, quoted in Barbara Lewalski, *Life*, Oxford: Blackwell, 2003, p. 295. A splendidly dramatic summary is in Mark Kishlansky, *Monarchy Transformed*, London: Penguin, 1997pp. 187-89

4 See my *The Satanic Epic*, Princeton UP, 2003, pp. 185-87.

14 Cromwell Protector

1 The case is quoted and discussed in James Holstun, *Ehud's Dagger: Class Struggle in the English Revolution* (London: Verso, 2000), pp. 279–86. I am grateful to Anna Beer's entertaining *Milton*, London: Bloomsbury, 2007, p. 259, for the reference.

2 Helen Darbishire, *Early Lives,* p. 7.

3 Barbara Lewalski, *Life*, p. 349, discusses Milton's *History* thoroughly, and I follow her account.

4 William Riley Parker was the first to argue for Mary Powell as the poem's 'late espoused Saint', *Review of English Studies* 21 (1945), pp. 235–8, repeated in his 1968 biography, pp. 475-76, and in the 1996 revision by Gordon Campbell, p. 1045. The key point is that Mary died three days after giving birth to Deborah, so the lines in the poem about being 'washed from child-bed taint' apply more closely to her than Katherine, who also died after childbirth, but some three months after. On the other hand, if indeed 'Purification in the old law' is taken seriously, at least 66 days would need to have passed (Leviticus 12:4–8) if she is saved, which applies to Katherine, not Mary, as Lewalski, *Life*, shows, p. 653, n. 136. Katherine means purity or chastity in Greek. John Carey collects all the pro and con references in his 1997 edition, pp. 347–48. I had thought that the scribe argument clinched it in favour of Katherine until it was pointed out that Jeremy Picard could simply have been copying out a poem written 6 years earlier for Mary. Oh dear! We fall back on the subjective, or perhaps on

our need to prefer Katherine, the wife he never saw. Parker denounces
the misogyny that has gathered over the years around Mary. Anna Beer's
feminist agenda inclines her toward Mary for similar reasons, p. 269;
she pokes fun at 'modern biographers' who want Katherine as Milton's
true love, Mary as his functional wife. It is true that my argument is not
conclusive either. The key lines are echoed in *Paradise Lost* but that could
point either way as well. One or two critics want a composite wife, which
is ridiculous in view of the singular 'late' in the first line.

5 French, ed., *Life Records,* New Brunswick, IV, p. 218.

15 A Long Argument to Prove that God is Not the Devil

1 The 'Columbia Milton' (*CM*), i.e. *The Works of John Milton*, ed. F. A
Patterson et al., New York: Columbia University Press, 1931–8, XIV, p. 86,
also translated in *YP,* VI, p. 185.

2 John Rumrich, 'Milton's Arianism: Why It Matters' in *Milton and
Heresy*, ed. Stephen Dobranski and John Rumrich, Cambridge: Cambridge
University Press 1998, pp. 75–92 is a forceful argument against any
thinner description of Milton's views on the Son. The figure of the Son,
understood in this way, is absolutely central in the two *Paradise* poems, as
we shall see.

3 In the orthodox view, the Son is 'consubstantial' with the father,
and thus shares in his divine essence. But Milton argues that, while God
did indeed impart to the Son as much as he wished of the divine nature,
and thus of the substance also, we should 'not take *substance* to mean total
essence. If it did, it would mean that the father gave his essence to his Son
and at the same time retained it, numerically inaltered, himself. That is not
a means of generation but a contradiction in terms' (212). The context
of this statement is a discussion of the generation of the Son, referring to
Hebrews 1:2–3.

16 Expiring Liberty

1 John Aubrey, *Brief Lives,* ed. Andrew Clark, Oxford: Clarendon Press,
1898, I, pp. 289-91.

2. Anonymous pamphlet entitled *The Censure of the Rota*. The argument
for Butler's authorship is made in Nicholas von Maltzahn, 'Samuel Butler's
Milton', *Studies in Philology* 92 (1995), pp. 482-95.

3 Gordon Campbell, *John Milton*, Oxford: Oxford UP, 2007, p. 66.

4 Anonymous pamphlet entitled *The Character of the Rump* quoted by
Parker, *Milton*, pp. 548–9, and by Lewalski, *Life*, p. 377. See note 2 above for
von Maltzahn on Butler's putative authorship of this pamphlet as well.

5 *The Censure of the Rota*, quoted by Lewalski, *Life,* p. 378.

17 With Dangers Compast Round

1 Barbara Lewalski, *Life*, p. 402.

2 All of this information and a great deal more can be found at http://www.british-civil-wars.co.uk/biog/regicides.htm.

3 Lewalski, *Life*, p. 401.

4 Most of these splendid details, together with the sources of the quotations, may be found in Lewalski, *Life*, pp. 400–3.

5 William Riley Parker, *Milton: A Biography*, Oxford: Clarendon Press, 1968, I, p. 577.

6 J. M. French, ed., *Life Records of John Milton*, New Brunswick, NJ: Rutgers University Press, 1949–58, p. 229.

7 I mostly follow the measured account of Lewalski, *Life*, pp. 408–9. All biographers have to blunder in to fill the gaps in the record, and thereby reveal themselves and irritate each other: there is, for example, an impassioned attack on William Riley Parker's 'patronizing misogyny' as 'positively offensive' in Ann Beer, *Milton*, who leaps to the daughters' defense, pp. 352–3, and who sees Milton as having lost control of his household and therefore his masculinity.

8 See for example, Ralph Houlbrooke, *The English Family 1450-1700*, London: Longman, 1984, p. 21.

9 Helen Darbishire, ed., *The Early Lives of Milton*, New York: Barnes and Noble, 1965, p. 289.

10 Darbishire, *Early Lives*, p. 33

11 Cyriack Skinner in Darbishire, *The Early Lives*, p. 32, and Thomas Newton, 'Life of Milton', prefixed to his edition of *Paradise Lost*, London, 1749, I, 252–3, n. 305.

18 The Plague, and *Paradise Lost*

1 See above, Chapter 10.

2 David Norbrook, 'Lucan, Thomas May, and the creation of a Republican Literary Culture' in *Culture and Politics in Early Stuart England*, ed. Kevin Sharpe and Peter Lake, Stanford: Stanford University Press, 1993, pp. 45–66, and *Writing the English Republic: Poetry, Rhetoric And Politics 1627–1660*, Cambridge, Cambridge University Press, 1999, pp. 23–62, 438–67. Norbrook is followed by Barbara Lewalski, *Life*, pp. 448, 460, but she makes clear how thoroughly Milton exploits the whole epic tradition.

3 Rachel Falconer, reviewing Norbrook's *Writing*, in *Milton Quarterly* 34 (2000) 27.

19 Fire and War

1 Barbara Lewalski, ed. *Paradise Lost* (Oxford: Blackwell, 2007), p. xvii.

2 I have discussed this in my *The Satanic Epic,* Princeton: Princeton UP, 2003, 'Signs Portentous', pp. 329–47.

3 Nicholas von Maltzahn, 'The First Reception of *Paradise Lost* (1667)', *Review of English Studies* 47 (1996), p. 490.

4 Lewalski, *Life*, p. 459.

20 Adam and Eve – and Satan

1 *Commentaries on the First Book of Moses called Genesis*, I, p. 172, on 3:16. trans. John King, 1578, Grand Rapids, Mich: Eerdmans, 1996. Available online at http://www.ccel.org/ccel/calvin/calcom01.html.

21 Milton's Womb: Chaos, Hell and the Ribs of Gold

1 Jonathan Richardson II, 1734. Quoted in Christopher Ricks, *Milton's Grand Style*, Oxford: Clarendon Press, 1963, p. 79.

2 Ricks, p. 79. Fowler's note on the passage wonderfully calls Bentley's objection a 'critical *felix culpa,* leading to later notice of Milton's mimetic syntax.'

3 Tom Furniss and Michael Bath, *Reading Poetry: An Introduction*, Harlow: Prentice Hall, 1996, p. 55.

4 See Stevie Davies, *Milton*, Hemel Hempstead: Harvester Wheatsheaf 1991, p. 129, and above, chapter 18. Philip Pullman's remarkable trilogy of fantasy novels, His Dark Materials, published in the UK by Scholar and the US by Knopf between 1995 and 2000, takes its title from the passage quoted, II 916.

5 See above, chapter 17, note 11.

6 Norman O. Brown, 'Studies in Anality' in *Life Against Death*, Middletown: Wesleyan University Press, 1959, pp. 179–304.

7 William Empson, *Some Versions of Pastoral*, London: Chatto and Windus, 1935, p. 176.

8 Stanley Fish, *Surprised By Sin*, London: Macmillan, [1967] 1997, pp. xv–xvi.

9 There is an anticipation of this idea in a marvellous passage in *Comus* (728–36), quoted above, Chapter Three, where the world of animal and mineral nature have the same tendency to grow unchecked.

22 Emptying the Desk

1 Helen Darbishire, ed., *Early Lives,* p. 185.

2 Darbishire, p. 76. For Howard, see French, *Life Records*, p. 450.

3 The question of date is reviewed by John Carey, who changed his mind, and therefore moved the placing of the poem between the two

editions of his *Complete Shorter Poems*, Longman: 1971; 1997. See pp.
349–50 of the second edition.

4 Gordon Campbell, *John Milton*, Oxford: Oxford University Press,
2007, p. 85.

5 Manfred Gerlach, *Introduction to Early Modern English*, Cambridge:
Cambridge UP, 1991, p. 86.

6 Judges 16.30. John Donne, *Biathanatos* III, v, 4. This is a long treatise
on the rights and wrongs of suicide, available in an edition by Michael
Rudick and M. Pabst Battin, New York: Garland, 1982: the quoted passage
is on pp. 181–2.

7 *Of Civil Power*, in YP VII, p. 246.

23 *Paradise Regained*

1 I have learned a great deal from Stanley Fish, 'Things and Actions
Indifferent: The temptation to Plot in *Paradise Regained*', *Milton Studies*
17 (1983) 163-85, reprinted in *How Milton Works* (Cambridge: Harvard
UP, 2001), pp. 349-90. I take the occasion to thank him for his inspiring
teaching.

2 This is one of the many generous assessments in Christopher Hill,
Milton and the English Revolution, New York: Viking (1978), pp. 425-27.

24 Final Accomplishment

1 Nicholas von Maltzahn, 'Samuel Butler's Milton', *Studies in Philology*
92 (1995), pp. 482–95.

2 Paul Hammond, 'Marvell's Sexuality', in Thomas Healy, ed. *Andrew
Marvell*, London: Longman, 1998, p. 54.

3 Elizabeth Sauer, 'Milton's *Of True Religion*, Protestant Nationhood, and
the Negotiation of Liberty', *Milton Quarterly* 40 (2006) pp. 1–19.

4 A. N. Wilson, *The Life of John Milton*, Oxford: Oxford University Press,
1984, p. 257.

5 Nicholas von Maltzahn, 'The Whig Milton, 1667–1700', in
David Armitage, Armand Himy and Quentin Skinner, eds, *Milton and
Republicanism*, Cambridge University Press, 1995, p. 231.

6 Helen Darbishire, ed., *Early Lives*, pp. 13, 72–3.

7 Barbara Lewalski, *Life*, p. 508.

8 John Dryden, *The State of Innocence*, II ii 52–5.

9 Andrew Marvell, 'On Mr Milton's *Paradise Lost*', lines 7–10.

10 Darbishire, ed., *Early Lives*, p. 33.

11 Sharon Achinstein, *Literature and Dissent in Milton's England*,
Cambridge: Cambridge University Press, 2003, pp. 256–7.

12 The story is told by Allen Walker Read, 'The Disinterment of

Milton's Remains', *Publications Of The Modern Language Association* 45 (1930), pp. 1050–68, and updated by Carol Barton, '"Ill fare the hands that heaved the stones": John Milton, A Preliminary Thanatography', *Milton Studies* 43 (2004), pp. 198–260.

Epilogue

1 Gordon Campbell, 'Life Records', in *A Milton Companion*, ed. Thomas Corns, Oxford, Blackwell, 2001, p. 483.

2 Campbell in 'The Life Records', pp. 486–87. See also Leo Miller, 'Milton's Clash with Chappell', *Milton Quarterly* 14 (1980), pp. 77–86. 3 Barbara Lewalski, *Life*, p. 21, sticks to 1626.

3 Since Daniel Skinner became, briefly, a fellow of Trinity College, Cambridge, in 1676, it is plausible tht it was he who gave the so-called Trinity Manuscript of Milton's early poems to the college.

4 T. S. Eliot, 'Milton I', in *On Poetry and Poets*, London: Faber and Faber, 1957, pp. 142–3.

5 F. R. Leavis, 'Mr Eliot and Milton', in *The Common Pursuit*, London: Chatto and Windus, 1952, p. 14.

6 Gordon Campbell, *John Milton*, Oxford UP, 2007, p. 92.

Index